fROM GUILt

FROM GUILT TO GLORY

VOLUME I
ROMANS 1-8

RAY C. STEDMAN

WORD BOOKS
PUBLISHER
4800 WEST WACO DRIVE
WACO, TEXAS
76703

FROM GUILT TO GLORY,
VOLUME I (Romans 1-9)

Discovery Books are published by Word Books, Publisher, in
cooperation with Discovery Foundation, Palo Alto California.

ISBN 0-8499-2826-5
Library of Congress Catalog Card Number: 77-92460

First Printing, April 1978
Second Printing, July 1978

Printed in the United States of America

Contents

29885

Preface

Paul's letter to the Romans is a description of the power of God let loose amidst the ruin of man. It is about the good news, the gospel of Jesus Christ. God has found a way, through the death and resurrection of Jesus, to justify the ungodly. That includes all of us, because we are all ungodly. Romans teaches us that as God sees and understands our hearts, he understands *all* that is there. As a result, no one is able to count upon his own righteousness in the presence of God. As Paul tells us, "There is none righteous, no, not one." There is no sweet little old lady, or strong virile man, or boy or girl who has lived a clean moral life, who is able to stand in the presence of the demands of the law and the love of God. We are all ungodly to start with.

If you understand that, then you can be justified—because we have a God who has found a way to justify the ungodly. To be justified means to be given the gift of righteousness, the gift of loving acceptance before God. That is where our lives start. As long as we remain self-righteous, we don't have a chance. If we are ungodly, we qualify.

In this book we are looking at only the first eight chapters of Romans. In bite-size sections, we will trace through

Paul's masterful logic, as he sets forth the process God takes
us through. His goal: to make us like his Son—while somehow also making us more completely unique in ourselves.

This process involves our entire person. Paul explains to
us what we have in Christ so that we will be able to actively
participate in his plan for us. We are not being acted upon
by some blind force. Rather, we are being prodded awake to
make us realize the almost incredible potential of our lives,
both now and in eternity.

An Expanded Outline of Romans

I. FROM GUILT TO GLORY—EXPLAINED (chapters 1–8)

   A. *Introduction: The Themes of Romans 1:1–17*

      1. Jesus Christ, our Lord, 1–6
      2. The Saints of God (at Rome and elsewhere), 7–12
      3. The Apostle Paul, 13–15
      4. The Gospel, 16–17

   B. *The Need for the Gospel, 1:18–3:20*

      1. The universal wrath of God, 18–32
      2. The sinfully moral, 2:1–13
      3. The unenlightened pagans, 14–16
      4. The religious moralist, 2:17–3:8 (Jew)
      5. Man's universal condition (total wipeout), 9–20

   C. *The Gift of Righteousness, 3:21–31*

      1. What is God's answer to man's failure? 21
      2. How is it obtained? 22–24
      3. How redemption works, 25a
      4. Why redemption provided, 25b, 26
      5. The results of the gift of righteousness, 27–31

Editor's note: For a more detailed outline consult the appendix at the end of Vol. 2 of *From Guilt to Glory*.

fROM GUILT TO GLORY

1

Introduction to Life

The letter to the Romans is unquestionably the greatest and widest in scope of all of Paul's letters. It is most intense and penetrating in its insight into the understanding of truth; therefore, it is one of the books of the New Testament with which every Christian ought to be thoroughly familiar. If you are not able to think through the Book of Romans without a Bible before you, then I urge you to set that as your goal. Master the Book of Romans—be so well acquainted with it that you can outline it and think of its great themes without referring to your Bible. That requires reading it, studying it, and thinking it through in careful detail.

It is safe to say that Romans is probably the most powerful human document ever written. During this country's Bicentennial celebration the Freedom Train traveled around the nation, bringing to many areas some of the great documents of our American history, such as an original copy of the Constitution and Thomas Jefferson's copy of the Declaration of Independence. We value these great documents of human liberty. In many ways, our freedom rests upon them and we Americans rightly honor and respect them. But even they cannot hold a candle to the impact the Epistle to the Romans has had upon human history.

To this letter we owe the conversions of some of the greatest church leaders of all time. St. Augustine, whose shadow has loomed large over the church since the fourth century, was converted by reading just a few verses of the thirteenth chapter. Later, Martin Luther came to an understanding of faith while studying the writings of Augustine. The sixteenth verse of the very first chapter of the letter spoke volumes to Luther's heart as he thought and meditated on the great phrase, "The righteous shall live by faith." This book's effect on Luther ushered in the Protestant Reformation, the greatest awakening our world has seen since the days of the apostles. John Wesley, listening one day to Luther's preface to his commentary on Romans, found his own heart "strangely warmed" and out of that came the great evangelical awakening of the eighteenth century. John Bunyan, studying Romans in the Bedford jail, was so caught up by the themes of this great letter that he wrote *Pilgrim's Progress*, which has taught many people how a Christian relates to the world in which he lives. In our own day, Karl Barth has been associated with studies in Romans that have shaken the theological world. We may not always agree with everything Barth writes, but one thing is clear: his arguments on the Book of Romans absolutely demolished liberal Christianity three or four decades ago.

Paul's letter to the Romans was written about A.D. 56–58, when the apostle was in Corinth on his third missionary journey. As you read this letter, you can catch glimpses of the conditions in the Greek city of Corinth. Located at the crossroads of trade in the empire, it was one of the most wicked cities in the Roman world. Much of that atmosphere is reflected in this letter to the Romans.

This letter was written only about thirty years after the crucifixion and resurrection of the Lord Jesus. The memory of it was still sharply etched in the minds of Christians all over the Roman Empire. This letter was sent to teach and instruct them, to bring to their remembrance the meaning of these fantastic events that had so startled and amazed men in that first century.

Bull's-Eye

The first seventeen verses of Romans constitute an introduction. In this introduction are the great themes of this epistle, the things that Paul returns to again and again as he boldly puts forth these concepts that have so fantastically altered the lives of men. There is both a literary and a logical order to these themes. The literary order, of course, follows the pattern in which they appear here in the Epistle to the Romans. The logical order is not quite the same, but I am combining the two. The progression forms a kind of target, as shown on page 5. The bull's-eye, the heart of the target, is the theme: Jesus is Lord. We can see this theme in the first seven verses of the introduction.

> Paul, a servant of Christ Jesus, called to be an apostle and set apart for the gospel of God—the gospel he promised beforehand through his prophets in the Holy Scriptures regarding his Son, who as to his human nature was a descendant of David, and who through the Spirit of holiness was declared with power to be the Son of God by his resurrection from the dead: Jesus Christ our Lord. Through him and for his name's sake, we received grace and apostleship to call people from among all the Gentiles to the obedience that comes from faith. And you also are among those who are called to belong to Jesus Christ.
> To all in Rome who are loved by God and called to be saints: Grace and peace to you from God our Father and from the Lord Jesus Christ (Rom. 1:1–7).

At the heart of Paul's argument is this central personage, Jesus Christ, our Lord. The Lordship of Christ is the theme of the Epistle to the Romans, as it is the theme of all Paul's writings and all of the New Testament. Our union with Christ as Lord is the central truth that God wants us to see, as Paul himself wrote in the letter to the Colossians: "Christ in you, the hope of glory" (Col. 1:27). That is the great

salvation truth from which all others flow. Some commentators and Bible teachers identify certain of the emphases
that come from that truth as being the central truth. For
instance, they emphasize justification by faith, or sanctification—that is, solving the problems of sin. But these themes
all stem from the great central theme: union with Christ.
That is why the person of the Lord Jesus is central in all of
the apostle's thinking, just as it is central in God's program
for mankind everywhere. We are not simply followers of a
philosophy, or even of a philosopher, but of a savior, a redeemer, a person—and he must be first in all things.

From this central point, Paul builds a logical progression
of concentric circles, like a target. The *gospel* of our Lord
Jesus Christ is the next theme flowing out from the central
personage of Jesus. Next, since the gospel is brought to us
through the apostle, Paul will speak of himself as the apostle to the Gentiles, through whom the gospel is spread.
Then, the recipients of that gospel are the Roman Christians
to whom this letter was written, as well as ourselves, the
twentieth century recipients of the letter to the Romans.
Then, as the final outthrust of this tremendous movement
which begins with the Lord himself and flows through the
apostle and the Christians, the gospel reaches out to the
nations of the world—Jew and Gentile alike. We will see
this logical order as we go through the introductory paragraph of this letter.

The Promised One

In his introduction, Paul points out that the Lord was
promised long before he came; he came as predicted in the
Old Testament. The gospel "was promised beforehand
through the prophets in the Holy Scriptures regarding his
Son." One of the most important things we can learn about
our faith is that it comes to us through the anticipation and
prediction of centuries of teaching and preaching. We are
familiar with the predictive passages in the Old Testament.
We remember that when Jesus walked with the two men on

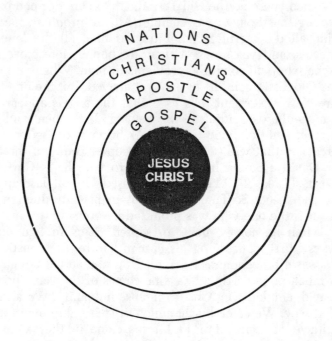

the road to Emmaus, "beginning with Moses and all the
prophets," he taught them the things concerning himself.
Jesus saw himself predicted in the Old Testament. We can
see clearly the great messianic passages in the Old Testament that point unerringly to Jesus.

When you read the Old Testament you are gripped by the
feeling that Someone is coming! All the prophets speak of
him, all the sacrifices point toward him, all the longings,
dreams, and yearnings of men are hoping for someone to
come who will solve the problems of man. When you close
the Old Testament, he has not yet arrived. But the first thing
the New Testament tells us is that the angels appeared to
the shepherds abiding in the fields at Bethlehem and sang
a great song of hope to them: "I bring you good news of
great joy that will be for all the people. Today in the town
of David a Savior has been born to you; he is Christ the
Lord" (Luke 2:10,11). The Promised One at last appears
on the scene. So Paul reminds us in his introduction that
Jesus is the one who was promised beforehand.

When he comes, he is presented to us in two unique
ways: First, concerning his human nature, the apostle says
he was a descendant of David. Now the actual Greek here
is much more earthy; it says he comes of the very sperm of
David, emphasizing Christ's intense humanity. We all came
that way. We came by the union of sperm and ovum in the
miracle of conception, and Jesus came in the same way,
through the sperm of David. Thus, his humanity is empha-
sized and underscored. But secondly, linked with that, is
his deity; "through the Spirit of holiness, [he] was declared
with power to be the Son of God." That phrase, "the Son
of God," unmistakably declares the deity of our Lord. He
was God. Paul emphasizes this several times throughout his
letter. But he also stresses the fact that in the uniqueness of
his personality he combined together all that was human
and all that was divine.

And yet, as we will learn in this letter and in other
passages of Scripture, Christ laid aside the exercise of his
deity—he did not come to act as God. He came to act as a

man filled with God. This is hopeful and helpful to us. If we are called on to act like God we might as well give up right now. We can't make it. But we are called on to be men possessed by God. That is the level on which Christ lived, and on which we too can live. That is the heart of the gospel. God has made it possible for us to live as he lived and to follow his example in that way. Paul will develop these thoughts much more thoroughly in this Epistle.

There were three things, Paul says, that marked the deity of Jesus. First, there was power; he came "by power." This is a reference to the miracles—all the displays of remarkable power that he manifested among men. These miracles were a sign that he was a man of God, a man fully indwelt and possessed by God.

Second, he came by the Spirit of holiness. I have always been concerned about this word "holiness" because people so often misunderstand it. We don't like the word holy. It is something that is bad—good, but bad. We don't like to be called holy ourselves. When we call someone a "holy Joe" we are using a term of disparagement. And yet it is a great word. I think its meaning can be recaptured for us if we will use a similar term that comes from the same root, the word "wholeness." Paul is saying that when Jesus came, he was a whole person. He demonstrated whole humanity—humanity exactly as it was intended to be. We, too, are called to be whole persons. The glory of the good news is that God's goal for us is to make us whole, so that we are capable, able to cope, to walk through the midst of the pressures and the turmoils and the tragedies of this world and handle them as whole persons—holy persons. That wholeness is what Jesus fully demonstrated.

The third great mark of Jesus' deity is the resurrection; his deity was authenticated "by his resurrection from the dead." That is where our faith ultimately rests. We can have confidence that God has told us the truth by the unshakable fact that he raised Jesus from the dead. No one can remove that fact from the annals of history. It happened, and our faith rests on it. Whenever anyone pursues you and tries to

shake your faith, ask them to explain the resurrection. Ask
them what they do with it, because it cannot be explained
away. It is the unshakable fact through which God has
broken into our time, and Paul rests the whole story upon
that great fact. This, too, will be explored further in this
letter.

Now, in the literal order of this letter, the apostle says
much about the Roman Christians. And what he says about
them also applies to us. In verses 6 and 7 he says:

> And you also are among those who are called to belong to
> Jesus Christ. To all in Rome who are loved by God and called
> to be saints: Grace and peace to you from God our Father
> and from the Lord Jesus Christ.

First, Paul says the Roman Christians, the saints, are
"called." We are not self-made saints, we are not man-made
saints; we are "called saints." God called us. Every one of
us can tell a different story of how it happened—how God's
voice was heard, how we felt the drawing and pulling of
God's Spirit in our life. We were called that way. This is
true of every Christian, and it reveals a remarkable thing:
God sought us! We really did not seek him—we thought we
did, but he sought us. That is why Jesus said to his disciples,
"All that the Father gives me *will come to me*, and who-
ever comes to me I will never drive away" (John 6:37, italics
mine). And thus we came, called of God, sought of God.

The remarkable thing about that calling is underscored
here by these words of Paul's: "We are loved by God." Paul
always starts his letters on the basis of God's love for us. He
may have to scold the saints he is writing to, he may have
to correct them, he may have to speak sharply to some of
them; but he always starts out by reminding them that they
are loved by God. Paul understands that this is the fundamental relationship we have with God. He loves us. We
ought to remind ourselves of that fact every day, as I am
sure these Roman Christians did.

The grace and peace God gives to his saints is proof of
his love for them. The word "grace" stands for all the em-

powerment and enrichment that God can give—all that he daily pours into human life. We do not earn grace, but it is given to us in view of our daily needs. All those moments when strength and courage are infused into our lives, when we are discouraged and God's word comforts and heals us— that is God's grace. And the result is peace, rest! Grace and peace are our inheritance as Christians. These two things ought to characterize Christians everywhere, all the time, so that we live differently before the world.

Startling Faith

Paul points out a second characteristic about the Roman Christians in verse 8:

First, I thank my God through Jesus Christ for all of you, be-cause your faith is being reported all over the world.

Notice: it was the faith of the Roman Christians that was being talked about—not the number of buses they operated or the size or cost of the organ, or the size or cost of the building in which they met. It was the faith of these Christians that startled the Roman world. These were vital Christians. Paul gives us a clue as to why that was true in the next verses:

God, whom I serve with my whole heart in preaching the gospel of his Son, is my witness how constantly I remember you in my prayers at all times; and I pray that now at last by God's will the way may be opened for me to come to you (vv. 9,10).

Their faith was reported all over the world because the apostle and other Christians were praying for them. Paul had never been to Rome; he had never met these people. He had met some of them elsewhere, but he had never known many of them. But he prayed for them constantly! "How constantly I remember you in my prayers at all times." That is why this church flourished. If there is one thing we need more than anything else today, it is to re-

cover again this sense of concern and prayer for one another. I think it would make all the difference in the world
if we began to uphold each other in prayer regularly.

The third characteristic that Paul points out about the
Roman saints is this: they were strengthened by gifts.

> I long to see you so that I may impart to you some spiritual
> gift to make you strong—that is, that you and I may be
> mutually encouraged by each other's faith (vv. 11,12).

The exercise of spiritual gifts in its midst is what makes a
congregation strong. When Paul says, "I want to impart to
you some spiritual gift," he does not mean that he has all
the gifts in a bag which he carries around like an ecclesi-
astical Santa Claus, doling them out to people. "Impart"
really means "share with you." The gift is not something
Paul gives to them; only the Holy Spirit can give spiritual
gifts. Paul wants to share with them the gifts God has given
him. He wants to minister to them, as they are expected to
minister to him with the spiritual gifts they have; thus they
will be mutually strengthened by one another's faith. That
is how God wants a church to function—the saints minister-
ing to each other, building up one another by their faith
and sharing, and exercising the gifts God has given them.

Set Apart

Going back to the logical outline of this epistle, remember that Jesus as Lord is at the center, followed by the gospel. Then comes Paul himself as the great apostle to the
Gentiles. It is through the apostle that the Christians are
being reached. What does Paul say about himself as an
apostle? In verse 1, he says he is called and set apart as an
apostle. "Called" is used as an adjective here. Paul is not
called to be an apostle—he is a called apostle. God did the
calling. This happened, Paul tells us in Galatians, before he
was born. This is the wonder of the God we serve. He does
not have to wait until we appear in human history. He
called us long before we were even conceived, long before

our family tree ever began to take shape. Then he sets us apart. That is the process of history, and that is what happened to Paul. All the events of Paul's young life, including his training under Gamaliel and his ascendancy among the Pharisees, even his antipathy toward the gospel, all this was part of God's process of setting him apart to be an apostle. And when the time came, God pulled the trap door and Paul fell through. He was caught. That is what happens to us all; that is the way God works in our lives.

What is an apostle? Paul tells us in verse 5: "Through him and for his name's sake, we received grace and apostleship to call people from among all the Gentiles to the obedience that comes from faith," or more literally, "the obedience of faith." An apostle is a man sent to call people out. As Paul himself tells us in verse 14, "I am obligated both to Greeks and non-Greeks, both to the wise and the foolish." Paul had a deep sense of an imperative to tell people the gospel because he knew they desperately needed it. If you were the sole possessor of a remedy for cancer, would you be quiet about it, or would you feel an imperative to share the secret with others? That is what Paul says urged him on —this constant consciousness that he had the secret of release which people desperately needed.

As an apostle, he journeyed out to carry that secret to them. He tells us how he does this in verse 9: "God, whom I serve with my whole heart in preaching the gospel of his Son. . . ." Here is a wholehearted man, single-minded, with his spirit fully engaged in this work. He tells us the final step in the process in verse 15: "That is why I am so eager to preach the gospel also to you who are at Rome." If Paul is going to reach the nations, why does he preach the gospel to the Christians at Rome? It is by means of the Christians that the nations are to hear. It will be the changes God works in the lives of his people that cause others to begin to take note. That is how true evangelism occurs. Paul says, "That is why I want to preach the gospel to you at Rome." By the gospel, Paul does not mean simply explaining how to become a Christian, as we often think. That is not

what Paul means here, because these Romans were already
Christians. Rather, the gospel includes all the great facts
about humanity and about God that God wants to impart to
us and that will enable us to be whole persons.

That brings us to the message itself—the gospel which the
apostle will preach to the Christians, and through them
reach all the nations. This is what Paul says of the gospel in
verses 16 and 17.

> I am not ashamed of the gospel, because it is the power of
> God for the salvation of everyone who believes: first for the
> Jew, then for the Gentile. For in the gospel a righteousness
> from God is revealed, a righteousness that is by faith from
> first to last, just as it is written: "The righteous will live by
> faith."

This quotation from Habakkuk ("the righteous shall live by
faith") is the scripture that gripped Martin Luther's heart.
Paul says this is the great fact he is expounding in the gospel. He is not ashamed of it, he says, which is a way of saying he is proud of it. He can't wait to get to Rome that he
might fully declare it.

Powerless Romans

Paul especially is not ashamed of the gospel in Rome because the Romans appreciated power, just as Americans do,
and the gospel is "the power of God." The Romans prided
themselves on their power. Their military power could conquer the nations standing in their path. They had tremendous power in road-building, and they had some of the
greatest law-makers of history. They also had the power to
write literature and create art. But Paul knew that the
Romans were powerless when it came to changing hearts.
They were powerless to eliminate slavery; half of the popu-
lation of the Roman Empire were slaves. They were
powerless to change the stubborn, hostile, hateful hearts
of men and eliminate violence. The Roman Empire was
full of violence and corruption, and the suicide rate was

extremely high. The Romans could do nothing about these problems. Paul says that is why he is so proud of the gospel: it is the power of God to do those very things that men cannot do. We never need to apologize for the gospel. It is absolutely without rival.

Not long ago I received a letter from Dr. Richard Halverson, pastor of the Fourth Presbyterian Church in Washington, D.C. He was writing to tell me of the book, *Born Again,* by Charles Colson, one of the men who went to prison in the Watergate scandal. This book is the story of the conversion of Charles Colson—how he became a Christian. Halverson said the story is so remarkable that it can only be compared with the conversion of the apostle Paul. It is so drastic and so different that even today people struggle with accepting and believing it. But he said there is no question but that this man is a changed person. Now what got hold of Colson's heart and changed him like that? The gospel of the blessed God—the good news about Jesus Christ—it is the power of God to salvation.

Second, Paul is not ashamed of the gospel because it reveals a righteousness from God. Righteousness is an old word that we don't understand very well. I would like to substitute "worth": a place of acceptance, or worth before God is given to us in the gospel. We cannot earn it and we certainly do not deserve it, but it is given. God really accepts us because of the gospel, because of the good news of the work of Jesus Christ on our behalf. Therefore, it is something that you, or I, or anyone else can have. It is complete, perfect, needing nothing from us to supplement it.

The last thing Paul says is that this righteousness is received by faith. We can never earn it, but we can take it anytime we need it, and that is good news. Our worth before God is not something we receive once, by faith, at the beginning of our Christian lives. It is something we remind ourselves of every time we feel depressed, despairing, discouraged, or defeated. God has loved us, restored us, and we have perfect value in his sight. He already accepts us

and loves us as much as he possibly can; nothing more can
be added to it. That is the righteousness revealed in the
gospel, by faith, to all who believe, no matter what his
background or training may be.

These are the great themes of Romans. Centering upon
the Lord, the gospel Paul preaches is the power of God to
release men from their vicious cycle of sin and to establish
them as whole people, filled by God and able to appropriate
by faith their true worth before God. I hope these themes
will have their effect upon our hearts as they did upon the
hearts of many in the first century church.

2

The Tragic Sense of Life

Paul's introduction to Romans concludes with the great statement, "I am not ashamed of the gospel, because it is the power of God for the salvation of everyone who believes; first for the Jew, then for the Gentile. For in the gospel a righteousness from God is revealed, a righteousness that is by faith from first to last" (Rom. 1:16,17). By that tremendous declaration, Paul sets in focus for us the great theme of this letter: the power of God to heal the hurts of men and to give us liberty and freedom from the bondage of evil in our lives.

Beginning with verse 18, however, a more somber note is sounded. This section introduces the most extensive, careful, and logical analysis of the human dilemma that has ever been found. It extends from chapter 1, verse 18, through chapter 3, verse 20, and is introduced thus:

> The wrath of God is being revealed from heaven against all the godlessness and wickedness of men who suppress the truth by their wickedness, since what may be known about God is plain to them, because God has made it plain to them. For since the creation of the world God's invisible qualities—his eternal power and divine nature—have been clearly seen, being understood from what has been made, so that men are without excuse (Rom. 1:18–20).

In the preceding verses, Paul has already spoken of the
Son of God—the key and the heart of the gospel. He declared the power of God that is released among men as they
believe the gospel; he declared the righteousness of God
which is granted to us as a gift which we cannot earn or
ever deserve, but which is ours, nevertheless, by faith. But
now Paul speaks of the wrath of God. It is the first negative
note sounded in this letter, yet it is very necessary because
it introduces this passage that tells us why we need the gospel of God. We need it precisely because men everywhere
are suffering from the wrath of God.

Judgment and Lightning

What do you think of when you hear this phrase, "the
wrath of God"? Most people think of the wrath of God as
something yet to come, something that follows death—the
judgment of God. It is true that hell and all that may follow
are an expression of the wrath of God. But that is not what
it means at this point. Others think of the wrath of God as
thunder, lightning, and judgment, fire and brimstone, and
the sudden destruction and catastrophes that come upon
obviously guilty sinners. Indeed these are all manifestations
of the wrath of God. But actually, the wrath of God is not
only something yet to come; it is present now. As the text
says, it is "being revealed from heaven"—that is, it is going
on right now. When something is "revealed from heaven,"
it does not pour down from the skies upon us. That phrase
means that it is everywhere present; it is coming from invisible forces at work in our lives. Therefore, it is absolutely
inescapable; everyone is confronted with and suffers from
the wrath of God—without exception. His wrath is everywhere present, and it is being manifested by the invisible
resistance of God to the evil of men.

In 1962, I visited Mexico City with a group of businessmen, and we were invited to hold witnessing sessions in
homes with some of the businessmen and wealthy leaders
of Mexico. To properly orient us to the culture of Mexico,

we had a session in a downtown hotel in Mexico City. Dr. Baenz-Camargo, a local Christian and a very wise university professor, instructed us in the uniqueness of Mexican culture. In a most beautiful and elegant way, he captured the heart of Mexican life and set it before us. He said there were five traits of Mexican society that he wanted us to understand. The first thing about Mexican people is that they have a sense of the dramatic; they love eloquence and oratory. With that comes a love of beauty and pageantry. Thirdly, and stemming from these first two characteristics, is a deeply embedded sense of inferiority—the Mexicans feel they are a small nation and an inferior people, and are desperately trying to catch up with the rest of the world. That sense of inferiority, of course, produces the fourth mark of Mexican society, a resistance to authority. Rebelliousness and revolution are close to the surface in Mexico. All these traits find their ultimate expression in a kind of fatalism, which is the fifth characteristic; a strong belief in the role of chance and a lack of a sense of responsibility.

As Dr. Baenz-Camargo developed the first characteristic for us, the awareness of the dramatic in life, he used the phrase, "the tragic sense of life." Mexicans are deeply aware of the tragic aspects of life. I have not forgotten that phrase because I find that it applies not only to Mexican people, but to people everywhere. We are continually confronted with this tragic sense of life. It is the wrath of God which Paul is talking about.

Why is it that tragedy is so close to the surface? Even in our moments of joy and gladness we experience it. We have all felt this bittersweet character of life, when, in the midst of the warmth and joy of the home circle there comes an underlying sense of fear, of the probability of the whole thing suddenly being turned into tragedy and sorrow. Why is it that at Christmas time, for instance, the season of the year when men are traditionally more glad and joyful, more mellow, perhaps, than at any other time of the year, that the suicide rate mounts alarmingly? Anyone who has experienced it knows that the loneliness which can be borne

throughout the year can be deeply etched in bitter symbols
upon our hearts during the Christmas season. Sorrow and
grief seem to be more foreboding then than at any other
time. Why is that? It is because of the wrath of God. God's
resistance against human evil is creating a sense of tragedy
and darkness that we must all live with. In Psalm 90, Moses
expresses this perfectly:

> For all our days pass away under thy wrath,
>   our years come to an end like a sigh.
> The years of our life are threescore and ten,
>   or even by reason of strength fourscore;
> yet their span is but toil and trouble;
>   they are soon gone, and we fly away (Ps. 90:9,10 RSV).

The shortness of life, the brevity of it, the sorrow of it, the
tragedy of it—this is all part of what Paul captures in
the phrase "the wrath of God . . . being revealed from
heaven." No one escapes God's wrath; it is revealed, and we
have to face it.

The rest of verse 18 reveals the cause of this wrath. The
apostle explains: it is "the godlessness and wickedness of
men who suppress the truth by their wickedness" that
draws forth God's wrath. The tragic aspect of life is caused
by the attitudes and subsequent actions of men; first godlessness and then wickedness. The order is never reversed.
It is the godless attitude that produces the wicked actions,
and that is why the wrath of God is being revealed constantly from heaven against man.

The Secular Attitude

What is godlessness? It is not necessarily atheism, the belief that God does not exist. Godlessness is *acting* as though
he doesn't exist, disregarding God. That attitude is widespread in our society today; it is what we call the "secular"
attitude. It does not necessarily deny that there is a God,
but it never takes any account of him; it doesn't expect him
to be active. It is that attitude of godlessness of which the
apostle speaks here.

As a result of godlessness, there is unrighteousness or wickedness, selfish and hurtful acts of men toward one another. Why do we act selfishly? Why do we hurt each other? Because we disregard God. That is Paul's analysis, and by means of these hurtful and selfish acts, the truth is suppressed. That is just the problem! The picture is that of a world in which truth from God is breaking out all around, but men are busy covering it up, hiding it, suppressing it, keeping it from being prominent and dominant in their thinking. Against that attitude of hiding truth, suppressing the truth, the wrath of God burns within the human family. The reason why life has turned tragic in so many cases is that the world is deprived of the truth necessary for life and liberty and freedom and godliness. It is being hidden and suppressed by men.

Verses 19 and 20 set before us the nature of the truth that is suppressed:

> . . . since what may be known about God is plain to them, because God has made it plain to them. For since the creation of the world God's invisible qualities—his eternal power and divine nature—have been clearly seen, being understood from what has been made, so that men are without excuse.

The truth that men labor to suppress is the greatness of God, that he is a God of eternal power and majesty. In Job 9, this very truth which the world hides is eloquently expounded:

> Then Job answered: "Truly I know that it is so: But how can a man be just before God? If one wished to contend with him, one could not answer him once in a thousand times. He is wise in heart, and mighty in strength—who has hardened himself against him, and succeeded?—he who removes mountains, and they know it not, when he overturns them in his anger; who shakes the earth out of its place, and its pillars tremble; who commands the sun, and it does not rise; who seals up the stars; who alone stretched out the heavens, and trampled the waves of the sea; who made the Bear and Orion, the Pleiades and the chambers of the south; who does great things beyond understanding, and marvelous things without number. Lo, he

passes by me, and I see him not; he moves on, but I do not
perceive him. Behold, he snatches away; who can hinder him?
Who will say to him, 'What doest thou?'" (Job 9:1–12 RSV).

There is an evident conspiracy among men not to mention
God. Don't talk about him; don't act as though God has
anything to do with our common affairs in life. Or, admit
that there is a God if you want to, but don't expect him to
interfere or to do anything with us. Do not, above all else,
mention his name in a serious way. Isn't that strange? An
unknown poet has put it this way in a little poem entitled
"The Humanist."

> He exists because he was created.
> He's here because he was placed here.
> He's well and comfortable because divine power keeps him so.
> He dines at God's table.
> He's sheltered by the roof that God gave him.
> He's clothed by God's bounty.
> He lives by breathing God's air which keeps him strong and
>   vocal to go about persuading people that whether God is
>   or not, only man matters.

There are times when men cannot evade the fact of God;
but when those times come, when they just have to speak
of God, people resort to euphemism. They don't use the
name of God; they call him something else. They may call
him "nature." "Nature" is responsible for the way we are.
Well this, of course, is because nature *is* what we are; nature
is the sum total of all the phenomena of the natural world.
To say that the sum total of the phenomena of the natural
world accomplishes what is the phenomena of the natural
world is nonsense. Yet everywhere this is the way men talk.
Sometimes men call God fate, or karma, or destiny. That is
simply a way to avoid recognizing that God is at work in
human affairs.

Yet, I think it is one of the ironies of life that God, who
sits above the heavens, has arranged it so that men can't
even rip off a round oath without mentioning his name. You
never hear people saying, "By nature, I'm going to do this."

You never hear them say, "Fate damn you!" In order to be emphatic, men must use the name of God. Though they will not acknowledge him in other ways, God sees to it that they recognize his presence when they swear.

Revelation in the Stars

How has God made truth plain? The Scripture says that God has revealed himself to man. Truth is not a vague, invisible, difficult thing to comprehend; it is clearly seen. God himself has insured that. How? The Scriptures say, "It is seen in that which is made," that is, creation. From the creation of the world it is visible; that is, it has been always and everywhere present. There is no one who is left out—all can read this revelation of God if they want to do so.

One night my daughter Laurie and I were walking at Forest Home in the mountains of Southern California. It was one of those beautiful evenings when the stars were out in all their glory—we were above the smog. We walked through the darkness and looked up at the stars and felt the sense of awe that comes upon the human spirit on occasions like that. I pointed out the Milky Way and explained to her that it was part of the galaxy to which our world belongs. There were millions of galaxies like that whirling on in their determined courses—never late, always on time, strange and almost unexplorable by man, I told her. I pointed out the Big Dipper, the North Star, the Pleiades, and we talked about the universe. Then, in a joking way, I said to her, "But remember dear, all this happened just by chance; all these things came together by accident." And she began to laugh. How ridiculous that in all this imposing display of beauty and light and order anyone should ever say it all happened by chance! Laurie sensed the nonsense of that claim. How can we say that a watch is built only by intelligence and wisdom and skill—but hearts beat and babies grow and roses smell simply by chance? It is ridiculous.

This argument from design and order has never been answered. Those who disregard God cannot explain it because truth about God is breaking out everywhere around us. Elizabeth Barret Browning wrote,

> Earth's crammed with heaven,
>   and every common bush aflame with God.
> But only those who see take off their shoes;
>   the rest sit round it and pluck blackberries.

Thus, says the Scripture, men are without excuse. No one who really wants to find God need miss him. One of the great verses that confronts the problem of what happens to those who never hear the gospel is Hebrews 11:6. It says, "And without faith it is impossible to please God, because anyone who comes to him must believe that he exists and that he rewards those who earnestly seek him." Just two things are necessary. First, he must believe that God is there. Everything in his life is telling him that. Everything about himself is yelling at him, shrieking at him, that God has planned all these things. The easiest thing in the universe to believe is that God is there. You must work hard at convincing yourself that he's not there, and it seems only the very intelligent are able to do it. The rest of us, who simply see facts and believe them, will readily accept the fact that God is there.

Those who never hear the gospel must first believe God is. Then they must diligently seek him. If men do not find God, it is because they do not seek him. The Scriptures promise us that if we seek after him he will give further light on himself, and that light will eventually lead to the knowledge of Jesus Christ; for without the Son, no man can come to the Father. There is no other name under heaven given among men whereby we must be saved but the name of Jesus. Knowledge about Jesus starts with where you are and the revelation that is in nature and in yourself about the majesty and the power and greatness of God.

To Suppress the Truth

In verses 21 through 23, the apostle tells us in detail how men suppress the truth about God.

For although they knew God, they neither glorified him as God nor gave thanks to him, but their thinking became futile and their foolish hearts were darkened. Although they claimed to be wise, they became fools and exchanged the glory of the immortal God for images made to look like mortal man and birds and animals and reptiles.

Paul tells us in detail how men suppress the truth about God. There are three steps traced for us here, with the effects they have upon the race. First, men neither glorify God nor give thanks to him. In other words, they ignore him. There is that obvious conspiracy of silence about God. That is why we are not allowed to sing carols in our public schools at Christmas time; that is why there is great resistance against having the Bible read on almost any public occasion today. No one wants to admit that there is a God. They do not glorify him as God, neither do they give him thanks.

The effects of this are immediate. Paul says two things are immediately created when this attitude prevails. The people's thinking becomes futile, and their hearts become darkened. Futile thinking means that clever ideas and procedures and programs will fall apart and come to nothing. In my own lifetime I have lived through the New Deal, the Fair Deal, the New Society, Peace with Honor, and the Great Recovery. All of them have failed dismally! They all started with brilliant promises, glowing words of hope and expectation; and every one of them came to the same futile end.

When hearts are darkened, human needs which ought to evoke emotions of pity and response are ignored. People lose compassion and awareness of the struggles and needs of others. Perhaps you have seen accounts in the newspaper of people in desperate need, calling out for help, while others walk right by and ignore them because they don't want to get involved. That is a sign of a darkened heart, and it is the result of ignoring God.

The first device men employ to suppress the truth, then, is to ignore God. The second device they use is to claim to be wise. In other words, they imitate God. They claim to know and to be able to know everything and to run anything. The result of that is put in one brief, blunt, pungent word: they become *fools!* Remember the old story of the sorcerer's apprentice who, picking up the magician's wand, loosens powers he doesn't know how to handle? Finally, he cowers in terror at the tremendous forces he has unleashed. Just read the intellectual magazines of our day and see how clever the secular writers are. They are masters at taking some simple discovery and making it sound impressive and profound, as though it were on a parallel with the creation of the universe as recorded by Moses. They claim to be wise, but they become fools.

Of Men and Snakes

The third device men employ to suppress the truth is that they exchange the glory of the immortal God for images made like mortal man. Thus men insult God. They exchange the glory of the undying God for images made like dying men, and birds, and animals, and reptiles. Notice the descending order. When idolatry begins, it begins first with men making images of men. The world is filled with statues, most of them reflecting the images of the ancient Greek and Roman world. These, of course, are merely symbols of ideas that men worship, and we still have such images today. But these images invalidate God; they debase him by substituting something for God that makes God seem to be less than what he is. That is what idolatry always does. It is a destructive force in human affairs. Idolatry is symbolized first with men, then birds (which are at least heavenly), then animals, and finally it winds up with reptiles. Man is at one end and a snake is at the other.

Do you think people don't worship images and bow down before idols now? What are movie stars and football heroes? They are dying men and women who are idolized and worshipped in our day. And I do not believe it is any accident that we tend to name our cars after animals. We once named them after men: Lincoln, Ford, Chrysler, and

Dodge. But now we are naming them after animals: Impala, Cougar, Mustang, Pinto, Jaguar, Rabbit, Panther, and there's even a Greyhound bus! It is God's ironic way of forcing men to reveal what is going on inside. We already have a car called the Cobra. And perhaps we will soon be naming our cars for the python, viper, and maybe, for the slower models, the crocodile!

These are our gods, aren't they? We worship rockets, planes, guns, bombs, tanks. We worship power, like military power; or forces like sex, ambition, and greed; or concepts like comfort, beauty, youth, adventure, life. We have exchanged the glory of the undying God in all his majesty and greatness for images. What are movies but images? What is television but images of mortal men, birds, animals, and reptiles?

The effect of idolatry upon a society is profound and terrible to contemplate. Paul analyzes our society for us as he analyzed the society of the first century, and we will find it exactly the same. We are right where they were. We will see what happens in a society when men everywhere begin to worship men and women, birds, animals, reptiles, and the ideas that these all represent.

The amazing thing in this account is that this description of the wrath of God is wholly and fully met by the righteousness of God. God's righteousness wipes out his wrath. Wouldn't you think, therefore, that men everywhere would be eager to discover this marvelous gift of the righteousness of God? That is what heals our hurts and corrects our errors and gives a sense of peace and joy and forgiveness to the heart. The wrath of God creates the hurts of life; all the pain and heartache and darkness, the death, the depression, the despair—all come from the wrath of God. They are the products of ignoring God, trying to imitate God, and invalidating God in our lives. Wouldn't you think that men everywhere would long to hear the good news of how to escape God's wrath? Yet the wonder of our times, and the revelation of the twisted, demoralized, distorted world in which we live, is that we cling to our hurts and refuse the healing of God.

3

The Deepening Darkness

It is evident to anyone reading Romans 1 that the moral climate of today is the same as the moral climate of the first century about which Paul wrote. That gives rise to the question, "Just how much progress have we made in twenty centuries of human existence?" The apostle says there were two characteristics of the civilization he lived in, and those characteristics also describe our society today. The first characteristic is godlessness; the second is wickedness. Godlessness is a disrespect of God, and this results in wickedness—injury and hurt done to other human beings. The fundamental thesis upon which this epistle to the Romans is built is that in every generation there is godlessness, which results in wickedness.

The apostle has traced for us how this godlessness came about. He begins with the self-disclosure of God in nature; God has spoken to this world and has shown himself in the natural scene. Nature includes mankind itself, for we are also part of nature. God has made himself visible in every age and place. The truth about God pours out toward us from every direction, if only we have eyes to see. This truth, the apostle says, has been met with an unspoken agreement among men to suppress it.

Paul goes on to explain that mankind follows a threefold

process in suppressing the truth. First, he ignores God. He does not glorify him or give thanks to him. The second step is that men imitate God, claiming that they are able to handle all the problems of life and that they understand all that has happened in human affairs. You may have seen the rather remarkable presentation by Jacob Bronowski and the Public Broadcasting System, called "The Ascent of Man." Here is a very clear example of man's attempt to trace all that has happened to mankind without a single reference to God. The third process by which man suppresses truth is to choose substitute gods to make God appear to be much less than he really is. By these means, men suppress the truth of God and have become wicked.

When Men Lose God

In verses 24 through 32 of Romans 1, the apostle traces the effect of this godlessness in human society—the wickedness which inevitably follows. When men lose God, they always lose themselves. They do not understand what is happening in human affairs and are not able to diagnose the sicknesses and problems that break out in society because they have lost God. In his book, *The Great Divorce*, C. S. Lewis says hell is made up of people who live at an infinite distance from each other. That alienation is the result of the loss of God in their lives.

Wickedness at Work

This wickedness at work among human beings also follows a three-step process which is identified for us in this passage by the thrice-repeated phrase, "God gave them over." This phrase identifies what is going on in our culture. The first reference is in verse 24:

> Therefore God gave them over in the sinful desires of their hearts to sexual impurity for the degrading of their bodies with one another (Rom. 1:24).

The first mark of wickedness in a godless society is widespread sexual immorality—the degrading, or the dishonoring, of the body. Note that the sentence begins with the

word "Therefore." This immorality is a result of the idolatry
into which men fall. Idolatry is common in our day. We do
not worship idols and images so much anymore, but concepts and ideas are idolized and deified as much as any of
the idols of the ancient world. The result of idolatry is widespread sexual immorality.

Many think this account describes God giving up on people because of the evil things men do. They think God
washes his hands of them because they are so filthy. That
certainly is not what this account says. But because men run
after other gods and refuse the testimony of their own
hearts and the world of nature around them, because they
run after other gods and do not glorify or thank the true
God, God removes his restraints from society so that what is
done in secret is allowed to break out into openness and
acceptability. That is the mark of the wrath of God at work.
The first sign of wickedness in a civilization is that sexual
immorality, which is always present in human life, becomes
widely accepted.

This means that God allows men to experience the full effects of their attempts to satisfy their hungers, cravings, and
desires apart from him. He allows us to discover that we do
not have the answer. God removes the societal restraints
to let these things come to the surface. By that means, he
forces us to experience the full effect of what we do. God
forces us to harvest the crop we insist on sowing. We like
to sow our wild oats; but when they begin to sprout and the
results begin to appear, we want to abandon our field and
run to another one, and just keep sowing our wild oats. But
God says you cannot do that. You are going to have to live
with the results. That is what Paul calls, "the wrath of God
at work among us."

The Supreme Vice?

You may ask, "Why is it that sex always seems to be
singled out as the sign of God's judgment? Why is sexual
immorality the first sign of a disintegrating civilization?"

There is a good reason. Many Christians have wrongly concluded that sexual sins are the worst kinds of sin. But that is not true. Sexual sins are not the worst kind of sins. C. S. Lewis has caught this fact very accurately. In his book, *Mere Christianity*, he says,

> If anyone thinks that Christians regard unchastity as the supreme vice, he is quite wrong. The sins of the flesh are bad, but they are the least bad of all sins. All the worst pleasures are purely spiritual. The pleasure of putting other people in the wrong, of bossing and patronizing and spoiling sport, and backbiting: the pleasures of power, of hatred. For there are two things inside me competing with the human self which I must try to become: they are the animal self, and the diabolical self; and the diabolical self is the worst of the two. That is why a cold, self-righteous prig, who goes regularly to church, may be far nearer to hell than a prostitute. But of course, it's better to be neither.*

Those words are true, and this passage in Romans bears it out. Wickedness begins with sexual impurity and then proceeds to sexual perversion. But the final result, in the climax of the chapter, is not sexual sins; it is the sins of the spirit. Widespread animosity and heartlessness—these are the worst sins.

There is good reason, however, why God allows perverted sexual practices to become publicly acceptable. He allows it to show us what is going on in our spiritual lives. This highlights the fact that sex is linked with worship. Any serious reading of the Scriptures will make this crystal clear. Sex is man's longing after worship. It is a desire to possess another body and to be possessed by another. It is a deep–seated craving inherent in every human being. We have all heard the statement, "Girls give sex in order to get love; boys give love in order to get sex." This is true, superficially. But what both are really after is not sex at all; they are after worship. They really want to worship and to be worshiped. They really want a sense of total fulfillment, a

* C. S. Lewis, *Mere Christianity* (New York: Macmillan, 1964), pp. 94, 95.

oneness, an identity. That is what they think they are getting when they indulge in illicit sex.

The Scriptures tell us that only God can give that fulfillment. Only God can satisfy that deep sense of longing for
complete identity and unity with another person. That is
what we call worship. When we worship, we are longing to
be possessed of God, and to possess him fully. That is why
the highest description of the relationship possible to a believer is found in the words of Jesus in John 15, "You in me,
and I in you." When men think that they are going to find
that fulfillment in sex, God, in effect, says to them, "Look, it
won't work. But you won't believe that until you try it out."
So he removes the restraints and allows immoral sexual
practices to become widely accepted, understanding that
men indulging in these things will finally find themselves
just as dissatisfied, empty, and hopeless as they were when
they started. Thus they will learn that God is trying to teach
them that sex is not the way by which men find fulfillment.
This is true even in marriage. Men find complete fulfillment
only in a relationship to God.

Shameful Lusts

This brings us to the second mark of a godless and wicked
society, found in verses 25–27:

> They exchanged the truth of God for a lie, and worshiped and
> served created things rather than the Creator—who is forever
> praised, Amen. Because of this, God gave them over to shame-
> ful lusts. Even their women exchanged natural relations for
> unnatural ones. In the same way the men also abandoned
> natural relations with women and were inflamed with lust for
> one another. Men committed indecent acts with other men,
> and received in themselves the due penalty for their perver-
> sion.

Homosexuality is the second mark of a godless and wicked
society. In the first step of this process, bodies were dis-
honored. In this second step, Paul speaks of shameful lusts
arising from inside, desires that are part of the soul of man.

The apostle describes the growth of widespread psychological confusion. Notice the irony of this. This is God's silent way of forcing men to demonstrate their sin so they can see what is going on in their lives. Paul says because they have exchanged truth for a lie and exchanged the Creator for created things, God allows them to exchange natural functions for unnatural functions—to use a man for a woman, and a woman as a man.

The restraints are removed, so homosexuality becomes widely accepted in society. In the first century world in which Paul lived and wrote, homosexuality was a common practice. All the great philosophers extolled it and practiced it, for the most part. Men like Socrates and other great thinkers of Greece were homosexuals. Of the first fifteen Roman emperors, fourteen were homosexuals, and some gave themselves blatantly and openly to this vice. It was common in the Roman world, as it is becoming common in our own day. Once again, the restraints are being removed, and these things are thrusting themselves into public view.

The truly awful thing about the rise of homosexuality today is that homosexuals are allowed to believe the lie that theirs is a biological condition which they cannot help, but to which they should adjust. Even churches are falling into this trap and consenting to this deceit. In a recent newspaper article reporting the inclusion of a homosexual church into the local council of churches, the arguments reported in the local papers were unbelievable. Pastors stood up and said they could not make a judgment as to whether homosexuality was good or evil. Yet I was also encouraged by a paper which was sent to me by a Christian who is an ex-homosexual. The paper was written by a group of Christians who were homosexuals, but who have been delivered by the grace and the gospel of the Lord Jesus, by the power of Christ in their lives. To help those still enmeshed in this vice, they are publishing a paper that makes a forthright plea to those trapped in homosexuality not to believe the lie so widely circulated that this is a biological condition and they cannot help themselves. This lie is what holds them in

a fatal grip. As long as homosexuals believe it, there *is* no
help for them. But if they understand that homosexuality is
a sin like other sins, that it can be forgiven and they can be
delivered and freed from this sin by the power and grace of
Jesus Christ, then there is tremendous hope in the midst of
their darkness.

Paul speaks of a "due penalty" for this perversion. Anyone
who has spent any time with those involved in this un-
fortunate condition knows what this penalty is. It is a loss
of one's sense of identity, an uncertainty as to one's role
and place in life. We see this manifested in considerable
degree in the Women's Liberation Movement, as well as in
dress styles and the emphasis on unisex in education. This
sexual confusion that abounds on every side is an attempt to
mar and defeat God's precise delineation in making us male
and female.

Desire to Exploit

The third and final mark of a godless and wicked culture
is given in verses 28–32.

> Furthermore, since they did not think it worthwhile to retain
> the knowledge of God, he gave them over to a depraved mind,
> to do what ought not to be done. They have become filled
> with every kind of wickedness, evil, greed and depravity.
> They are full of envy, murder, strife, deceit and malice. They
> are gossips, slanderers, God–haters, insolent, arrogant and
> boastful; they invent ways of doing evil; they disobey parents;
> they are senseless, faithless, heartless, ruthless.

This is a terrible list of sins, but it is the mark of a civilization nearing collapse—this growing spirit of contemptuous
and arrogant disregard for other human beings. In one
word, this describes a desire to *exploit* other people. Godlessness eventually brings us to the place where these things
will be evident in society. The term, "depraved mind,"
literally means an unacceptable mind, a mind that cannot
be lived with, that simply will not fit into any kind of civilization or culture or society. A depraved mind destroys,
rends, and fragments everything it touches. It is an unac-

ceptable mind, and its public hostility is marked by increasing cruelty and violence. Probably the most vivid demonstration and documentation of this in our day is given in Aleksandr Solzhenitsyn's book, *The Gulag Archipelago,* in which you find an entire culture characterized by this terrible, senseless cruelty. But we in the Western world are not escaping, either. Every day our newspapers report the skyrocketing rise of senseless vandalism, of vicious and unprovoked attack upon innocent and often helpless people. The rise in child abuse is a symptom of this in our society. It culminates, as Paul makes very clear in verse 32, in an attitude of callous disregard:

> Although they know God's righteous decree that those who do such things deserve death, they not only continue to do these very things, but also approve those who practice them.

Knowing that harm is coming from their wickedness, nevertheless they attempt to spread it more widely. They invade the field of education; they dominate the media; they seek legal status for their wickedness and defy all attempts at control. As you can well recognize, this is what is going on today. Thus the apostle Paul traces the deepening darkness of his own day—and it is spreading in our day as well.

But though this is an honest record, it is also clear that God does not turn his back on man. This account is not a record of what God despises, so that he turns aside with contempt. Man is never here as an object of contempt or as a worm. Rather, God's concern underscores this whole passage. He is at work to try to bring men to their senses, to wake up a civilization as to what is going on in its midst, and to show it how desperately it is in need of deliverance, which can come only as a gift of righteousness from God's hands.

You may ask, "Why does God give a civilization over to this kind of thing?" He does it because it is only when darkness prevails, and despair and violence are widespread, that men are ready to welcome the light. Remember Isaiah's prediction:

The people who walked in darkness
    have seen a great light;
those who dwelt in a land of deep darkness,
    on them has light shined (Isa. 9:2 RSV).

In the first century, mankind was sunk in the darkness of despair. Idolatry had penetrated the whole world; men had turned from the true God, whom they could have known. Hopelessness and rank despair lay like a heavy blanket upon the earth.

In that hour, in the darkness of the night, over the skies of Bethlehem, the angels broke through and a great light of hope shone forth. From that hope all light streams. The angels' message is the coming of the Lord Jesus, the availability of the gift of righteousness from God. It is against the growing darkness of our own time that we need to make this message as clear as we possibly can—by our testimony, by our lives, by the joy and peace of our heart. God has found a way to break through human weakness, arrogance, despair, and sinfulness to give us peace, joy, and gladness once again. Just as Jesus was born in Bethlehem so long ago, so he can be born in your heart now. This is the good news of the gospel. In this decaying world in which we live we can see again the glory of this truth as it delivers people from their sins. "Thou shalt call his name JESUS; for he shall save his people from their sins" (Matt. 1:21 KJV).

4

Sinful Morality

There are many people who would say they do not belong in the picture of degraded society Paul has been describing. I am sure there were thousands in Paul's day, and I know there are millions today who feel they are not described in Romans 1. "That isn't talking about us. We're not like that. It may describe them, but it does not describe us." Whenever you read this first chapter of Romans, that division immediately becomes evident: "them" and "us." "They" are the obviously gross, wicked people; "we" are not. Many people would say, "We're law-abiding, home-loving, clean-living, decent people." Many have been church members most of their lives. Others perhaps do not go to church at all, but nevertheless pride themselves on their moral standards, their ethical values, and their clean, law-abiding lives. They believe the world is in its present condition because of the wickedness of gangsters, radicals, revolutionaries, prostitutes, pimps, and perverts of our day; but they themselves are the salt of the earth.

It is on these people that the apostle turns his spotlight in chapter 2. We will see his argument developed in three separate steps. The first is given in verse 1.

> You, therefore, have no excuse, you who pass judgment on
> someone else, for at whatever point you judge the other, you
> are condemning yourself, because you who pass judgment do
> the same things (Rom. 2:1).

Here Paul talks about those who pass judgment on others.
If anyone reading this book does not belong in that category, he is free to go on to the next section. I want to ad-
dress myself to those who have, at one time or another,
passed judgment on someone else. The apostle makes two
points about these people. First, he says that they know the
difference between right and wrong; otherwise they would
not presume to be judging. They have a clear understanding
of a standard. They know that one thing is wrong and
another thing is right. They are clearly aware, therefore,
that there are things that are wrong, and which merit the
judgment and wrath of God released in society.

Guilty Judges

Paul's second point about these people who have a clear
view of what is wrong in society is devastating. He says
they are guilty because they are doing the same things
themselves. The judges are as guilty as the ones they have
in the dock.

As a practiced, self-righteous hypocrite, I am always surprised at that statement. "What do you mean? How could
this be?" This reminds me of our Lord's account of his return, when all the nations are to be judged before him. He
will separate them into two bands, the sheep and the goats.
The test of judgment is made on the basis of how people
treat others. He will say to the sheep, "When I was thirsty,
you gave me to drink, when I was hungry you fed me, when
I was naked you clothed me, when I was in prison you
visited me." To the goats he will say, "When I was thirsty
you did not give me to drink, when I was hungry you did
not feed me, when I was naked you did not clothe me, and
when I was sick or in prison you did not visit me." Both

groups are taken by surprise and say, "When did this happen? When did we see you thirsty or hungry or naked? We don't remember that!" This feeling of surprise is highly indicative of how little we understand ourselves and why we need a passage such as this. We are all guilty.

Blind Spots

If my attitudes are typical of us all, then I see three ways by which I try to elude the fact that I am guilty of the actions of which I accuse others. First, I am congenitally blind toward many of my own faults. I am just not aware of them. I do not see that I am doing the same things that others are doing, and yet other people can see that I am. I don't see it, and neither do you see it in yourself. We all have these blind spots. One of the greatest lies of our age is the idea that we can know ourselves. We often argue, "Don't you think I know myself?" The answer is, "No, you do not know yourself. You are blind to much of your life." There can be very hurtful and sinful areas of which you are not aware.

I stayed with a pastor and his delightful family not long ago. They had three children, two boys and a girl. The oldest boy was about sixteen and, like all sixteen-year-olds, he was very concerned about the undisciplined life of his twelve-year-old brother. One day he came in all upset at something his brother had done, his mother told me. He said, "Who does he think he is? Why, he acts as though he's as good as the rest of us!" What a typical example of the attitude we all have—only this boy was honest enough to say it.

I caught myself the other day saying to someone, "Relax! Take it easy!" It was only afterward that I heard my own voice and realized that I was not relaxed, and I was not taking it easy myself. Have you ever lectured your children on the sin of procrastination and then barely got your income tax report in on time, if at all? How blind we are! We are congenitally blind toward many of our own faults. We just do not see them. In that way we can indeed be guilty, as the verse says, of doing the very things we accuse others of doing.

A second way is to accuse others by conveniently forgetting what we have done that is wrong. We may have been aware of our sin at the time, but somehow we just assume that God is going to forget it. We do not have to acknowledge it in any way—he will just forget it. As the sin fades from our memory, we think it fades from his as well.

For example, let's consider our thought life. Much of this passage in Romans must be understood in the light of our Lord's revelation in the Sermon on the Mount. Jesus says that God, who looks at the heart, sees what is going on in the inner attitude and judges on that basis; he doesn't judge as men judge, according to what is observable from the outward life. In the Sermon on the Mount we learn that if we hold a feeling of animosity and hatred against someone, if we are bitter and resentful and filled with malice toward an individual, then before God we are guilty of murder, just as if we had taken a knife and plunged it into that person's breast. If we find ourselves lustfully longing to possess the body of another, if we play with this idea over and over in our mind, and treat ourselves to a fantasy of sex, we have committed fornication or adultery. If we find ourselves filled with pride, yet we put on the appearance of being humble and considerate of others, we are guilty of the worst of sins. Pride of heart destroys humanity.

We think these things will go unnoticed, but God sees them in our hearts. He sees all the actions that we have conveniently forgotten. When we cut people down, or speak with spite and sharpness, and deliberately try to hurt them, he sees it. He sees it when we are unfair in our business tactics, when we are arrogant toward someone we think is on a lower social level than ourselves. When we are stubborn and uncooperative in trying to work out a tense situation, he sees that, too. All these things God notices. We, who condemn these things in others, find ourselves guilty of the same things. Isn't it remarkable that when others mistreat us we always think it is most serious and requires immediate correction? But when we mistreat others, we say to them, "You're making so much out of a little thing! Why, it's so trivial and insignificant!"

The third way we try to elude our guilt in the very things we accuse others of doing is by cleverly renaming things. Other people lie and cheat; we simply stretch the truth a little. Others betray; we are simply protecting our rights. Others steal; we borrow. Others have prejudices; we have convictions. We cry, "Those people ought to be stoned!" Jesus says, "He that is without sin among you, let him cast the first stone." Yes, we are all guilty of the same things we accuse others of doing.

Only One Standard

In verses 2–4 Paul develops the second step of his argument. He asks two questions; here is the first:

> Now we know that God's judgment against those who do such things is based on truth. So when you, a mere man, pass judgment on them and yet do the same things, do you think you will escape God's judgment?

What a ridiculous ground of hope! How tenuous to hope that God, who sees all men openly and intimately, who sees not only what is on the outside but also what is on the inside, will pronounce judgment on these other people but not on us. People will say, "How can a just and loving God permit the injustice and vileness that takes place in this world? How can he allow a tyrant like Hitler or Stalin to arise and murder millions of innocent people? How can he allow these godless regimes to come into power and crush people, usurp their rights, put thousands in prison, and spread destruction and sorrow across the land? Why does he allow these things to go on year after year? Why doesn't God judge these men?"

The question we ought to ask is, "Why didn't he judge

me yesterday, when I said that sharp, caustic word that plunged like an arrow into a loved one's heart and hurt him badly? Why didn't he judge me? Why didn't he shrivel my hand when I took a pencil and cheated on my income tax? Why didn't he strike me dumb when I was gossiping on the phone this morning, sharing a tidbit that made someone look bad in someone else's eyes? Why didn't God judge that?" The God of truth and justice sees the one as well as the other. Paul asks, "Do you think that you will escape the judgment of God?"

Then Paul asks the second question, the other horn of the dilemma.

> Or do you show contempt for the riches of his kindness, tolerance and patience, not realizing that God's kindness should lead you to repentance? (Rom. 2:4)

First Paul asked, "Why are you acting this way? Why do you judge others so critically and so constantly, yet never seem to judge yourself? Surely it can't be that you think you are going to escape! If you know that God judges according to truth, you must be included in that judgment as well." But now he says in verse 4, "If it is not that you think you'll escape his judgment, then it must be that you are treating with disdain the opportunities God gives you to repent." Why are you allowed to live? Why are you permitted to experience life, to find a new year lying ahead of you, with all its chances to correct these wrong attitudes and conditions? God's goodness, tolerance, and patience are exhibited in his giving you a chance to change, a chance to acknowledge your sins and to be forgiven. We have to see all our life in this respect. A faithful God, judging the inner part of life, does give us these opportunities. He knows we are blind. He knows that we often struggle at recognizing what is wrong in our lives, and so he gives us these opportunities to repent and change. These moments of truth are extremely important.

In Romans 2:5 through 11, the apostle presents the last

step of his argument and describes what lies ahead for those who refuse to face the actual condition of their lives.

> But because of your stubbornness and your unrepentant heart, you are storing up wrath against yourself for the day of God's wrath, when his righteous judgment will be revealed. God "will give to each person according to what he has done." To those who by persistence in doing good seek glory, honor, and immortality, he will give eternal life. But for those who are self-seeking and who reject the truth and follow evil, there will be wrath and anger. There will be trouble and distress for every human being who does evil: first for the Jew, then for the Gentile. For God does not show favoritism.

I am amazed to see in my own heart how often I expect God to show favoritism. Even as a Christian, I expect him to overlook areas of my life without my having to acknowledge that they are there. I expect him to forget them without revealing to me what their true nature is. Yet the Scriptures tell us that God is constantly bringing us times when we see ourselves clearly, and what valuable times they are!

Treasures of Wrath

Paul says that when we refuse to judge these areas we are storing up wrath for ourselves. In the King James Version the word is "treasurest." We are laying up treasures, but the treasure is wrath. This is the same word that Jesus employed when he said, "Lay up treasures for yourselves in heaven." We are constantly making deposits in a bank account which we must collect one of these days. In his wrath, God allows us to deteriorate as human beings. We become less than what we want to be, and it is because we are receiving back the deposit of wrath we have laid up for ourselves. I think C. S. Lewis has described this very accurately. In his book, *Mere Christianity*, he says,

> People often think of Christian morality as a kind of bargain in which God says, "If you keep a lot of rules, I'll reward you; and if you don't, I'll do the other thing." I do not think that's

the best way of looking at it. I would much rather say that
every time you make a choice, you are turning the central
part of you, the part that chooses, into something a little different than what it was before. And, taking your life as a
whole, with all your innumerable choices, all your life long
you are slowly turning this central thing either into a heavenly
creature or into a hellish creature; either into a creature that
is in harmony with God and with other creatures and with
itself, or else into one that is in a state of war and hatred with
God and with its fellow creatures and with itself. To be the
one kind of creature is heavenly, i.e., it is joy and peace and
knowledge and power; to be the other means madness, horror, idiocy, rage, impotence, and eternal loneliness. Each of
us, at each moment, is progressing to the one state or the
other.*

In eloquent terms that is saying the same thing Paul brings
out here. God is a righteous God. He judges men and he
assesses wrath against those who do wrong. No matter how
the outward life may appear, he sees the inward heart and
judges on that basis. There is righteous judgment waiting.
It comes, in part, all through life, because we experience the
wrath of God even now. But a day is coming when it will
all be manifested, one way or the other.

The question Paul brings out here is this: What do you
really want out of life? What are you seeking? If you are
"by persistence in doing good seeking glory and honor and
immortality," i.e., if you want God's life, you want to be his
kind of a person, you want to honor him and be of value to
him—if that is what you really want above everything else,
then you will find it. God will give you eternal life. In the
context of the whole Scripture, this means you will find
your way to Jesus Christ, for he *is* life eternal. You will find
him as your Redeemer and Lord and Savior. You will grow
increasingly like him, as you judge these evil areas of life,
and honestly confess them, not assuming that God will pass
over them. But what do you really want? If what you really
want is not God, truth, life, glory, and immortality—if you
really want pleasure, fame, wealth, power, and prominence,
if you want to be the center of things and have everyone

* Ibid., p. 95

thinking of you and looking at you and serving you—then, according to this passage, "there will be trouble and distress for every human being who does evil: first for the Jew, then for the Gentile."

Consistent with Love

God plays no favorites. Church member or pagan, civilized or savage, white, brown, red, black or yellow, it makes no difference before God. Now if all this sounds harsh, if it sounds unloving, it is because you have not read the passage in its context. For this is not inconsistent with the picture of a loving God, who loves humanity and wants to restore it. It is a picture of a loving God who loves us so much that he tells us the truth, and that is true love. He will not allow us to deceive ourselves, to be tricked and trapped by falling into self-deceit. He tells us the truth. There is no way out, except one, and that is what he wants us to see. God's love is helping us to see that there is only one way to deal with sin: admit it is there, and recognize that God has already dealt with it in Christ. On that basis, God offers us full and free forgiveness. There is no other way.

Any person who thinks he will escape by taking another route, or listening to some of the other voices that try to trap us into ways of rationalizing these feelings, and accepting them on other terms rather than dealing with them as ugly sins before God, will discover ultimately that he has stored up a treasure house of wrath. That is why God tells us the truth now. God, in great love and at tremendous cost, has provided a way out. It is that we surrender self. We must give up self-seeking and living for ourselves and begin to live for the God who made us. By the power of the Lord who forgives us and restores us and makes us his own, we will have heaven instead of hell. Again C. S. Lewis says the principle of giving up self runs all through life, from top to bottom:

Give up yourself, and you will find your real self. Lose your life, and you will save it. Submit to the death of your ambi-

tions and your favorite wishes every day, and the death of
your whole body in the end, submit with every fiber of your
being, and you will find eternal life. Keep back nothing.
Nothing that you have not given away will ever be really
yours. Nothing in you that has not died will ever be raised
from the dead. Look out for yourself and you will find, in the
long run, only hatred, loneliness, despair, rage, ruin, and decay. But look for Christ, and you will find Him, and with
Him, everything else thrown in.*

This is the gospel at which this tremendous passage is aiming. We are to realize that there is no hope, none whatsoever, except in a day-by-day yielding to the plan and the
program of God, as we find it in Jesus Christ our Lord.

Perhaps you have seen yourself in a new light. Perhaps
you have seen that you need to stop justifying and excusing
yourself, that you are in need of forgiveness from God just
as much as if you were a cold-blooded murderer. We all are.
Perhaps there are many Christians reading this who have
realized that when we protect and allow areas of our life
to be given over to this kind of judgmental condemning and
criticizing of other people, we are blocking the flow of the
life of God to our lives, keeping back the joy and peace that
he would have us enjoy. These areas need to be judged in
the Christian life as well as in the unredeemed life. Above
all else, this process is designed to make us take seriously
God's way of escape. There is a way of escape: admit your
sins freely, and receive the forgiveness of God, on the basis
of the work of Jesus Christ in his death on the cross and his
resurrection life available to us.

* Ibid., p. 96.

5

According to Light

Men and women everywhere desperately need the gospel. In the gospel, God has found a way to condemn our sin and to destroy it without destroying us. No man can do that. When we want to correct evildoers, we have to punish them by imprisoning them. Sometimes, to protect society, we have to take their lives. But God does not do that. Jesus, the center and heart of the gospel, changes people. He has found a way to change our most fundamental urges from self-centeredness and selfishness, to loving concern for others, so that the basis of our behavior has been altered. In the gospel God has made divine power available to us. God has promised to us and provided for us an ultimate destiny that is mind-blowing, beyond all our wildest dreams. And yet it is amazing that when people hear this good news, they often resist it and stubbornly hold out against accepting it.

So far in Romans Paul has shown us the obviously wicked man, who defies God, and the self-righteously moral man who deludes himself. Now we come to the last two types of people who resist the truth. One of these is the unenlightened pagan. Here we will deal with the question of what to do about people who have not heard the gospel. What about those who live where the Bible is unknown, or those who are in a different religion where there is no knowledge of the facts of the life, death, and resurrection of Jesus Christ? In this passage Paul will show that their problem is that they defile their consciences. And the last type is the religious devotee who seeks deliverance from the judgment of God by religious practices, rituals, performances, and knowledge of the truth.

By Their Own Standards

These two types of people are introduced by a statement of the universal lostness of mankind:

> All who sin apart from the law will also perish apart from the law, and all who sin under the law will be judged by the law. For it is not those who hear the law who are righteous in God's sight, but it is those who obey the law who will be declared righteous (Rom. 2:12,13).

This is probably the strongest statement Paul makes, and it answers the question non-Christians ask Christians more often than any other, "What about the people who have never heard of Jesus Christ?" Usually they are thinking of naked savages in jungles. They seldom think of the savages in the concrete jungles of our cities, but both are in the same condition, as we will see. Paul's answer to this question is that they will be judged by their own standards. God judges men, not according to what they do not know, but according to what they do know.

So far in Romans, Paul has made three great statements about the basis of judgment. In Romans 2:2 Paul says that God's judgment is according to truth, i.e., it is realistic. He only deals with that which is actually there. God does not falsely accuse anyone, but he judges according to truth. Then in Romans 2:6 he says God judges according to works. Now that is interesting, because it shows God is patient. God, who does see what is going on in our inner lives and who could judge immediately on that basis, nevertheless

waits patiently until our inner attitude begins to work itself
out in some deed, speech, or attitude that we manifest
openly. Therefore, God will allow men to be their own
judge, to see for themselves that what is coming out is a
revelation of what is inside.

In Romans 2:9 and 10 Paul also says that the judgment
of God is according to light. That is, God is not going to
summon all mankind and tell them they are going to be
judged on the basis of the Ten Commandments. Rather, he
will say to each individual, "What did you think was right
and wrong?" And then, "Did you do the right, and not the
wrong?" By that standard, of course, everyone fails. Paul
makes clear that this is true. He says, "All who sin apart
from the law will also perish apart from the law. . . ." The
fact that such men never heard the Ten Commandments, or
anything else that is in the Bible, does not mean they will
be acceptable in God's sight. They will perish, not because
they did not hear, but because they did not do what they
knew was right.

Now Paul goes on to take up the case of the unenlightened pagan:

> (Indeed, when Gentiles, who do not have the law, do by na-
> ture things required by the law, they are a law for themselves,
> even though they do not have the law, since they show that
> the requirements of the law are written on their hearts, their
> consciences also bearing witness, and their thoughts now ac-
> cusing, now even defending them.) This will take place on
> the day when God will judge men's secrets through Jesus
> Christ, as my gospel declares (Rom. 2:14–16).

Verses 14 and 15 are in parentheses so as not to distract too
much from the main flow of Paul's argument, which is that
a day is coming when God will judge the secrets of men
everywhere and all that is hidden will be revealed. Jesus
himself spoke of that day: "What you have said in the dark
will be heard in the daylight, and what you have whispered
in the ear behind closed doors will be proclaimed from the
housetops" (Luke 12:3). Now there were some in Paul's
day who said that because the Jews possessed the law and

knew God's truth, they would not be condemned in that
final judgment. But Paul is saying, "Look, if your knowledge
of truth is what saves you, then everyone will be saved,
even the savages and the pagans, for they show they have
a law, too. They know a great deal about the law; it is written on their hearts, and their consciences act as judges
within them, just as they do within those of us in the more
civilized world." On that basis, you see, everyone would be
saved. But God does not judge that way.

Written on Hearts

Now here we have a revelation of what goes on in the
primitive world. Men and women who have never heard
anything about the Bible, Jesus Christ, Moses, the Ten
Commandments, or any standard that we are familiar with,
nevertheless are subject to judgment because they have
truth written in their hearts. They do know what is right
and wrong—they show it in their own lives.

Recently I read an amazing book called *Peace Child* *
(which has since been made into a movie). It is a remarkable story of some missionaries who went to the island of
New Guinea, to live among a tribe of people who were so
degraded, so sunken in immorality, that they actually ad-
mired treachery. They highly regarded the man who could
win someone's love, friendship, and trust, and then betray
and murder him. Such a man was held up as an admirable
person to follow. When the missionaries first came to these
people they despaired of ever reaching them, for there
seemed to be no ground of appeal to a people who had so
reversed the moral standards of life.

As they lived among them and became better acquainted
with their culture, however, they discovered that this moral
reversal was not quite universal. There was one situation in
which they recognized that men and women were bound
to a moral standard, and that was in the case of an exchange

* Don Richardson, *Peace Child* (Regal Books Division, G/L Publi-
cations, Glendale, Ca., 1974).

of a peace child. If a tribe gave a baby or a child from their tribe to another, then that other tribe would be bound to keep its agreements and to honor its treaty with the first tribe. If they did not, they would lose face and be regarded as despicable. It was at this point that the missionaries were able to introduce the gospel, for they pointed out that God had given us a peace child in Jesus Christ. Thus these people were bound to honor God. It is a remarkable story, but it shows clearly how God had prepared the way for the gospel by building into this culture a concept that would be ready and waiting when the gospel came.

Now the Romans were living according to the rule of conscience; and the conscience, as Paul points out here, never brings a settled peace. These tribes are a continual testimony to that fact. People say, "Let your conscience be your guide." That is a recipe for unhappiness. If that is all you have, you are certain to have a life that alternates between momentary peace and fear.

An interesting article in *Christianity Today* by Rachel Saint, sister of one of the five men who were cruelly murdered by the Auca Indians on the banks of the river in Ecuador twenty years ago, describes the way the Aucas lived before the gospel came:

> The Aucas have been thoroughly acquainted with demons and devil worship for many generations. The result of this is a religion of terror. The witch doctor is the central authority, and he controls the tribe. Any death is supposed to be caused by the witch doctor. Then that death has to be avenged and the feuding starts. They are afraid that they might be speared at night in their own houses. Everyone is a potential enemy. If a father loses a son, he feels he must kill his daughter. If the group loses a marriageable girl, a grandmother is killed. Why should a worthless old woman live if a marriageable girl has died? This kind of thinking permeates their culture.

This sort of thinking goes on not only in the jungles of South America and other primitive places, but it happens wherever people are governed only by the law of conscience. Yet even under their own law they will perish, just

as certainly as do those who are judged by God's law, for
they do not obey their own consciences.

Religious Braggarts

Paul goes on to take up the case of the religious devotee
of his day, the Jew. Today we need only substitute the title
"church member" to bring it up to date. We American
church members are in the same condition as the Jew was
in the culture of Paul's day. We have a great body of truth
in which we delight, and we feel proud of our knowledge
and our understanding of it. But unfortunately, we often
hope and think that that knowledge in itself will deliver us
in the sight of God. This is how Paul handles such thinking:

> Now you, if you call yourself a Jew; if you rely on the law
> and brag about your relationship to God; if you know his will
> and approve of what is superior because you are instructed
> by the law; if you are convinced that you are a guide for the
> blind, a light for those who are in the dark, an instructor of
> the foolish, a teacher of infants, because you have in the law
> the embodiment of knowledge and truth—you, then, who
> teach others, do you not teach yourself? You who preach
> against stealing, do you steal? You who say that people should
> not commit adultery, do you commit adultery? You who abhor
> idols, do you rob temples? You who brag about the law, do
> you dishonor God by breaking the law? As it is written:
> "God's name is blasphemed among the Gentiles because of
> you" (Rom. 2:17–24).

Paul lists here the five great advantages which the Jews of
his day had and on which they relied for their position before God. First, they relied on possessing the law. There are
many people in the churches of America today who rely
upon the fact that the Bible is available to them. We have
the Bible in twenty-five different versions and many take
great pride in owning a specific version. "I am a King James
Christian! If it was good enough for the apostle Paul, it's
good enough for me!" Or "We're liberated! We have the
American Standard Version!" You hear people bragging

about this! Well, that is exactly what the Jew was doing in Paul's day.

Second, they bragged about their relationship to God. The Jew made it clear that he had a special inside track with the Almighty. You hear people talking like that today. "God, Billy Graham, and I were talking the other day. . . ." We make it clear that we have a special standing with the "Good Lord," as he is usually called, and in some way we brag about our relationship to him.

Third, the Jews were people who knew the will of God. They had the Scriptures, they had the Ten Commandments, and the knowledge of what God wanted. There are many today who boast about their knowledge of the Word of God and who rest upon that fact.

Fourth, these Jews approved of what was superior, i.e., they rejected certain attitudes and actions in life and chose only that which was regarded as morally superior. Many, many church members do this. They take pride in the fact that they do not do certain things. I am amazed at how many people think God is going to be impressed by the things they do not do. "We don't dance, we don't drink, we don't go to the movies, we don't go to theaters, we don't play cards, we don't drink coffee," and on and on.

Finally, the Jews were instructed in the law. There were many who could quote great passages of Scripture, and they took pride in that. Now, there is nothing wrong with any of these advantages except that the Jews, and many of us today, depend on them for righteousness. We feel we have a special standing with God because of them; and that is where we fail.

Paul goes on to list four privileges which the Jews felt were theirs because they had these advantages. First, they felt they were a guide to the blind. Today we have people who are always ready to correct those around them, to impart truth to those unfortunates who have not learned anything yet. Second, the Jews felt they were a light to those in the dark. Every now and then we run into people who are quite ready to dazzle us with their knowledge of the

Scriptures. They know all about the antichrist, they know when Christ is coming again, they know all the elective decrees of God, they are thoroughly acquainted with the supralapsarian position of people before the Fall, and so on, and they take great pride in this knowledge.

Third, the Jews felt they were instructors of the foolish. A lady came up to me after a service one time and told me a long, painful story of how she had injured her wrist in an auto accident. The doctor who took care of her in the emergency room happened to let a couple of curse words slip while working on her. She lectured him at great length about how she was a Christian, how she wouldn't listen to this kind of language, and how terrible it was that he took the name of God in vain. This attitude is typical of many who feel they are instructors of the foolish, because they have a knowledge of the Scriptures. The fourth privilege which the Jews possessed was that they were teachers of children. I am amazed at how many want to teach Sunday school classes for the wrong reason. Now there is a right reason, but many want to teach simply to satisfy their own egos.

Paul's judgment of such people is, "You are guilty yourself." This attitude of the Jew is the same one Paul condemned earlier in the moral Gentile. "You are outwardly righteous and correct, but inwardly you are doing the wrong thing." They were envious, proud, covetous, lustful, bitter, dangerous people. Religious zealots are dangerous people. The Jews were notorious in the Roman Empire for being over-sharp in business deals. That is why Paul says, "You who preach against stealing, do you steal?" They were not above a little hanky-panky with the slave girls they had to deal with. Paul says, "You who say that people should not commit adultery, do you commit adultery?" They were ready to profit from trade with pagan temples. He says, "You who abhor idols, do you rob temples?" They bragged about the law, but Paul says, "God's name is blasphemed among the Gentiles because of you."

That was the ultimate judgment upon the Jews. To them

blasphemy was the worst of sins. Yet Paul says, "Though
you claim to have so much, and to be so knowledgeable,
yet what you have done is to blaspheme God. People have
been turned away from God because of you." I do not think
I have to detail how true that is of American Christianity as
a whole. Not only in this country, but around the world,
Christians have caused people to turn from God because of
our attitudes and the way we approach people. I have often
thought it is amazing how the people who keep close
records on how many they win to Christ never keep any
records on how many they drive away!

Resting on a Symbol

Now Paul seizes upon and singles out the supreme symbol of Jewish separatism, circumcision:

> Circumcision has value if you observe the law, but if you
> break the law, you have become as though you had not been
> circumcised. If those who are not circumcised keep the law's
> requirements, will they not be regarded as though they were
> circumcised? The one who is not circumcised physically and
> yet obeys the law will condemn you who, even though you
> have the written code and circumcision, are a lawbreaker
> (Rom. 2:25–27).

The Jews, of course, prided themselves (and still do today)
on the rite of circumcision, the symbol that they were God's
people. You only need to substitute baptism, confirmation,
or church membership to apply that to the twentieth century, to Protestant or Catholic Americans. So many Americans rest upon the fact that they have been baptized,
confirmed, or accepted as members of a church, as the sign
that they belong to God. Paul says that is useless and worthless unless something has happened in the heart.

Paul's conclusion about the religious man is in verses
28 and 29:

> A man is not a Jew if he is only one outwardly, nor is circum-
> cision merely outward and physical. No, a man is a Jew if he

is one inwardly; and circumcision is circumcision of the heart, by the Spirit, not by the written code. Such a man's praise is not from men, but from God.

That last phrase is a play on words. The word "praise" is taken from the word "Judah," from which we get the word "Jew." Paul says the true Jew is not praised by men but by God; but he also makes clear what constitutes a true Jew in God's sight. Now this is one of the most hotly debated questions in the state of Israel today. The Israelis are constantly trying to decide what is the basis of Jewry. What makes a Jew? Is it religion? Is it observing the Old Testament Law; keeping a kosher kitchen? Many Jews are atheists, who have no use for the Old Testament, and yet they claim to be Jews because their ancestry is Jewish; their ancestors, as far back as they know, were Jews. Is that the basis on which to claim Jewishness? There are black Jews who are petitioning to belong to Israel. But other Jews say you have to be white to be a Jew. What makes a Jew?

Paul says that nothing outward makes you a Jew. One becomes a Jew when his heart is changed. As with Abraham and Jacob, you become a Jew when you believe in Yeshua Hamashiach, Jesus the Messiah. The Jews for Jesus group is telling people this today. What makes you a Jew is not the culture from which you came, the ritual through which you have gone, the circumstances of your life, or your background, ancestry, or history: but the fact that you have come to know the Lord Jesus Christ. That is what makes you a Jew. Paul wrote in Galations 3:29, "If you belong to Christ, then you are Abraham's seed, and heirs to the promise."

Paul's conclusion to Romans 2 is that man without Christ is hopelessly lost. He defies God, deludes himself, defiles his conscience, and denies what he himself teaches; thus he is absolutely, hopelessly lost until he comes to know the Lord Jesus and lives on the basis of that relationship. That is what makes a Christian. It is not a question of whether you are baptized, galvanized, sanforized, or pasteurized. The question is, do you have faith in the Lord Jesus Christ and have you received the gift of righteousness which God gives to those who do not deserve it, cannot earn it, but receive it by his love and grace? We will see what additional problems this raises with the Jews in the next section of the Book of Romans.

6

Total Wipeout

Notice as we go through this letter to the Romans, how logically and powerfully the apostle Paul develops his subject. Evidently he possessed a vivid imagination which, as we shall see, he used skillfully to illustrate and illuminate what he wanted to say. I never fail to be delighted at how the mind of the apostle Paul works as he sets this truth out for us.

The first twenty verses of chapter 3 divide easily into two parts. The first eight verses are an imaginary dialogue that the apostle holds with the Jews. The second part, verses 9 to 20, are his powerful description of the condition of mankind before God.

The dialogue with the Jews grows out of the end of chapter 2, in which Paul declares that the only thing that makes a man a Jew is faith in the Messiah. It is here that Paul's vivid imagination comes into play; he sees an imaginary Jew standing up and arguing with him at this point. Perhaps this actually happened many times in the course of Paul's travels throughout the Roman Empire. He would have stated these things in many synagogues and surely at one time or another some knowledgeable Jewish rabbi would stand up and argue with him. That is what he is sharing with us now.

Paul imagines three arguments from this Jewish objector. In our own culture, you can place any religionist in place of the Jewish objector—a Mormon, a Christian Scientist, a Hindu, a Buddhist, a Mohammedan, a Baptist, a Presbyterian, a Catholic. Anyone who counts on religion will offer the same kind of argument.

The Supreme Advantage

Paul first imagines a Jew standing up and saying, "Now, hold it! Wait a minute! These things you say don't count are the very things God himself has given to us." Circumcision came from God; God asked it of the Jews. And the Law was given by God to the Jews. It was God who called them his chosen people. The argument is, "Paul, you're setting aside what God has established. If these things don't count, what advantage is there in being a Jew?" That question and Paul's answer are phrased in the first two verses of chapter 3.

> What advantage, then, is there in being a Jew, or what value is there in circumcision? Much in every way! First of all, they have been entrusted with the very words of God (Rom. 3:1,2).

When Paul says "first," he does not mean first in a long list of advantages, though he did see many advantages in being a Jew. What Paul means by "first" is supremely, chiefly. The great glory in being a Jew in Paul's day was that the Jews had the Law. They possessed the written Word of God. Paul says that is a tremendous advantage. Already he has shown that everyone is under law; nobody is without a moral standard. The conscience lays hold of that law written in the heart to tell people whether they are doing right or wrong. So light is given to everyone. No one lives in darkness.

But even though everyone has that light, the Jews had an additional degree of light. They were given the written Word on stone, so that it was permanently preserved. Thus they had a knowledge of the mind and will and character of God that other people did not possess. They had a greater opportunity to know and obey God than anyone else in that day; they had a tremendous advantage, but they failed to make use of it, and therefore it did them no good at all. They were no better off than if they had never known the law at all because they did not put it to its intended use.

To Hunt for Needles

Just imagine an island in darkness, populated with people. There is only one way to escape the island, a narrow bridge over a deep chasm, but the darkness is so great that only a few find their way over that bridge. Everyone on that island has been provided with a little penlight that enables them to dimly illuminate a small space around them, barely enough to avoid the more obvious obstacles in their path. But a certain group of people is given a powerful searchlight that can shine thousands of yards into the darkness. It is given to them not only so that they can find the bridge, but also so they can show others the way out.

Yet these people, who have so much more light than the others, spend their time using this powerful searchlight to look for needles in a haystack. That, in essence, was what the Jews were doing. The rabbis were arguing constantly over infinitesimal theological differences. Jesus called this "straining at a gnat, but swallowing a camel." They argued over how many steps constituted a violation of the Sabbath and whether spitting on a rock is permissible on the Sabbath, or whether spitting on mud is a violation. One would be right, and the other wrong. This is what they used the law for. Though the Jews had a tremendous advantage in having the law, Paul says, they failed to use it properly.

Now the imaginary rabbi comes back with a second objection:

What if some did not have faith? Will their lack of faith nullify God's faithfulness? Not at all! Let God be true, and every man a liar. As it is written:

"So that you may be proved right in your words, and prevail in your judging" (Rom. 3:3,4).

The Jewish rabbi asks, "Paul, are you suggesting that if some of the Jews did not believe (he is ready to admit that as a possibility), then God would forget his promises to all the Jews? Are you saying that just because some of us didn't measure up to what God required in the law, everyone in Israel has lost the promise that God gave them? You seem to suggest that God is not interested in the very rituals which he himself instituted. Are you saying that circumcision and all these things mean nothing to God? Are you saying that God is upset by the disbelief of just a few Jews and so he has canceled all Israel's prerogatives?"

Paul's answer uses the strongest words in the Greek language to say a thing is false. "By no means! Not at all!" (Literally, May it never be! Or, as it is translated in some versions, God forbid!) That would suggest that God is the failure. It would suggest that God gave a promise and then did not keep his words, just because a few people failed to measure up. So God would be at fault. Our human hearts always tend to blame God for what goes wrong in our lives, for our inability to fulfill what God demands. Paul says, "Never let that be! Let God be true, and every man a liar." God is going to keep his Word no matter how many fail.

Let God Be True

Paul then quotes from Psalm 51, the second half of verse 4. When David repented of the twin sins of murder and adultery, he wrote this beautiful psalm, in which he confesses his sins to God:

Against thee, thee only, have I sinned, and done that which is evil in thy sight, so that thou art justified in thy sentence and blameless in thy judgment (Ps. 51:4 RSV).

For a year and a half, David tried to hide his sins and refused to admit them to God or anyone else. He went on acting as though he were righteous, letting people think he

was still the godly king of Israel. He let that hypocrisy go
on for eighteen months; then God sent Nathan the prophet,
who speared him with his long, bony finger, and said, "Thou
art the man!" David's sins were exposed; he admitted them
and confessed to God. He said, "It is not you who are to
blame, God; I did it." So Paul says, "Let God be true and
every man a liar," i.e., even if all the Jews fail in their belief,
God will still fulfill his promise.

How can God do this? God has said that some will believe. If everyone fails to believe, how can he keep his
word? Paul says, "That's your problem; it's not God's problem." When certain of the Pharisees boasted to John the
Baptist that they were "children of Abraham," John said,
"Don't you understand that God can raise up from these
stones children unto Abraham?" (see Luke 3:8). If men
fail, God has unlimited resources to fulfill his promise. So
there is no objection at this point. God will still judge the
Jews, and all religionists, despite the failure of some.

A third objection is raised in verse 5 and Paul responds in
verse 6. The Jew asks,

> But if our unrighteousness brings out God's righteousness
> more clearly, what shall we say? That God is unjust in bring-
> ing his wrath on us? (I am using a human argument.) Cer-
> tainly not! If that were so, how could God judge the world?

As Paul says, this is a common human argument. You still
hear it today. People say, "If what we're doing makes God
look good because it gives him a chance to show his love
and forgiveness, how can he condemn us? We've made him
look good. We've given him a chance to reveal himself, and
that's what he wants. So he can't condemn us for our sins.
In fact, let's sin more and make him look all the better!"
People today say, "If God is glorified by human sin and
failure, as the Scriptures say, then let's sin all the more."

Locked into Evil

Paul's answer is, "Let's carry that out to its logical conclusion. If everyone lived on that basis, then nobody could

be judged and God would be removed as judge of all the world." It would demean God. God would be no better than the worst of men. God himself could not act as a judge if he actually arranged things so that sin would glorify God. If God cannot judge, he is demeaned; if he does not judge, the entire world is locked into perpetual evil. There would be no way of arresting the awful flow of human evil in this world. Therefore, this is a ridiculous argument.

The fact is, sin never glorifies God. Sin always has evil results; it does not produce good. As the Scriptures say, "The one who sows to please his sinful nature, from that nature will reap destruction; the one who sows to please the Spirit, from the Spirit will reap eternal life" (Gal. 6:8).

This is an ordained law of God which no one can break. Paul strengthens this argument with a personal illustration in verses 7 and 8.

> Someone might argue, "If my falsehood enhances God's truthfulness and so increases his glory, why am I still condemned as a sinner?" Why not say—as we are being slanderously reported and as some claim that we say—"Let us do evil that good may result"? Their condemnation is deserved.

The NIV text adds the words, "Someone might argue," but that does not belong here. If your text does not add this, it is more accurate. Paul is saying that he includes himself in the circle of condemnation. He says, "If my falsehood . . ." If you look back in Romans you can see how he has narrowed this circle. In chapter 1 he talks about what "they" do. "They are without excuse." Chapter 2 comes down to "You O man, who judge another, you are without excuse." Then in chapter 3 it is "our unrighteousness," and finally, "my falsehood." I love this because it means that Paul does not consider himself, even as a believer, beyond the possibility of sin. He is just as capable of falsehood as anyone else. When that happens, that area of his life is subject to the condemnation of God, the same as for anyone else. Paul does not hold himself up as better than anyone else.

Paul continues, "Let's go on to say the logical thing: Let's do evil that good may come." What a ridiculous argument, he concludes. Why, that removes all difference between good and evil. This is what people are saying today. "There's no such thing as good or evil. Whatever you like is good; whatever you don't like, that's evil. It's only in your mind that there's any difference between good and evil." You see how up-to-date this argument is? Paul says it is ridiculous. The logical conclusion to that thinking is moral chaos and anarchy. Nobody could judge anything. We would simply plunge into a tremendous abyss of immorality in which anyone could do anything, and no one would dare to raise a hand in opposition. This would produce moral anarchy. So, Paul says, the condemnation of this kind of reasoning is well deserved.

In verses 9 through 20, Paul introduces another question and answers it:

> What shall we conclude then? Are we any better? Not at all! We have already made the charge that Jews and Gentiles alike are all under sin (v. 9).

I think it would be a little better to change this phrase from, "Are we any better?" to "Do we have any standing at all?" for that is what Paul is really saying. He has looked over all of mankind and says, "Is there any ground by which a man or woman can please God apart from faith in Christ? Is there any way you can try to be good and make it?" His answer: None at all. No one can make it on those terms.

Already he has demonstrated the universal condition of both Jews and Gentiles. He showed that the blatantly wicked people end up defying God, therefore they cannot make it. The morally self-righteous people, who pride themselves on their good conduct and clean living, simply delude themselves, so they cannot make it. The unenlightened pagans in all the jungles of the world defile their own consciences; they do not make it because they do not live up to their own standards. The religious zealots deny in deeds what they teach in words, and so they cannot make it. They are all wiped out.

Scripture Summary

Now comes the final touch, in which Paul gathers up what the Scriptures say on this subject. We are living in a day when what men say is considered the final word. The Scriptures may be considered, but not really taken as authoritative. But the apostles never treated Scripture that way. They listened to what men said, but when it came to the final authority, they said, "What Scripture says, that's it!"

Paul gathers up a compilation of scriptures from the Psalms and Proverbs and Isaiah to show that what he has described, God has already said. The scriptures he uses divide into three very clear groups. First, there is the character of man, as God sees it; then the conduct of man, in both speech and action; and finally, the cause of all this. Here is man's true character:

> As it is written: "There is no one righteous, not even one . . ." (v. 10).

Isn't that an astounding statement? Think of all the nice people you know. They may not be Christians, but they are nice people—good neighbors, kind and gracious people who speak lovingly and do kind things. Looking at them, God says, "There's not one among them that is righteous, not even one." Surely the total depravity of the human heart is revealed by the fact that when we read this kind of statement, "There is no one righteous, not even one." we mentally add, "except me." Right?

> . . . there is no one who understands. . . .

Think of all the people today who are searching to understand the mystery of life. All over the world, in temples, schools, universities, in the jungles, before idols, people are

searching to find the answer to the mystery of man: Why
are we like we are? And in all that vast array of searchers,
God says there is not one who understands, not even one.

. . . no one searches for God.

What a claim that is! Here are all these religious people
going to temples, going through various procedures, observing rituals, flocking to churches, filling up places of worship
all over the world. What are they looking for? We would
say they are looking for God, but God does not say so. He
says there is no one searching for God. They are looking for
a god, not *the* God. They are not looking for the God of
truth and justice, who is behind all things.

> All have turned away
>   and together become worthless.
> There is no one who does good,
>   not even one (Rom. 3:10–12).

That could hardly be made any clearer. There is no one who
does good, not even one. Do you struggle with this? Then
imagine that someone has invented a camera that records
thoughts. Imagine that at a Sunday morning service you
were to pass through a security system like those at airports,
and all your thoughts would be recorded. During the service, the camera would be scanning, picking up your
thoughts. What you thought when you sat down, what you
thought when the person next to you sat down, what you
were thinking during the hymn, and what you were thinking during the prayer. Then it is announced that the next
Sunday, instead of the regular service, a screening of the
film from that camera would be presented. I wonder how
many would show up? But this is the stark revelation from
Scripture of what God sees when he looks at the human
race. There is no one who does good, not even one.
  Then he details why. First, their speech:

> Their throats are open graves;
>   their tongues practice deceit.

The poison of vipers is on their lips.
Their mouths are full of cursing and bitterness (vv. 13,14).

This covers the whole realm of human speech. It begins deep down in the throat, it comes to the tongue, then the lips, and then the whole mouth. From the inward to the outward parts it moves. Deep down, Paul says, God sees an open grave with a stinking, rotten corpse and a horrible stench coming up from it that reveals itself, ultimately, in vulgarity.

Do you ever wonder why children love toilet talk? Or why adults like words with double meanings? You hear them on television all the time. What is down in the heart comes out in the speech—not only vulgarity, but hypocrisy. "Their tongues practice deceit." Those little white lies, the way we erect façades, the way we claim to feel one way when we actually feel another; we think all this deceit is harmless and unnoticed. But God sees it. "The poison of vipers is on their lips." This is a picture of the tongue used to slander, to plant poison in another person's heart: the putdown, the sharp, caustic words, the sarcasm that cuts someone off and depersonalizes another being. We are all guilty. This is what is inside, and this is what God sees with the realism of his eye.

"Their mouths are full of cursing and bitterness." If you do not believe that, just step out on the street and hit the first fellow who comes by right on the mouth and see what comes out—cursing and bitterness! Cursing is blaming God; that is profanity. Bitterness is reproaching God because of the way he has run your life. This is what we hear all the time, even from Christians. We hear complaints about their circumstances, where God has placed them, and what he is doing with their life—cursing and bitterness.

Look now at the deeds that follow.

> Their feet are swift to shed blood;
> ruin and misery mark their paths. . . .

Wherever man goes, ruin follows. Do we need any documentation of that today? Why do cities always develop ghettos and slums? Why do our beautiful mountains and streams become polluted? It is because of the heart of man.

> . . . ruin and misery mark their paths,
> and the way of peace they do not know (vv. 15–17)

I have often thought this would be an appropriate slogan for the United Nations! "The way of peace they do not know." The United Nations is helpless to stop the cruel wars that continue to flare up all over the world because "the way of peace they do not know."

The cause of this follows, in just one sentence:

> There is no fear of God before their eyes (v. 18).

That brings us right back to chapter 1, verse 18 of Romans: "The wrath of God is being revealed from heaven against all the godlessness . . . of men. . . ." When men reject God, they lose everything. All these things follow because "there is no fear of God before their eyes."

In the last two verses we have a clear vision of why God gave the law. Since the Jews were so convinced that their possession of the law gave them special privileges in God's sight, Paul now returns to that subject.

> Now we know that whatever the law says, it says to those who are under the law, so that every mouth may be silenced and the whole world held accountable to God. Therefore no one will be declared righteous in his sight by observing the law [That was a fantastic statement to make.]; rather, through the law we become conscious of sin (Rom. 3:19,20).

When we read this terrible description of the human race as God sees it, it is almost impossible for us to believe that God does not say, "Enough! Wipe them out!" If all he sees is wretchedness, misery, evil, deceit, hypocrisy, vulgarity, profanity, slander—in every heart, every one without exception, our natural instinct is to conclude that God doesn't want us. But the amazing thing is that across this kind of verse he writes, "God so loved the world that he gave his only begotten Son." God did not send the law to destroy us (and this is very important); he sent the law to keep us from false hope.

The Wrong Road

The worst thing that can happen is to be going down a road to an important destination thinking you are on the right track, only to discover the road peters out into nothingness. You find you have been on the wrong track and it is too late to go back. That was what was happening. So God, in his lovingkindness, has given us the Law to keep us from taking a false path. Though the law condemns us, it is that very condemnation that makes us willing to listen, so that we find the right path.

Paul says the law does three things to us. First, it stops our mouth. We have nothing to say. You can always tell someone is close to becoming a Christian when he shuts up and stops arguing back. Self-righteous people are always arguing, "But I . . . yes, but . . . I do this . . . and I do that." But when they see the true meaning of the law, their mouth is shut. When you read a statement like this, there is really nothing left to say, is there?

I had a friend who was given a traffic ticket one day. She was guilty of doing what she was charged with, but she felt there was some justification for it, so she thought she would go to court and argue it before the judge. She imagined in her mind how she would come in and the judge would ask her if she was guilty. She would say, "Yes, but I want to explain why." She would proceed to convince the judge and all the court that what she did could hardly be avoided and that she was justified in doing it. Her argument was ready. But, she said, "When I came into that court and stood up there all alone, and the judge was there on the bench, dressed in his robe, and he looked over his glasses at me and said, 'Guilty or not guilty?', all my arguments faded. I just said, 'Guilty.'" Her mouth was stopped. That is the first thing the law does: it shuts you up, and you do not argue with God anymore.

Second, Paul says, "The whole world is held accountable

to God." That makes us realize there is no easy way, no way by which death suddenly is going to dissolve all things into everlasting darkness, forever forgotten. The whole world has to stand before God. Hebrews puts it so starkly, "Man is destined to die once, and after that to face judgment" (Heb. 9:27).

Finally, the law clearly reveals what sin is. What does the law want of us? Jesus said that all the law is summed up in one word: love. All the law asks us to do is to act in love. All these things the law states are simply loving ways of acting. When we face ourselves before the law we have to confess that many, many times we fail to love. We do not love. That is what the law wants us to see. Because then, when all else fails, we are ready to listen to what follows.

Now we are ready for verse 21: "But now a righteousness from God . . . has been made known." That is what Paul wants us to hear. When we take that one way, we find we have learned to love—not by the law, but by the provision of the Son of God.

7

But Now

In the opening words of Romans 3:21, "But now . . . ," you can almost hear a sigh of relief. Now, after God's appraisal of man's efforts to achieve some standing before him, come God's words of relief. God's total answer to man's total failure.

> But now a righteousness from God, apart from the law, has been made known, to which the Law and the Prophets testify (Rom. 3:21).

This is God's great "nevertheless" in the face of man's failure. In the subsequent paragraphs, the apostle Paul develops this in his usual reasoned and logical style. For a little guide to this section, here is the way it breaks down: in verse 21 we have God's answer to man's failure. In verses 22–24 he tells us how that gift of righteousness is obtained. Verses 25 and 26 tell us how and why it works; and in verses 27–31, the results that follow are given. Let us turn now to this great statement beginning with verse 21, which is one of the great declarations of the gospel.

> But now a righteousness from God, apart from law, has been made known, to which the Law and the Prophets testify.

69

That is what Paul elsewhere calls "the glorious gospel of the blessed God," the good news that God has to announce to us, which consists of a gift that God gives us—the righteousness of God himself. We have already seen that this word "righteousness" is greatly misunderstood in our day. Often it is associated with behavior. If people are behaving in a right way, we say they are behaving righteously. But in this part of the Book of Romans, righteousness does not directly touch on behavior. It does not refer to what you do, but to what you are. The gift Paul is talking about, the gift from God, is that of a righteous standing before him.

The real meaning underlying this word, as I have already pointed out, is found in the word "worth." People everywhere are looking for a sense of worth. In fact, psychologists tell us that this sense of worth is the most essential element in human activity, and that without it you cannot function as a human being. Therefore, whether we know it or not, or describe it in these terms, we are all looking for a sense of worth. But the gospel announces that it is given to us. What people strive all their lives to achieve is handed to us right at the beginning, when we believe in Jesus Christ. According to the gospel, we cannot earn it but it is given to us. That is the good news. What a wonderful statement that is.

The other day, in reading an article on some of the movements of our day, I came across these words by Dr. Lewis Smedes, a professor at Fuller Theological Seminary:

> Anyone who can see the needs of people today must recognize that the malaise of our time is an epidemic of self–doubt and self-depreciation. Those whose job it is to heal people's spiritual problems know that the overwhelming majority of people who seek help are people who are sick from abhorring themselves. A prevailing sense of being without worth is the pervasive sickness of our age.*

That comes from a man who spends a great deal of time trying to help people with emotional problems and personality difficulties in their lives. He says the basic need is a sense of worth. There are millions of people today who are

* From an article entitled "God's Noble Lad" in *The Reformed Journal*, 1973.

openly acknowledging that they need help, and who come
looking for help. There are others who never ask, but behind their smiling façades and confident airs there are insecure hearts and a consciousness of deep self-doubt. This is
the basic problem of mankind.

This gospel, therefore, is dealing with something tremendously significant. It does not have to do only with what
happens when you die. This is one of the reasons why
hundreds of churches today are half-empty; so many people
do not know that self-worth is what the gospel is all about.
Young people today are looking for a ground of worth. They
want to be loved. All of us do. Well, far, far deeper than the
need to feel that some human being loves us is our need to
know that God loves us, and that we are acceptable in his
sight, that we have standing, value, and worth to him.
Something about us (that bit of eternity planted in our
hearts by God himself) bears witness to us that this is the
ultimate issue. Somehow life can never be satisfying if that
question is not settled. Therefore this good news comes
with tremendous relevance today. What God is offering is
a gift of righteousness—his own perfect righteousness, that
cannot be improved upon, a perfect value. By faith in Jesus
Christ he gives us a sense of worth and acceptance, and
there could be no better news to mankind.

Paul adds two things to this, so as to make it clear to us.
First, this righteousness is apart from the law. That is, it is
not something you earn; it is a gift. You cannot earn it by
doing your best to be pleasing to God, and anyone who approaches God on those terms has already failed. There is
no way anyone can measure up to God's standards. The
sweetest, dearest little old lady you know cannot make it,
because God knows her heart. Nevertheless, God has found
a way to give us that gift, and therefore it is apart from the
law; it is not something we can earn.

Known from of Old

Second, Paul says, it is witnessed by "the Law and the
Prophets." This gift is not something entirely new in history,

something that only Jesus Christ brought to light. He did make it known, so that we understand it far more clearly because of his coming, but it is found in the Old Testament as well as in the New. The saints who lived before the cross knew and experienced the wonder of this gift just as much as we do today, although they came to it by a different process.

The law bore testimony to this righteous gift of God by providing a series of sacrifices. The Jews knew, somehow, that they did not measure up to God's standards, so the law itself provided a system of offerings and sacrifices that could be brought and offered on the altar. This system pictured the death of Jesus; the whole sacrificial system of the Old Testament is a witness to mankind that One is coming, the Lamb of God who takes away the sins of the world. They bear witness to this righteous gift.

The prophets also—these well-known names of the Old Testament: Abraham, Moses, David, Isaiah, Jeremiah, and others—not only talked about this gift, but experienced it themselves. In one of the psalms, referred to in the next chapter, David is quoted as saying, "Blessed is the man whose transgression is forgiven, to whom the Lord will not impute iniquity, whose sins are covered." David understood that God had found a way to give the gift of worth to a man, even before the cross occurred in history. This is not new, Paul says; nevertheless, it is clearly explained and made fully available to us in the cross of Jesus.

In the next division Paul tells us how to obtain this gift. Perhaps you are looking for this sense of worth, this sense of value, of being loved and wanted by God. How do you get it? Here is Paul's answer.

> This righteousness from God comes through faith in Jesus Christ to all who believe. There is no difference, for all have sinned and fall short of the glory of God, and are justified freely by his grace through redemption that came by Christ Jesus (Rom. 3:22–24).

There is one way—expressed here in four different aspects, but only one way: through faith in Jesus Christ. Notice first how Paul's answer centers immediately on the person of the Savior, not only on his work or his teaching, but on his person. It is by faith in Christ himself that you come into this standing. He is the Savior; it is not what he taught, not even what he gives; but it is he who saves us. Therefore the gift involves a relationship to a living person. That is why in John's gospel he does not say, "Believe in what Jesus did" but rather, "As many as received him, to them he gave power to become the sons of God." That means there must come a time when you open your life to Christ, when you ask him to be what he offers to be: your Lord. Later in this epistle Paul will say, "If you confess with your mouth, 'Jesus is Lord,' and believe in your heart that God raised him from the dead, you will be saved [another term for this gift of righteousness]. For it is with your heart that you believe and are justified, and it is with your mouth that you confess and are saved" (Rom. 10:9,10). In the Book of Revelation Jesus himself said, "Here I am! I stand at the door and knock. If anyone hears my voice and opens the door, I will go in and eat with him, and he with me" (Rev. 3:20). There is no other way. No way can be found in all the religions of earth that can bring men into a sense of value and standing in God's sight, and of worth and love before him, except this way—by faith in Jesus Christ.

The Hand That Takes the Gift

Second, Paul stresses the fact here that it is all who believe who are saved; righteousness is not automatically and universally applied. Today many are teaching that the death of Christ was so effective that whether people hear about it or not, they are already saved. They do not even need to know about it, for they are saved by the death of Jesus. But Paul is careful to make clear that this is not true. You are saved when you personally believe. Faith, therefore, is the hand that takes this gift that God offers. What good is a gift if you do not take it? Gifts can be offered, but they cannot be used until they are taken. When that occurs, then the gift becomes effective in the life of the one who takes it.

The third element that describes how we obtain this
gift is in the phrase, "Justified freely by his grace." Do you
see what that says? It is God who does this. If you try to
say, therefore, that there is anything man must do to be
justified, you will destroy the gift, because it is all of God.
We are justified, made righteous, declared of worth in God's
sight, by his grace. If you add baptism to that, or church
membership, or anything else, then you destroy the grace of
God. It is God who freely and completely and wholly saves
us. We do not contribute a thing. Have you ever sung the
hymn, "Nothing in my hand I bring; simply to Thy cross I
cling"? That is one beautiful way of expressing this truth.

The last word in this section is this: The gift comes
"through the redemption that came by Christ Jesus." That
is, Christ is the one who accomplished the work of redemption. Here we are brought face-to-face with the cross, with
the death of Jesus. Many churches are given over to following the teachings of Jesus but hardly ever refer to his cross.
If you find a "Christianity" that does not emphasize the
cross, you are listening to "another gospel" which is not the
true gospel. The real gospel is based only upon the redemption which Jesus accomplished in his cross.

Paul now gives a brief explanation of how and why this
redemption works. "How" is found in the opening words of
verse 25, and "why" in the verses that follow.

> God presented him as a sacrifice of atonement, through faith
> in his blood. He did this to demonstrate his justice, because
> in his forbearance he had left the sins committed beforehand
> unpunished—he did it to demonstrate his justice at the pres-
> ent time, so as to be just and the one who justifies the man
> who has faith in Jesus (Rom. 3:25,26).

This is the heart of the gospel, and the ground of assurance.
Many people, even though they become Christians, struggle with assurance. They do not rest upon the fact that these
words are true, so they often struggle with doubts and uncertainty. They have a sneaking suspicion, deep inside, that

perhaps, despite all these wonderful words, God is still not quite satisfied; if something should happen to them, they might be lost. Pay careful attention to Paul's argument here. He gives a full answer to that struggle.

First, he says that God has accomplished a propitiatory sacrifice. God presented Jesus as a "sacrifice of atonement" through faith in his blood. The words, "sacrifice of atonement," are really translating a single word in Greek, *hilasterion*, which is translated "expiation" in some versions, and "propitiation" in others. I know those words are theological terms, and may not make much sense; however, it is important for us to understand their meaning, for herein lies the heart of the gospel.

To Release Love

Expiation is that which satisfies justice; propitiation is that which releases love. Both of these terms are involved in the death of Jesus, but expiation does not go quite as far as propitiation. Propitiation carries us clear through to the releasing of God's love toward us. That is why I think "propitiatory sacrifice" is a better translation than "expiation." Let me illustrate the difference. In these days we often read of industrial accidents. Let us say that someone has been injured in the course of his work and has been partially paralyzed. His company is at fault, having neglected to provide safety equipment, thus creating the conditions that put this man in danger. So the company is held accountable for the man's injury and subsequent paralysis. Therefore the court awards this man a tremendous sum of money, to be paid by the company. When the money is paid, the company has expiated its wrongdoings; it has satisfied the demands of justice. No longer does it have any responsibility toward this man; it has paid its costly debt. That is what expiation means.

But that does not say anything about how the man feels toward the company. He may yet be filled with resentment, bitterness, even hatred. He may spend the rest of his life

abhorring the name of that company, even though it has
given him all the money he could possibly use. The debt
has been expiated, but he has not been propitiated.

What Paul is saying here is that human sin has injured
God, just as that man was injured by the negligence of the
company. Our sin has hurt and injured God, and justice
demands that we be punished for that sin in some way. In
the death of Jesus that punishment was accomplished, so
that God's justice was satisfied. If you read this as expiation,
that is all the cross means. In a way, it means that it paid
God off, so that he no longer holds us to blame. But that is
not all Paul is saying here. The word means also that God's
love has been awakened toward us; he reaches out to love
us, and grants us the feeling of worth, acceptance, and
value in his sight. That is what propitiation means, and that
is what the death of Jesus does. It did satisfy God's justice,
but it went further; it released his love, and now he is
ready to pour out love upon us.

Paul shows us *why* this had to happen, beginning in the
middle of verse 25: "He did this to demonstrate his justice,
because in his forbearance he had left the sins committed
beforehand unpunished. . . ." What is he talking about?
He is referring to all the centuries when God apparently
had done nothing about the wrongdoings of men. People
are still questioning this today. They say, "Where is the
God of justice? How is it that a just God lets tyrants rise up
and murder millions of people? How can he let people live
in poverty and squalor and filth? He never seems to do anything about oppressors. Where is the justice of God?" Those
questions have been raised for centuries; in fact, we even
find them in the Psalms.

The last time in history that mankind got a clear idea of
God's holy justice was the event of the Flood. In response
to the wickedness of men toward other men, God wiped out
the whole human race except for eight people. The Flood
was a testimony to God's sense of justice, but there has
never been a manifestation of it to that degree since that
time. So the question arises in human hearts, "Does God

really care? It doesn't matter whether you do wrong or not,
God will let you get away with it. God won't do anything
to you." David writes, "Why do the wicked flourish, and
the righteous suffer? Where is the God of justice?" Now,
God has been patiently restraining his hand in order that
the human race may continue to exist, but people do not
see that. Therefore the justice of God seems to be com-
promised by his self-restraint.

No Compromise

But the cross settles that. The cross says that God remains
just. All the stored-up punishment amply deserved by the
human race is now poured out without restraint upon the
head of Jesus on the cross. God did not spare his Son one
iota of the wrath that man deserves. Though Jesus was his
beloved Son he did not lessen the punishment a single degree. All of it was poured out on him. That explains the cry
of abandonment that comes from the cross, "My God, my
God, why hast thou forsaken me?" In the Garden of Gethsemane, Jesus faced the possibility of being shut away from
all love, all beauty, all truth, all warmth, all acceptance,
the possibility of being forever denied all that makes life
beautiful. There he faced the eternity of emptiness in the
judgment of God, and this is what he experienced on the
cross; it was all poured out on him.

Paul's argument is that God did this to demonstrate his
justice at the present time—so as to be just, and yet free to
extend love to us who deserve only his justice. That is the
glory of the gospel. God's love has been freed to act toward
us, and his justice satisfied, so that it is no longer com-
promised by the fact that he forgives sinners.

In the closing paragraph, Paul gives us the results of this
forgiveness:

Where, then, is boasting? It is excluded. On what principle?
On that of observing the law? No, but on that of faith. For
we maintain that a man is justified by faith apart from observ-

ing the law, Is God the God of Jews only? Is he not the God
of Gentiles, too? Yes, of Gentiles too, since there is only one
God, who will justify the circumcised by faith and the uncircumcised through that same faith. Do we, then, nullify the
law by this faith? Not at all? Rather, we uphold the law
(Rom. 3:27–31).

Paul raises and answers three simple questions to show us
the natural results of this tremendous acceptance that God
gives us in Jesus Christ. First, who can boast? No one,
absolutely no one. How can we boast when everyone receives the gift of grace without merit on his part? This
means that all ground for self-righteousness is done away
with. This is why the ugliest sin among Christians is self-
righteousness. When we begin to look down on people who
are involved in homosexuality, or greed, or gambling, or
whatever—when we begin to think that we are better than
they are—then we have denied what God has done for us.
All boasting is excluded. There are no grounds for anyone
to say, "Well, at least I didn't do this, or this, or that." The
only ground of acceptance is the gift of grace.

Then, second, no one is excluded from grace, Jew or Gen-
tile. No special privilege or favor counts in God's sight. He
has no "most-favored nation"; they are all alike before him.
Paul argues, "Is God the God of Jews only? Then there must
be two Gods—one for the Jews and one for the Gentiles.
But that cannot be; there is only one God; God is one."
Therefore he is equally the God of the Gentiles and the
God of the Jews, because both must come on exactly the
same ground. This is the wonderful thing about the gospel.
All mankind is leveled; no one can stand on any other basis
than the work of Jesus Christ on his behalf.

Paul's third question is, "Does this cancel out the law or
set it aside? Do we no longer need the law?" His answer
is no; it fulfills the law. The righteousness which the law
demands is the very righteousness given to us in Christ. So
if we have it as a gift we no longer need to fear the law—
because the demands of the law are met. But it is not something we can take any credit for; indeed, whenever we act

in unrighteousness after this, the law comes in again to do its work of showing us what is wrong. That is all the law is good for. It shows us what is wrong, and immediately, all the hurt and injury accomplished by our sin must be relieved again by the grace of God, the forgiveness of God.

Receiving God's forgiveness is not something we do only once; it is something we take again and again. It is the basis on which we live, constantly taking fresh forgiveness from the hand of God. John's letter puts it this way: "If we confess our sins, he is faithful and just, and will forgive our sins and cleanse us from all unrighteousness" (1 John 1:9 RSV). That is God's gift, and we need all the time to take it afresh from the hand of God. When we find ourselves slipping into self-righteousness, when we find ourselves looking down our noses, when we find ourselves filled with pride and acting in arrogance, being critical, calloused, caustic, and sarcastic toward one another, or feeling bitter and resentful—and all these things are yet possible to us—our relationship to a holy God is not affected if we acknowledge that we have sinned. We can come back, and God's love is still there. He still accepts us and highly values us. We are his dearly loved children, and he will never change.

That is what God's gift of righteousness means to us. It is wonderful good news indeed, that we never need fear the condemnation of God. The God of ultimate holiness, the God who lives in holy light, whom we cannot begin to approach, has accepted us in the Beloved, and we stand on the same ground of worth that he himself does. We can remind ourselves, as I seek to do every day, of three things: I am made in God's image; therefore I am able to act beyond the capacity of any animal on earth. I am not an animal; I am a man made in God's image. Second, I am possessed of God's Spirit. That means I am forgiven, I am freed, and I am filled. Third, I am part of God's plan. I am part of the working out of his purposes in the world today, and God will make everything I do fit into his plan. Therefore, I can go on with purpose, and with confidence, and with love; without guilt, nor any sense of inadequacy or fear. I have perfect freedom to concern myself with the problems around me, and not be all wrapped up with the ones inside. Those are all taken care of. That is truly wonderful freedom.

8

The Father of Faith

In chapter 4 of Romans Paul uses Abraham as an illustration of a man who found the fantastic gift of righteousness, this gift of worth and standing and acceptance and significance before God. Abraham is one of the great names of all history. Few names are known and honored throughout the world in the entire record of human history, but Abraham is known, revered, and honored by three faiths—Judaism, Islam, and Christianity. Here is a man who, by any reckoning at all, stands head and shoulders above most of the human race. Paul uses Abraham as an example especially for the Jewish readers of his letter.

In the first twelve verses of chapter 4 Paul discusses three important questions about Abraham: How was Abraham made righteous? When was Abraham made righteous? And why was Abraham made righteous? Paul introduces the first question in verses 1–3:

> What then shall we say that Abraham, our forefather, discovered in this matter [that is, in regard to being acceptable before God]? If, in fact, Abraham was justified by works, he had something to boast about—but not before God. What does the Scripture say? "Abraham believed God, and it was credited to him as righteousness" (Rom. 4:1–3).

Paul says that Abraham our forefather discovered two ways
to gain a sense of worth. One, Paul suggests, is by works.
Abraham was a man of good works. Genesis, the very first
account of Abraham, when he was living in the city of Ur
of the Chaldees in the Mesopotamian Valley, describes
him as a religious man. Abraham was an idolator and worshiped the moon goddess, but he was not deliberately seeking to evade God. He worshiped the moon goddess in
ignorance. It was in the midst of that condition that God
appeared to him and spoke to him. Abraham believed God,
responded to his call, and set out on a march without a map.
He trusted God to lead him to a land he had never seen before, to take care of his family, and to lead them into a place
that would fulfill the promises of God. So Abraham appears in the Scripture as a man of great works.

Something to Boast About

But Paul says, "If in fact Abraham was justified (i.e.,
made righteous) by works, he had something to boast
about." Abraham discovered early in his life one way of
gaining a sense of significance, importance, or self-respect—
performance. If you can give a good performance in any
endeavor you will be highly thought of, you will gain a
sense of being appreciated, you will have a feeling of self-
respect, and you will be able to function on that basis. If
Abraham was righteous because of works, he had something to boast about. Works always give one something to
boast about. If we can look at the record and show people
what we have done and why we ought to be appreciated—
it helps! We may not boast openly, but we all have subtle
ways and clever tricks of getting it out into the open so
people can see what we have done. We drop a hint, hoping
that people will ask some more about it. Somehow we man-
age things so that people will know we have significance.
That is the way the world is today, and the way it was in
Abraham's day.

"But," says Paul, "that may work before men, but not before God." God is never impressed by that kind of performance. In fact, God, who sees the heart, is not looking at
outward performance; he knows what is going on. He knows
the selfishness, the greed, the grasping, the self-centeredness, the ruthlessness with which we cut people out and
harm those we profess to love. He sees all the maneuvering
and manipulating, the clever arranging that goes on in our
lives and in our hearts. Therefore, for the purposes of God,
that outwardly beautiful performance is utterly invalid,
worthless. That is why the sense of righteousness that results from our performance before men never lasts. It is but
a temporary shot in the arm that we need to repeat again
and again, almost as though we were addicted to it. But it
will always let us down in the hour of crisis. It is only the
righteousness that comes from God that is lasting and will
work—not only in time, but for all eternity. That is what
Abraham discovered: righteousness which comes from performance is worthless.

How did he discover this? Paul says, "What does the
Scripture say?" He refers to the fifteenth chapter of Genesis,
where God appeared before Abraham. He took him out one
night and showed him the stars in the heavens. "Abraham,
look up!" Abraham looked up into the stillness of that
oriental night, with the stars blazing in all their glory. God
said to him, "Even if you can number those stars, you cannot number your descendants. Their number will be far
more than all the stars of heaven" (see Gen. 15:5). And,
Paul says, "Abraham believed God, and it was reckoned to
him as righteousness"—self-worth, standing before God, acceptance, a sense of love and value in the sight of God was
his, by faith!

Fill in the Blanks

When the Scripture says that "Abraham believed God,"
we have to be careful. These Old Testament accounts are

highly condensed versions. They do not give us the details, so we have to fill them in from elsewhere in Scripture, and often we need to use a bit of sanctified imagination, guided by what the passage gives us. From other passages we know that God did not just say, "Abraham, see the stars? So shall your seed be." But we learn that God explained to Abraham what he meant by "seed."

In the letter to the Galatians Paul tells us that God made it clear to Abraham that when God said, "so shall your seed be," he was talking about Jesus Christ, who would be the seed of Abraham. God evidently explained to Abraham that there was One coming who would fulfill all the promises and that Abraham would have a heavenly seed as well as the earthly seed of his physical descendants. With regard to his spiritual descendants God said his seed would be Jesus. It is through Jesus that all Abraham's heavenly seed would be brought forth.

That is why, on one occasion, when Jesus was talking to the Pharisees, they said to him, "Abraham is our father." Jesus said to them, "Your father Abraham rejoiced at the thought of seeing my day: he saw it and was glad" (John 8:39,56). God evidently explained to Abraham and Abraham understood by faith that the seed of righteousness, Jesus the Lord, was coming and that he would die on the cross to remove the penalty and guilt of man's misbehavior and to settle the question of the justice of God. He would rise again from the dead as a living Lord to give his life to men and women everywhere, thus fulfilling the promise to Abraham. And Abraham believed God. He believed God's promise about the seed, and so he was justified, made righteous, given the gift of worth.

Interestingly enough, when James quotes this passage from Genesis 15 he says (in James 2:23), "Abraham believed God, and it was credited to him as righteousness," then he adds, "and he was called God's friend." That is acceptance, isn't it? Abraham became God's friend—not because he behaved so well, or because he was a godly man and obeyed God—he became the friend of God because he believed God's promise about the seed. Abraham is a beautiful example of what Paul is talking about here in Romans. Paul illustrates this in verses 4 and 5:

> Now when a man works, his wages are not credited to him as a gift, but as an obligation. However, to the man who does not work but trusts God who justifies the wicked, his faith is credited [or reckoned] as righteousness (Rom. 4:4,5).

Here is an illustration taken from common life, and it is very up-to-date. There is a tantalizing regulation in the income tax law that awakens my cupidity every year. The rule says that if money is given to you as a gift, it is not taxable. I keep looking for ways that will make it appear to the IRS that all the money I receive from my various functions as a pastor is really a gift. But the IRS will never buy it. They insist that if you work then what you are given is not a gift, but wages, and must be reported.

This is exactly the argument Paul uses. If you work for something, then what you get is never a gift, it is what you have earned. You have it as a result of your labor; it is an obligation that must be paid. Therefore you yourself can take the credit for having earned it. But then Paul draws a conclusion in verse 5: "However, to the man who does not work but trusts God who justifies the wicked, his faith is credited as righteousness." He is reckoned righteous—not because he earned it, but as a gift. Who is Paul talking about? From the context it is clearly Abraham. This could read: However, to this man Abraham, who does not work, but trusts God who justifies the wicked (the ungodly), his faith is credited to him as righteousness—worth, acceptance, standing, and love from God.

This is an amazing declaration of the gospel. It is startling to think that Abraham was a wicked man, but he was. Anyone who tries to earn acceptance, to earn God's love, to earn a place of respect and standing before God by trying hard to do things for him, is a wicked person. That is what the Scriptures say. He is trying to gain something by his own merit that can never be gained that way. Therefore it is the height of wickedness.

Many, many Christians fall into this trap. Having once accepted Christ and believed on him for their eternal destiny, they spend the rest of their lives trying to gain a sense of God's approval and love by hard, exhausting, committed, dedicated labor. But you can never win God's love that way. You will never know when you have done enough. You cannot earn the gift of love, but it is yours if you take it by faith in Christ, fresh every morning. That is what Abraham did.

In the Midst of Evil

Paul now brings in another illustration from the Old Testament to confirm this. He says David expressed the same idea when he spoke of the blessedness of the man to whom God credited righteousness apart from works. Paul says David is another man who gained this wonderful gift of righteousness—not by his performance, but by his faith. In verses 7 and 8 Paul quotes David:

> "Blessed are they whose transgression is forgiven,
>   whose sins is covered.
> Blessed is the man to whom the Lord imputes
>   count against him" (Ps. 32:1,2).

The remarkable thing is that David found this gift of self-worth before God when he was tortured by a guilty conscience. His hands were red with the blood of Uriah the Hittite and he was troubled with a wrong spirit that had plunged him into deep evil as the king of Israel.

Paul thus points out that Abraham failed to find righteousness by being devout and moral; he found it when he believed in Jesus, the seed. He was called the friend of God, not because he was such an obedient servant, but because he believed in what God said. And the bloody-handed, lustful king, David, failed to find righteousness by being the king of Israel. In the midst of his evil he found it in Christ when he believed God; he believed that God did not require the sacrifice of animals, but a broken spirit that trusted in what

God had to say about the great sacrifice that was yet to
come. Thus David is called "a man after God's own heart."
Now, would you like to be a friend of God, a man or a
woman after God's own heart? There is a way—not by your
performance, but by your trust in Jesus' life and death and
what that means for you every day.

The apostle moves on to take up the question of *when*
this happens:

> Is this blessedness only for the circumcised, or also for the
> uncircumcised? We have been saying that Abraham's faith
> was credited to him as righteousness. Under what circum-
> stances was it credited? Was it after he was circumcised, or
> before? It was not after, but before! And he received circum-
> cision as a sign and seal of the righteousness that he had by
> faith while he was still uncircumcised (Rom. 4:9–11a).

Many people today are embarrassed by God's emphasis
upon circumcision. Because of their upbringing these people
feel that sex is dirty, and that our sexual organs are never
to be discussed or mentioned. They apparently think bodies
end at the waist! That, of course, represents a twisted view
of human sexuality. God frequently discusses circumcision.
He chose it as the symbol of this marvelous truth that we
are talking about, and he gave it to the Jews for a specific
purpose. God is not in the least embarrassed by that fact,
and I don't think we should be either. If we will think
through this whole matter of circumcision we will gain
some powerful insights into human life.

No Saving Value

Paul makes two points here. First of all, Abraham was
circumcised fourteen years after he was pronounced righteous
by faith, fourteen years after he was called "the friend of
God." Therefore the ritual of circumcision cannot have any
saving value whatsoever. Abraham was already God's friend
fourteen years before he was circumcised. You can see how
effectively that wipes out the arguments of the Jews from
Paul's day on, who claim that it is the ritual that makes you

acceptable. This, of course, also cancels out the modern equivalent of circumcision, baptism. People are justified, made righteous, accepted in God's sight—not by being baptized, but by faith in the Lord Jesus, in his work and in his death.

I will never forget a young man who came into my study one day, Bible in hand, and announced that he had been reading the Bible. He didn't know a lot about it, but he asked, "Would you circumcise me?" I blinked three or four times, then asked, "Why?" He said, "I've been reading in this Bible that if you want to know God you have to be circumcised. I want to know God, so I want to be circumcised." So I patiently explained to him what circumcision meant, that it was simply a sign of something that was already true by faith. That boy became a Christian and is still growing in the Lord. As Paul made clear, it is not circumcision which saves, but faith in Christ.

The second point that Paul makes is that not only is ritual valueless in saving anyone, but that the real purpose of circumcision was twofold: It is a sign and a seal. I do not want to offend anyone, but I want to point out how much God thinks this is highly important. God personally chose the place on a man's body where this sign, this rite of circumcision, would be placed. God chose to put it on the male sex organ, and a little thought will tell us why. God wants men to remember what this ritual stands for. The most important thing you will ever remember is where love, self-acceptance, standing, and significance before God is to be found. So God placed it, (out of all the parts of the body he could have chosen) on this organ, because a man must handle it several times a day. It is a sign, therefore, that would be impossible to overlook.

Furthermore, Paul says, it is not only a sign, but a seal. A seal is a guarantee of permanency. Once again, the rite of circumcision, which removes the foreskin of the male organ, is an unchangeable act. Once it is done it cannot be undone. Therefore it is a guarantee of the continuity of this great truth. It is God's expressive way of saying with visible force,

"This is the ground of your life, the secret of your functioning as a human being, this great truth of acceptance before me. It will never change." Of course we no longer observe the physical sign of circumcision today (except for health reasons) but now it is "the circumcision of the heart" which applies to both male and female.

To Make Him Father

In verses 11 and 12 Paul discusses the question of *why* Abraham was made righteous. Beyond the personal salvation of Abraham himself, God had another reason.

> So then, he is the father of all who believe but have not been circumcised, in order that righteousness might be credited to them. And he is also the father of the circumcised who not only are circumcised but who also walk in the footsteps of the faith that our father Abraham had before he was circumcised (Rom. 4:11b–12).

The words "so then" really should be, "it was to make him" a father. Paul is not saying that circumcision made Abraham a father; he is talking about what circumcision stands for: the gift of being made acceptable before God, being loved by God, a gift of worth from God. That was given to Abraham, not only for his own personal salvation, but to make him a father of many more yet to come. Remember the stars in the heavens? That promise was yet to be fulfilled.

Perhaps you are not a physical descendant of Abraham. I happen to be. I learned several years ago from the genealogist of the Stedman tribe that the Stedmans go back to Abraham—through Ishmael! That makes me a physical descendant—but I am not boasting of that. However, we all are spiritual sons and daughters of Abraham when we have received worth and self-respect by believing, as Abraham did, that God meant what he said. He gives us this gift in Jesus Christ, quite apart from any merit on our part. Thus we become sons of Abraham, by faith, and he is thus the father of all who believe.

Jesus illustrated this use of the word "father" when he said to the Pharisees of his day, "You belong to your father, the devil" (John 8:44). Now Jesus did not mean that in some way the devil had been involved in their conception. What he meant is that they were following the philosophy of the devil. They were agreeing with and controlled by the philosophy of the devil, so they were sons and daughters of the devil.

Likewise, we think and act like Abraham when we trust that the basis of our acceptance by God is what Jesus is and has done for us and not anything that we are doing. In this way Abraham is our father and we are his spiritual descendants. Paul says this is true for those who are uncircumcised, and yet who keep on believing in Jesus; and it is true of those who are circumcised (the Jews) who also walk in the footsteps of the faith of Abraham. So Jews are not saved by being circumcised; they are saved by trust in God.

This is the great secret of life. What a change this makes in our motivation if we know that we do not have to earn God's love, God's favor, God's forgiveness. It is already ours. We do not have to earn it, it is ours every day. Nothing I know will set us more free than that. We do not need to take our sense of worth from other people. We do not need to maneuver and manipulate and cleverly show ourselves as people of some significance. We are set free from that. We already have the only standing that ever counts—our standing before God. So we can relax and give people love without demanding anything back. That is what Christianity is all about.

9

The Faith of Our Father

Faith is a simple thing, but hard for many to comprehend. Many people are confused on the subject. Some think that faith is nothing but mental assent to a truth—that if you believe a thing is true, then you are exercising faith. But faith is more than simply believing something is true.

Others believe that faith is a feeling, a feeling of confidence. If you happen to have confidence, you have much faith; if you do not have confidence, then you have little or no faith. Your faith depends upon how much feeling you can generate. But that is not true faith, and that definition of faith deceives many people.

There are some who think that faith is actually a type of self-deception. Someone has said that faith is a way of believing what you know is not true. There are people who actually try to believe something they know is not true. And they talk themselves into believing it and call that faith.

If you really want to know what faith is, you have to see it in action. That is why the apostle Paul, in Romans 4, brings in Abraham, the man of faith. He is by no means the only man who has faith, but he is preeminently qualified as a man of faith. Looking at Abraham you can learn what faith is. In the first part of Romans 4, we looked at the righteousness of Abraham. Now we are going to look at the faith of Abraham.

The apostle Paul points out four things about the faith of Abraham. First, we will look at the opposite of faith—what faith is not. Sometimes the best way to learn what a thing is, is to learn what it is not. Second, we will look at the effects of faith—what faith does, what it accomplishes. Then we will look at what faith actually is—the nature of faith. Last, we will consider the beneficiaries of faith, or those whom faith helps.

The Worthless Promise

Let us begin with what faith is not.

> It is not through law that Abraham and his offspring received the promise that he would be heir of the world, but through the righteousness that comes by faith. For if those who live by law are heirs, faith has no value and the promise is worthless, because law brings wrath. And where there is no law there is no transgression (Rom. 4:13–15).

Here Paul tells us that faith is not trying to obey and fulfill some kind of law. It is not doing our best to try to live up to some standard. That is the law, and no matter what the law is or where it came from, trying our best to live up to it is not faith. In that case, Paul points out, we are not living by faith, we are living by works. It is not faith to expect God to accept and love us simply because we have tried our best to obey some standard. In fact, if we live on those terms, we will find that we cannot receive what God wants to give us. Abraham is proof that this method will never bring the gift of righteousness. If we think that God is going to accept, love, and forgive us because we have tried hard to do what we think is right, we are on the wrong track. It will never work, and Paul tells us why.

First, notice that Abraham received the gift, the promise of righteousness, long before the law was ever given. "It was not through the law," Paul says, "that Abraham and his offspring received the promise." In fact, if we look at Galatians 3:17 and 18, we find that Abraham received the gift of righteousness 430 years before the law was given. So righteousness did not come by law, that is clear.

Second, the law renders the promise worthless. "For if those who live by the law are heirs [of the promise], faith has no value and the promise is worthless." Now it is important to understand that. Suppose someone says to you, "If you will get up off that chair and start flying around the room, I will give you a thousand dollars." You would have to say, "Forget it! No one can fly by their natural strength. You are asking of me something that I cannot do."

What does the law require of man? Basically, it requires something that he cannot do. It asks us to love. That is all that the law asks. It asks that we love God with all our heart, strength, and mind, and our neighbor as ourselves. That is all the Ten Commandments ask, that I act in love all the time, without fail. Simple, isn't it? Jesus said that love is the fulfillment of the law. When I love people, I am doing what the law demands. Don't say that by not being angry with them or not hurting them I am loving them. Love is a positive thing. Love is reaching out, and the law requires that I reach out in love.

Now, if I cannot do that, the promise that comes with the law is useless. The promise is: "Do this and live." If I obey the law, God will accept me as righteous; worth, value, and approval will be given to me because I earned them by doing what the law demanded. But if I cannot, then the promise is worthless. And we cannot love everybody, and we do not. We cannot love God as we ought. It is not only that we will not, but we cannot. Therefore the law is worthless in obtaining the promise.

But Paul does not stop there. He says there is another reason why you will never be able to gain righteousness by trying to meet the requirements of the law. The law brings wrath. It actually subjects you to punishment if you do not measure up. And this is what we find in experience; the law brings wrath. Wrath, as we saw in the first chapter of Romans, is God's removal of all divine protection so that we can do what we want. Wrath is the removal of restraints from human beings so they are free to have their own way. C. S. Lewis said, very wisely, that the whole world consists of just two kinds of people: those who say to God, "Thy will be done" and those to whom God is saying, "Thy will be done."

When God removes the restraints we begin to fall apart. Therefore, wrath always results in the disintegration of the human personality. Emptiness, meaninglessness, loneliness, and worthlessness possess us because we feel abandoned and lost. We do not know where to turn, and despair and depression press down on us heavily. That is always the case when wrath comes in. The law brings wrath. Thus when we seek to live by law we experience human disorientation (wrath) as a result.

Paul amplifies this by saying, "Where there is no law, there is no transgression." Where there is no law, people do not deliberately disobey God; they disobey in ignorance. Nevertheless they experience death but without knowing why. There are many people today who fall into this category. I find young people who are living in immorality, living together without marriage, in all innocence of any transgression. I believe that many of them actually have no idea that there is anything damaging or destructive or wrong about this. Some of them are so ignorant of reality they really think their action is not hurting them or anyone else. This attitude is widespread in our day. What these people lack is light. They have not yet learned that what they are doing is causing them to experience a disintegration of personality. They do not see that it is destroying them in many subtle and effective ways and that ultimately it will lead them into death and hell. What Paul means when he says, "Where there is no law, there is no transgression," is that death and hell are taking their toll on men whether they know it or not. He will expand this idea in chapter 5, for there he says that sin reigned from Adam to Moses, even over those who had not yet transgressed (according to Adam's transgression). By that he means they were acting in ignorance, and yet they were falling apart.

When the law comes in, it makes me aware of what is wrong. In one sense, that only makes it worse, because then I may deliberately begin to disobey what God says, and that will bring more wrath. But the law also brings hope, because when things get bad enough we are ready to turn to the one who can deliver: faith in the work of Jesus Christ. That is why the law will never bring us righteousness. So sincere, dedicated attempts to obey the law are not faith. Abraham is proof of that.

Fulfilled by Faith

Next, let us look at verses 16 and 17, which tell us what faith does:

> Therefore, the promise comes by faith, so that it may be by grace and may be guaranteed to all Abraham's offspring—not only to those who are of the law but also to those who are of the faith of Abraham. He is the father of us all. As it is written: "I have made you a father of many nations" (Rom. 4:16,17).

Here is faith in action. If law cannot achieve righteousness, what does faith do? First, the promise comes by faith. We actually obtain what we desire, this sense of being approved and loved and wanted and accepted before God himself. We are a part of his family and we are forgiven of all the past. All that is achieved by faith, not by seeking to earn it. The promise comes by faith. What works could not do, faith does.

As we have already seen in verse 13, the promise includes not only personal self-worth before God, which Abraham achieved, but it also makes one the heir of all the world. The apostle Paul says, "All things are yours . . . and you are of Christ, and Christ is of God" (1 Cor. 3:21,23). The promise also says you will be indwelt, as Abraham was, with the Holy Spirit of God. Galatians 3 makes clear that Abraham received that promise by faith, and we receive it the same way Abraham did. So faith obtains the promise.

The second thing that faith does is to introduce the principle of grace. Law and grace are opposed to one another in certain ways. They do not cancel each other out; they simply do two different things. We need both; we need law and we need grace. Do not ever say, "I am under grace, therefore I have no need for law." The Bible never takes that position. It is law that helps me to come to grace, and without it I never would come. But law and grace do not have the same functions. It is grace that guarantees the promise.

Now what is grace? There are many ways to define it. I love the one that says it is enrichment that we don't deserve: God's Riches At Christ's Expense. It is all the richness of life—love, joy, peace, and the fulfillment of the heart's longing—all that enriches our life but that we do not deserve. It is given to us; therefore it is a gift. There is an old hymn that puts it well:

> "Do this and live!" the law demands,
> But gives me neither feet nor hands.
> A better word his grace doth bring.
> It bids me fly, but gives me wings.

The law condemns; grace enables. If you and I had to earn the standing that we have before God—not only at the beginning of our Christian life, but every day through it—we would certainly fail somewhere along the line. If it depended upon us, somewhere we would blow it and lose the whole thing. But if it comes by grace, if it is purely a gift, and does not depend upon us at all but upon God alone, then it is guaranteed to all Abraham's offspring. So faith brings in the principle of grace which guarantees the promise to all who believe.

Now we come to the heart of the passage in verses 17 through 20. We are ready now to consider what faith actually is.

He [Abraham] is our father in the sight of God, in whom he believed—the God who gives life to the dead and calls things that are not as though they were. Against all hope, Abraham in hope believed and so became the father of many nations, just as it had been said to him, "So shall your offspring be." Without weakening in his faith, he faced the fact that his body was as good as dead—since he was about a hundred years old—and that Sarah's womb was also dead. Yet he did not waver through unbelief regarding the promise of God . . . (Rom. 4:17–20).

Paul gives us three things that tell us what faith is. The key, he says, is the *object* of faith. Next, he shows us the *obstacles* to faith. And then he tells us the *objectives* of faith—where faith will bring us.

The Quality of Our Faith

Abraham, Paul says, believed God. God was the object of his faith. The quality of our faith depends upon the object in which faith has placed its trust. The amount of faith I have has nothing to do with it. That is why Jesus told us that even if we have a little tiny faith, like a grain of mustard seed, it will work. The object of our faith is the important thing.

I may leave for work tomorrow and go out to the driveway with the utmost faith that when I get into my car and drive into the street my car will work just as it was working today. But it may be that while it was parked someone took off the hubcaps and removed the lug bolts from the front wheels and then put the hubcaps back on so I cannot see any difference. That may have happened. And though I have the utmost confidence that my car is going to work properly, when I get onto the street and turn the corner, sooner or later the front wheels are going to fall off. I might end up dead—killed by faith!

On the other hand, I may have become worried a bit by what I have just said, and perhaps I will go out to my car and take off the hubcaps and examine the lug bolts to make sure they are there. And even then I may not be too confident; I may start my car and drive it rather timidly down the driveway, still thinking that something might go wrong. But if no one has tampered with it I am perfectly safe— even though I have little faith—because the *object* of my faith is strong. That is why we should not talk about our faith; we should talk instead about the God in whom our faith is fixed. That is what Abraham looked at. It is not a question of how little or how big our faith is; it is a question of how big our God is! What kind of a God is he?

Two things about this God helped Abraham tremendously. First, he is the God who gives life to the dead—the God who makes dead things live, who takes things that once were alive, vibrant, full of life, but have died and become hopeless, and brings them to life again. And second, he is the God who "calls things that are not, as though they were." He calls into existence the things that do not exist. He is a creative God. In the Book of Genesis it is recorded that God said, "Let there be . . ." and there was. Over and over, for a week, God said, "Let there be . . ." and there was. Until, after six days, he rested. That is the kind of God whom Abraham had—the God who gave life to the dead and who called into existence things that did not exist. It was that God in whom he fixed his faith. Abraham's faith worked because the object of his faith was capable of doing whatever he said.

Obstacles

Now let us look at the obstacles to faith. Whenever we are called to exercise faith, there will be obstacles. Abraham teaches us this. There are horrendous obstacles, and Abraham faced two of them. First, there were hopeless circumstances. "Against all hope, Abraham in hope believed . . ." And it also says in verse 20, "Yet he did not waver [or stagger] through unbelief regarding the promise of God. . . ." That is, the promise itself was the second obstacle to faith because it had such staggering possibilities. It was too good to be true! That God would make him heir of all the world

and give him a standing before God that he did not deserve
was beyond belief. It was too good to be true, so that was
an obstacle to faith. Isn't that interesting? There are two
obstacles to faith: hopeless circumstances and staggering
possibilities. Let us see what Abraham did with them.

What were the hopeless circumstances Abraham faced?
Paul tells us there were two: Abraham's body and Sarah's
womb. Abraham's body was a hundred years old and was
sexually dead. The promise of God hung on the fact that
there must be a child born to Abraham and Sarah. Through
that child would come all the descendants of the nations of
the world that would be blessed by Abraham. And, more
important yet, through that child would come the Seed,
which was Jesus Christ, whom Abraham saw and rejoiced
in, and who would make possible the gift of righteousness.
Everything hung on the birth of a baby. Abraham looked at
the circumstances and saw his hundred-year-old body and
the barrenness of Sarah's womb. She was ninety years old
and had never had a baby. They had been trying for years
and years and no baby had come. These were the hopeless
circumstances.

Now, here is the beauty of Abraham's faith. Paul says
that he faced the facts. I love that. In the NIV translation it
says that "without weakening in his faith, he faced the fact.
. . ." Many of us think that faith is evading the facts—
escapism, some kind of dreamy idealism that never looks at
facts, a kind of unrealistic adventuring in which you hope
everything is going to work out. It is never that! Abraham
looked at the facts. He faced them head-on. There were
his dead body and the barrenness of Sarah's womb. He sat
and thought about it, and he saw how hopeless the situation was. There was no chance at all! His body was a hundred years old and Sarah's womb was ninety years old and
had never borne children. She was far past the age of child-
bearing. It was hopeless.

There was no hope, yet Abraham believed in hope. How?
Because when he looked at his dead body he remembered
that he had a God who raises the dead. And when he

thought about Sarah's barren womb, he remembered that
he had a God who calls into existence the things that do
not exist. That would take care of everything, wouldn't it?
And so, against all hope, he believed in hope, because of
the God in whom his faith was fixed.

Then he did one other thing. It is not mentioned here,
but this has always intrigued me. He told Sarah what God
had said. I have often wished I could go back in history
and observe certain times, and this is one of them. I would
have loved to have been a bug on the tent wall when Abraham came in to tell Sarah this news! As he comes in, she
says, "Well, dear, your eggs are ready. What have you been
doing?" He says, "Oh, I've been having devotions, and
what a wonderful time I had! God told me something." She
says, "Well, what was it?" Abraham says, "Well, I don't
really know how to put this; you'd better sit down. God told
me something very startling that is going to happen to us."
"That's interesting," she says. "What is it?" Then, just like a
man, he blurts it out: "You're going to have a baby!" And
Sarah says, "*What?*" Abraham says, "That's what God said.
You're going to have a baby." "What, *me?*" "Yes, you."
"Why, how can it be? Abraham, did you stop at the wine
shop on your way home this morning?"

And Sarah laughed. It says so in Genesis. Sarah laughed,
"Ha! God said that I'm going to have a baby!" But then
Sarah did something else. God had said something to Abraham that also applied to Sarah, and Abraham must have
told her. I am convinced that Sarah must have made a little
plaque and put it over the kitchen sink and meditated on
what God said. He said: "Is there anything too hard for
God?" When God says that he will do something, is there
anything too hard for God? And you know, when Sarah
began to feel pregnant, her faith laid hold of that promise
again. And when the baby came, Sarah was a woman of
faith, because she had been thinking of the God for whom
nothing is too hard. There is the faith of Abraham. That is
how he handled the hopeless circumstances.

How did he deal with the staggering possibilities? It is

unbelievable that all nations should be blessed through him. He would be heir of the world, he would be called the friend of God. Could it be? But Abraham remembered that he had a God who gives life to the dead and a God who calls into existence things that do not exist. And so he believed. Staggering as the possibilities were, they did not stagger Abraham because of the God in whom he believed.

Faith Grows

In verses 20 through 22 we find the *objectives* of faith. The first is in verse 20:

> . . . but [he] was strengthened in his faith and gave glory to God. . . .

His faith was made strong. Faith grows, just as Jesus said it would. If you have faith like a tiny grain of mustard seed, but the object of your faith is trustworthy and has promised to do something, then exercise your faith and it will grow. Obey! Abraham did; and as he believed and obeyed, he was strengthened in his faith and he gave glory to God. Faith never glorifies man; it glorifies God. It is God who acts, not man. What is accomplished is not something we do on behalf of God; it is God who does it by us and through us, on his own behalf. God, therefore, is thanked; and God is glorified. So faith grows, and faith glorifies. In verse 21 Paul says Abraham also was . . .

> . . . fully persuaded that God had power to do what he had promised. This is why "it was credited to him as righteousness."

Faith grounds us on the truth, as it did Abraham. He was fully persuaded. This is the faith that was credited to him as righteousness. Faith grasps the promise. Faith lays hold of what God has offered. As Abraham's faith grew, he grasped the promise and found himself loved and accepted by God, a friend of God.

Finally, verses 23 through 25 deal with the beneficiaries of faith:

The words "it was credited to him" were written not for him alone, but also for us, to whom God will credit righteousness—for us who believe in him who raised Jesus our Lord from the dead. He was delivered over to death for our sins and was raised to life for our justification (Rom. 4:23–25).

This happened two thousand years before Paul, but Paul says God did not write those words for Abraham alone. For whom were they written then? For us, today. We look at the faith of Abraham and say, "That was extraordinary faith." Paul says it wasn't; it was ordinary faith. Anyone can exercise such faith if they want to.

I can have righteousness, too. I can be a friend of God, accepted before him, with worth and value in his sight—not just once as I begin my Christian life, but every day, taking it fresh from his hand. I am forgiven of my sins, restored, every day afresh and anew—a thousand times a day if I need it. All that Abraham had—the promises of being heir of the world, the indwelling of the Spirit—all are ours as well. This verse says the gift of righteousness is for those "who believe in him who raised Jesus our Lord from the dead." He is still the God of resurrection, the God who can raise from the dead. "He was delivered over to death for our sins and was raised to life for our justification." So we live by his death and by his life. Now if we believe in the God who raised Jesus from the dead and we are ready to live on the basis of his death and his life for us, we, like Abraham, are heirs of all the world. All these things are yours, Paul says. The indwelling of the Spirit is granted to us moment by moment, and day by day, all our life long. And we, like Abraham, are the friends of God.

If I have a God who can raise things from the dead and who can call things into existence the things that do not exist, I am going to be a very exciting person to live with. I will never know when a thing that is dead and dull and lifeless may be touched by the grace of God and brought to life again. When something that I cannot possibly hope for —something which does not now exist, but which will be called into existence by the God who calls into existence the things that do not exist—when such a thing is promised by a God like this, life is an adventure. That is faith, when all things are ours. Do we have that kind of faith?

10

Rejoicing in Hope

In Romans 5, the apostle Paul traces the results of having been justified by faith. We can see this from the opening word of the chapter: "Therefore. . . ." Obviously, as a result of what he has already said, Paul is coming to certain conclusions.

> Therefore, since we have been justified through faith, we have peace with God through our Lord Jesus Christ, through whom we have gained access by faith into this grace in which we now stand. And we rejoice in the hope of the glory of God (Rom. 5:1,2).

That little word "rejoice" is the key to this whole fifth chapter. We find it again in verse 3: "Not only so, but we also rejoice in our sufferings . . ." Have we gone that far yet? That is a higher stage of Christian growth and development. Finally, in verse 11 we find that the apostle, with his very logical mind, says, "Not only is this so, but we also rejoice in God. . . ." This is the third level of Christian growth.

There is the outline of the whole chapter—learning to rejoice at these various stages; rejoicing in the hope of glory, rejoicing in present sufferings, and rejoicing in God. As a

Christian, if I really understand my theology, I will be rejoicing, even in the midst of suffering. As I look around at
Christians, sometimes I wonder if we ever grasp this idea.
Some of us look like we have been marinated in embalming
fluid. We never seem to rejoice. But Christian teaching and
doctrine is designed to produce a spirit that cannot help but
rejoice. It is not something artificial—screwing on a smile
and pretending that I am happy when I am not. When we
really understand Christianity, it will produce a truly rejoicing spirit. If I am a glum bum, I should study the fifth
chapter of Romans and it will turn me into a glad lad!

First, we learn to rejoice in our spiritual position; then, to
rejoice in our present troubles; and finally, we come to the
place where we rejoice in God himself, our powerful Friend.
For the moment, we will look at the first two verses only.

> Therefore, since we have been justified through faith, we have
> peace with God through our Lord Jesus Christ, through whom
> we have gained access by faith into this grace in which we
> now stand. And we rejoice in the hope of the glory of God.

The first thing we learn as a Christian is that we are justified
by faith. To help us understand what that actually means
the apostle brought in the example of Abraham, who was
justified by faith. Those two terms, "justified" and "faith,"
are explained to us and demonstrated for us in the person of
Abraham. To be "justified" means that Abraham was declared to be the friend of God. What we need to understand
is that Abraham didn't earn that. He was given that right
at the beginning of his relationship with God, when he believed God about the coming of a promised seed.

The War Is Over

Then, Paul says, there are three ways by which you can
test whether you really do believe God's promise and have
been justified by faith. Since we have been justified by faith,
the first result is that we have peace with God. As we think
about our lives and our relationship with God, if we really

have believed that God justifies the ungodly, we will have peace with God. I am a Christian. That means I am in the family, I belong to the family of God. The war is over. All the conflict between me and God is ended; I am at peace with him.

I was in Honolulu when World War II ended. We had gone through the excitement and joy of V-E day some months before, when the war had ended in Europe, but that was a long way from the South Pacific. Though we were glad that the fighting in Europe had ended, we still had a war to fight. Out in the South Pacific there were many bloody battles yet to come. But I will never forget the day it was announced that peace with Japan had been signed in Tokyo Bay. All over the world, World War II was at an end. In Honolulu the people simply poured out into the streets. All over the city lights that hadn't burned for years went on. There was dancing and shouting and music and laughter, with thousands of people jamming the beaches and streets of the city, rejoicing because they were at peace.

That is something of what happens in the heart when we understand that we have been justified by faith. The war is over, we are at peace with God. All conflict has ceased. I think there are at least four things that are true immediately when we are at peace with God.

Lost Fears

The first is that we lose our fear of God. There is something in all of us that instinctively fears God. I remember how awesome the person of God seemed to me as a boy. I thought of God as a heavenly policeman, always watching me, a stern and forbidding judge, ready to correct me and straighten me out. I will never forget the joy that came into my heart when I realized that God was no longer my judge—he was my Father. When one has been justified by faith, he no longer fears God as a judge because, according to this book and the promises of Scripture, it is no longer necessary that God function as a judge in relationship to him. He is now a loving, tender-hearted, compassionate father. As a father, of course, he does discipline. That is what love does. But God is no longer a judge. That beautiful picture our Lord gave us in the story of the prodigal son is the picture of God as we learn to see him. Having been justified by faith, we immediately lose our fear of God.

Second, we lose our fear of death. If we have been justified by faith, we are no longer afraid to die. When I was young I lived for a while in the Red River Valley of North Dakota in a little Scottish settlement named after Ayr, Scotland—Ayr, North Dakota. It was a Presbyterian settlement and held to the old custom of ringing the bell of the church when someone died. I can still remember lying in my bed, listening to the tolling of the bell, knowing that someone had died and feeling the cold clutch of fear on my own heart as I faced the possibility of my own death. Someday I would die. It could even happen while I was a boy. I knew it could, because a friend of mine had died. I knew it could happen to me, and I felt the fear of death.

Certain psychologists and psychiatrists are now admitting that the basic fear behind all other human fears is the fear of death. The conflict with which we constantly live is this shadow of the end that hangs over us all, this awareness that some day this life is going to come to a close for us. Hebrews speaks of that. It says, Jesus came ". . . so that by his death he might destroy him who holds the power of death—that is, the devil—and free those who all their lives were held in slavery by their fear of death" (Heb. 2:14,15). So when I come to understand that I have been justified, given a righteous acceptance by a loving father, I immediately lose that fear of death. I am no longer afraid of what lies beyond. I know it is not judgment, but glory.

Third, when I have peace with God, I have the answer to the attacks of doubt and fear the devil is still able to bring into my life. Surely this is one of the things that troubles many young Christians. They start out their Christian life with a sense of rejoicing and an experience of peace. But after a while there will come a time when all they have been believing and resting on and rejoicing in seems to turn dull and cold and unbelievable. They don't know what has happened. They think they have just been kidding themselves about Christianity, and now they have awakened to the cold reality of life. They do not understand that the devil, through his angels, has access to us through our thoughts. He can insert these troubling doubts and fears into our minds without our being aware of it—even against our will, at times.

I know there are some who think that after one has been a Christian awhile he should reach a point when he never again has any doubts. But we never do. Some people think that pastors never have any doubts about their salvation or their relationship with God. On my own experience that is not true.

When I first came to Palo Alto there was a dear old Presbyterian pastor, Dr. Francis Russell, who was a tremendous help to me as a young pastor. Just a couple of years before Dr. Russell died I received a call from him, asking me to come and see him. I found him in deep distress over his personal salvation. He told me, "I feel like God is angry with me. If I were summoned into his presence now there is nothing I could offer to him." I had to help that dear, godly old man, and remind him again that he had been justified by faith in the work of Christ. I reminded him that his salvation had nothing to do with what he was like, but with Jesus, and what *he* had done. This is how we can deal with these doubts and fears if we have believed in our justification by faith.

If you do not have that sense of peace, the way to get it back is not by working on your feelings, but by reviewing your justification. Go over the facts again, remind yourself of what God has declared, and what kind of a God he is— Abraham's God, who can raise the dead to life and call into existence things that do not exist. He is able to perform what he has promised. Then your faith will be restored and you can handle these doubts and fears.

Fourth, if we have peace with God, we have an answer

to the accusation of our own consciences when we sin. I know that many young Christians, in that glory and first flush of love in their relationship with the Lord really think they are not going to sin again. Sin seems to them an impossible thing. Their hearts are so caught up with the love God has shown to them, that they cannot imagine themselves going back and doing some of the things they once did. But sooner or later they will be back doing some of those things. Old habits will reassert themselves; old ways of thinking will return. Perhaps they will not go back to all that they did formerly, but they will go back to some. They will sin again. Or it may be that after years of Christian life and service, they will fall into some terrible sin they thought they never would or could do again.

What do you say then to your accusing conscience when it asks, "Are you a Christian? Could you possibly be a Christian and act like this?" That is where justification by faith comes in. You remind yourself at that time: "My standing and my acceptance by God does not depend upon me. Even my sin does not cancel it out. The whole essence of this truth is that God has found a way to put aside my sin, in the work of his beloved Son on my behalf." That is why you read, at the close of the chapter, "He was delivered over to death for our sin and was raised to life for our justification" (Rom. 4:25).

These are the ways you can test whether you really have believed it: Do you have peace with God? Are you freed from the fear of God and the fear of death? Do you have an answer to the doubts and fears and attacks that come from the enemy, those "fiery darts of the wicked one" that Paul speaks of in Ephesians 6? Do you have an answer to the accusations of your own guilty conscience when you fall, or sin? Here is where the answer lies: You have been justified by faith.

Notice that Paul is careful to remind us again that our justification is through the Lord Jesus Christ. It is never through ourselves. We have no merit before God ourselves. We never deserve this, we never earn this, and no matter

how long we have served God as a Christian and have lived
a clean and moral life, we can only stand on the ground of
the work of the Lord Jesus on our behalf. That is why Paul
insists on saying this again and again. He knows our prideful flesh. He knows that after we have cleaned up some of
the bad areas of our lives we will begin to take credit for it
and think that we have deserved something from God. So
he faithfully reminds us that we are not deserving in this
matter at all. The first mark of our justification by faith,
then, is that we have peace with God.

Access to the King

The second mark is found in the next verse:

> . . . through whom we have gained access by faith into this
> grace in which we now stand (Rom. 5:2).

We have access to continued grace, to enable us to stand in
the midst of pressures, problems, trials, and difficulties. This
is a constant supply, because we have instant access to God
himself, the God of all grace. That is the second way we
know we are justified by faith—we see that we have this
instant access to the grace of God—to the throne of grace,
as the writer of Hebrews puts it.

A beautiful picture in the Book of Esther illustrates this.
Esther, a lovely Jewish maiden, was a captive in the land of
Persia. The king, seeking a bride, found her and made her
his queen. After Esther ascended to the throne as queen,
a plot was hatched against the Jews. Unwittingly, the king
signed a decree that meant death for all Jews in the land
of Persia. Esther's godly uncle, Mordecai, said it would be
necessary for her to go to the king and tell him what he had
done. Esther knew that was a dangerous thing, because it
was the law that no one could come before the king without first being summoned by him. There were no exceptions
—even for a queen—for this was the law of the Medes and
the Persians which could not be changed. Unless the king
extended his golden scepter to that person, he must die.

Yet Esther knew that she must dare to take her life in her hands and go before the king.

The story tells us that she fasted for three days and three nights before she went. I am sure that was to prepare her heart and her courage. It does not say what else she did during that time when she was getting ready to come before the king. With a wife, four daughters, and a mother-in-law in my home, I have observed women getting themselves ready for some years now, and I'm sure that one of the things Esther was doing was fixing her hair. It probably took three days and three nights to get it ready! Then we are told that she dressed herself in robes of beauty and glory, and stepped into the audience hall of the king, appearing all alone before him. The king was so smitten with her beauty that his heart went out to her. He stretched forth his scepter and accepted her. She had abundant access to the king.

This is a picture of what Paul is telling us. Who would dare stand before the God of all the earth, the God of majesty and power and greatness and glory, unless he had been given access to the King? The wonder of this promise is that by being justified by faith, we have been given access into his presence. Esther received from the king's hand all that she needed to handle this problem which was a threat to her life. That is what this portrays for us. Dressed in robes of beauty and glory that do not belong to us—for they are the garments of Jesus—we have access to the King, to receive from him all that we need to handle any threat that has come into our lives. We have continual acceptance before him. Our strength does not come from our circumstances; we get it from our continual access to the power and presence of God in our lives in the midst of danger or difficulty, trouble or pressure. The writer of Hebrews puts it this way:

> Therefore, brothers, since we have confidence to enter the Most Holy Place by the blood of Jesus . . . let us draw near to God with a sincere heart in full assurance of faith . . . Heb. 10:19,22).

Something Beyond

Now look at the third thing that comes as a result of being justified by faith:

And we rejoice in the hope of the glory of God (Rom. 5:2).

That means that as we look at life ahead, even though life comes to an end—and it will—that is not the end of the story. There is a confident anticipation that something is beyond. We rejoice in the hope of the glory of God.

Hope here is not a word that means a mere possibility, a good chance. Hope, as it is used in the Scriptures in this way, is speaking of a ringing certainty, based upon the words of Jesus himself. "If I go and prepare a place for you, I will come back and take you to be with me that you also may be where I am. . . . Because I live, you also will live" (John 14:3,19). That is the certain hope of everyone who has been justified by faith. If you really have been justified by faith you know that you have the promise of God that he will do this, and that he is able to do what he has promised.

That promise is given to us regardless of what our conditions here on earth may be. It may be tough here. For some people it is tough. There are some Christians in other parts of the world who know nothing of the freedom and the joy of relationships that we experience together in this country. They are under persecution, they are in danger, they wake up every morning with the dreary expectation of living one more day under the watchful eye of some hostile person. Life may be cold and hard, it may be filled with pain and sorrow, but the minimum promise to all who are justified by faith is that there is a glory beyond death that is absolutely certain.

I have a friend who lives in the Midwest. He lives in the country, and one stormy morning, in the dead of winter, he looked out his window and saw the mailman drive up and leave something in his mailbox. Wanting to see what it was, he dressed warmly and went out into the bitter cold. With the snow swirling about him, he walked about a quarter of a mile down the lane to where the mailboxes were located. He opened the mailbox and, to his disappointment, saw that all that was there was a seed catalog. But he opened it and began to thumb through it.

You know, there is nothing like a seed catalog to capture the beauty and brilliance of flowers and vegetables. As he stood there in the snow, suddenly he felt as though spring had come. He could taste the crunch of a cucumber and smell the fragrance of those red roses and feel the juice of a red–ripe tomato running down his chin. It seemed as though winter faded away for the moment and he was caught up into the beauty of spring and summer. Surely that is something of the experience that we get at times when we read the Scriptures. Here in the midst of "the winter of our discontent," something of the glory that is waiting beyond, the hope of the glory of God, breaks through.

I will never forget reading, as a young Christian, the words of Samuel Rutherford, that dear old seventeenth century Scottish Covenanter who lived at a time when the English church was persecuting the believers in Scotland. He was a dear and godly man who had come to know and love the Lord Jesus and to understand these great truths in the Scriptures about the inner strengthening that can come through faith. As he was lying on his deathbed, he received a summons from the king of England to come to London and appear on trial for his life. He knew he was dying, and he sent back this word by the messenger of the king: "Go and tell your master I have a summons from a Higher Court; and ere this message reaches him, I'll be where few kings and great folks ever come." That was the spirit of the man. He wrote many letters that reflect the glory of his faith and expectations. Anne Cousin has gathered them up for us. Some of them are arranged as hymns. One was D. L. Moody's favorite hymn, and it is mine also:

> The sands of time are sinking,
> The dawn of heaven breaks,

The summer morn I've sighed for,
The fair sweet morn awakes.
Dark, dark hath been the midnight,
But dayspring is at hand,
And glory, glory dwelleth
In Emmanuel's land.

O! Christ He is the Fountain,
The deep, sweet well of love!
The streams on earth I've tasted,
More deep I'll drink above;
There to an ocean fullness
His mercy doth expand,
And glory, glory dwelleth
In Emmanuel's land.

The bride eyes not her garment,
But her dear Bridegroom's face;
I will not gaze at glory,
But on my King of grace;
Not at the crown he giveth,
But on His pierced hand;
The Lamb is all the glory
Of Emmanuel's land.

—Anne R. Cousin

That is the first stage of the Christian life—just the beginning. That is what we get, without fail, when we believe that we are justified by faith. But it is just the start. Then we go on to handle life and its suffering, and finally, we end up rejoicing in God. But everyone who has put faith in what Jesus Christ has done on his behalf—not in what he himself has done—has come to a place of complete assurance, continual acceptance, and confident anticipation. When we know we have been justified by faith we will have these in our life.

11

Rejoicing in Suffering

We have just seen the first stage, or level, of Christian growth—the rejoicing in hope that comes as a result of being justified by faith before God. That rejoicing comes immediately. We rejoice because we are going to be with the Lord. We have a hope for the future, a hope beyond death. But Paul goes on:

> Not only so, but we also rejoice in our sufferings, because we know that suffering produces perseverance; perseverance, character; and character, hope. And hope does not disappoint us, because God has poured out his love into our hearts by the Holy Spirit, whom he has given us (Rom. 5:3–5).

It is clear from this that Christians are expected to experience suffering. We do not like that; nevertheless, it is a fact. In his letter to the Philippians, the apostle Paul puts it very plainly, "For it has been granted to you on behalf of Christ not only to believe on him, but also to suffer for him" (Phil. 1:29).

So those who think that becoming a Christian will remove them from suffering have been seriously misled and self-deceived, for the Scriptures themselves teach that we are to expect suffering. The Greek word for "suffering" basically means tribulation, something that causes distress. It can range from minor annoyances that we go through every day to major disasters that come sweeping down out of the blue and leave us stricken and smitten.

According to Romans 5, the proper Christian response to suffering is to rejoice. "Not only so, but we rejoice in our sufferings." Here is where many people balk. They say, "I can't buy that! Do you mean to say that God is telling me that when I am hurting and in pain, going through mental and physical torment, I am expected to be glad and happy and rejoice in that? What kind of a nut is this Paul, anyway? It's not human, not natural!"

There are many who feel this way. I think we can easily identify with the attitude of the lady whose pastor went to see her when she was going through trouble. She kept complaining and grousing and griping about it. He stopped her and said, "I don't think you should talk that way. Christians are not to do that." She was very upset. "Why, I don't understand, Pastor. When God sends us tribulation, I think that he expects us to tribulate a little bit!"

Unanimous Testimony

Most of us would feel the same way. We feel like tribulating, and we do. But it is instructive to note that it is not only Paul who tells us to rejoice, but this is the unanimous testimony of every writer in the New Testament. We are told by all to rejoice in our suffering. First Peter 4:12 says, "Do not be surprised at the painful trial you are suffering, as though something strange were happening to you. But rejoice. . . ." It is not strange, it is normal. James 1:2 says, "Consider it pure joy, my brothers, whenever you face trials of many kinds." There is that word again: joy, rejoicing. Even the Lord Jesus told us, in the Sermon on the Mount, "Blessed are you when people insult you, persecute you and falsely say all kinds of evil against you because of me." What does he say? "Rejoice and be glad, because great is your reward in heaven . . ." (Matt. 5:11,12). Paul's call to rejoice in suffering is found everywhere in Scripture.

Let us take a closer look at what this really means. Despite what many people think, there are certain things it does not mean. First, it is clear from Scripture that rejoicing in suffering is not a form of stoicism. It is not simply a "grin-and-bear-it" attitude, or tough it out and see how much you can take, or just hang in there until it's over and don't let anything get you down, or keep a stiff upper lip. Many people feel that if they do that, they are fulfilling the Word and "rejoicing in suffering." But that is not it. There are non-Christians who can do that. Many people pride themselves on how much they can take. Sometimes people who are not Christians will put us to shame by the things they can bear without complaining. Rejoicing in suffering is not merely being stoical.

Furthermore, we are not expected to enjoy the pain. There are some people who think "rejoicing in suffering" means that you are to enjoy your pain and hurt, that somehow Christians ought to be glad when terrible tragedy occurs and their hearts are hurting. That is not what Paul is saying. The people who feel that way are called masochists. They like to torture themselves. You have met people like that, who are not happy unless they are miserable. If you take their misery away from them, they are really wretched, because it is their misery that gives them a sense of contentment. That is a twisted, distorted view of life. That is not what Paul is saying.

Nor is he saying that we are to pretend that we are happy. Some think this passage is saying that when you are out in public, you should put on an artificial smile and act happy, when inside your heart is hurting like crazy. But Christianity is never phony. Phoniness of any kind is a false Christianity. Neither the apostles nor the Scriptures ever ask us to be unreal in our responses. This scripture clearly tells us to have a genuine sense of rejoicing.

However, you may not be able to rejoice right at the moment of trial. Hebrews 12 helps us there. It says plainly,

"No discipline seems pleasant at the time, but painful. Later on, however, it produces a harvest of righteousness and peace for those who have been trained by it" (Heb. 12:11). Right at the moment of hurt you are not going to feel like rejoicing, but it should soon follow that you rejoice in your suffering.

I heard a man some years ago put this very clearly. He had gone through great physical trouble, and one of his legs had been amputated. That did not arrest the course of his disease, and he ultimately died because of it. Just a few days before his death I visited him in the hospital and he said something to me that I never forgot because it so perfectly expresses what Christian rejoicing in suffering means. He said, "I never would have chosen one of the trials that I've gone through, but I wouldn't have missed any of them for the world!" Now that is saying it. There is an awareness that this suffering has done something of supreme value; therefore, you wouldn't have missed it. But you wouldn't have chosen it, either! That is rejoicing in suffering.

Inside Information

How do you get to the place where you can rejoice in suffering? The apostle's answer is, "We rejoice in suffering because we know. . . ." We are to rejoice because we know something. It is not just because it is such a great feeling to be hurt, it is because of something our faith enables us to know, a kind of inside information that others do not share. Worldlings lack it totally. Something that we know will cause us to rejoice in our suffering. What do we know? Paul says, "Knowing that suffering produces. . . ." Suffering does something, accomplishes something. It is productive. It is of value. We know it works, and that is what makes us rejoice.

Watch a woman in labor; watch the expression on her face. If you have any empathy in you, you cannot help but feel deeply hurt with her because she is going through such pain. And yet, there is usually joy in the midst of it because she knows that childbirth produces children. It is the child that makes it all worthwhile. Suffering produces something worthwhile.

Then what does suffering produce? The apostle says there are four things that suffering produces. First, suffering produces perseverance. In some versions the word is patience. The Greek word literally means "to abide under, to stay under the pressure." Pressure is something we want to get out from under, but suffering teaches us to stay under, to stick in there and hang with it. These are some of the expressions that we use today, and I think they are appropriate. Perseverance is the opposite of panic, of bailing out. The best translation I can think of is the English word "steadiness." Suffering produces steadiness.

When I was a boy in Montana, I used to help a man break horses, working in a corral with three-year-old horses that had never had saddles on their backs. I was always interested in watching the horses when they first felt a saddle thrown on their back. That must be a frightening experience to an animal. They don't know what in the world is happening to them. Some horses will react with anger, rearing back and trying to get away—even striking out with their forefeet at their trainer. Their nostrils flare, their eyeballs roll, and they panic! Others will just stand there trembling, shaking like a leaf. They won't move, they're so afraid. They do not know what is happening to them.

I think Christians respond that way, too. Do you remember when you became a Christian and first went through a trial? How easily you panicked and cried out to the Lord, "What's gone wrong?" You were in a panic over what was happening, fearful that it would wreck everything and destroy your hopes and dreams. You were just like the disciples in the boat on the Sea of Galilee when the storm was raging. They panicked. They came to the Lord and shook him and said, "Wake up! Don't you know we're about to perish?" And the Lord did as he does with some of us. He stood up and said, "Don't panic." Then he said to the storm, "Peace, be still." And quiet came.

That is what suffering does. It steadies us. We go through a time like that and we're all panicky; then the Lord stills the storm and we think, "Thank God that's all over. I'll never have to go through that again! I've learned my lesson!" And two weeks later, there is another storm. But this time we've been through it once, so we steady up a bit. We do not get quite so panicky.

We learn something—we learn about ourselves, first. We learn that we are not as strong as we thought we were. We learn that we do not have the stick-with-it we thought we had. We wanted to bail out much sooner than we thought we would.

Then we learn something about the Lord—we learn how gracious he is. We learn that he can handle events in ways that we could not dream of nor anticipate. We see him work things out in ways that we could never have guessed. So the third and fourth times a trial comes up, we are steadier. We don't panic; we don't bail out. We stay under and let it work itself out. That is what Paul is saying here. Suffering produces steadiness. If we did not suffer, we would never learn that quality.

Proven Reliability

Second, not only does suffering produce steadiness, but steadiness, Paul says, produces character. The Greek word for "character" carries with it the idea of being put to the test and approved. It is the idea of being shown to be reliable. Steadiness produces reliability. We finally learn that we are not going to be destroyed, that things will work out. Steady up, and people start counting on us. They see strength in us, and we become more reliable people.

We have all seen the tire advertisements on television in which a car is equipped with four tires and put through horrendous tests—driven through desert sands, bogs, swamps, and marshes, driven over rough, hard, cobblestone roads, over roads with holes and chuckholes, over boards studded with nails. The tire is twisted and pulled and stretched in every direction, and we are amazed at what that tire can take! After the test is over, they hold the tire up and it looks as though it has never been out of its wrapping! Then the ad comes: "Buy Sock'em Tires! They're tested, proven!" Now that is what this word "character" means. God is building me up so he can hold me up and say, "He's approved, he's tested."

God is in the process of making veterans. A veteran has been through something and has been tested and proven. Here is a passage I have always loved from the *Living Bible:*

> I think you ought to know, dear brothers, about the hard time that we went through in Asia. We were really crushed and overwhelmed, and feared we would never live through it. We felt we were doomed to die and saw how powerless we were to help ourselves; but that was good, for then we put everything into the hands of God, who alone could save us, for he can even raise the dead. And he did help us, and he saved us from a terrible death; yes, and we expect him to do it again and again (2 Cor. 1:8–10).

Now, this is a veteran speaking. He has been through some tough things, but he knows that God can take him through anything, and he will. He is not saying, "It's all over." No, he is saying, "There's more coming, but God will take us through." That is a veteran.

Years ago I asked a nine-year-old boy, "What do you want to be when you grow up?" I'll never forget his answer. He said, "I want to be a returned missionary." He did not want to be just a missionary, but a returned one—one that has been through it and it is all behind him. Here Paul tells us that God is in the process of building returned missionaries.

Third, we find that reliability also produces something. Suffering produces steadiness, steadiness produces reliability, and reliability produces hope. So now we are back to hope again. In verse 2, Paul spoke of "rejoicing in hope," the hope of sharing the glory of God, a hope for the future beyond death. But here is hope that we will share the glory of God—which is God's character—*right now.* We have the hope that God is producing the image of Christ in us right now. That is a great thing! This hope is a certainty, not just a possibility.

We are being changed; we see ourselves changing. As we grow more like Jesus, we become more thoughtful, more compassionate, more loving. We are being mellowed. We are becoming like Christ—stronger, wiser, purer, more patient. To our amazement, a certainty grows in our hearts that God is doing his work just as he promised. He is transforming us into the image of his Son.

Confidence from Hope

That brings us to the fourth step Paul mentions here, and it is that hope does not disappoint us. I like the King James translation better. It says, "hope does not make us ashamed." That is a figure of speech called "litotes," which is the use of a negative to express a positive idea. Paul does this in Romans 1:16 when he says, "I am not ashamed of the gospel of Jesus Christ because it is the power of God. . . ." What does he mean? He means he is proud; he is confident and bold. I think that is the term we ought to use here. Hope makes us confident. Hope, or certainty, produces confidence and boldness.

I met a man who had gone through the terrible trauma of having been shot by his own son. He survived this awful time, and then began to stand up before groups of men to tell them how God used that situation to get his attention, and he began to study and to grow. Hearing him, I could understand that a man who previously had been ashamed to speak of Christ was now confident and bold. What the Lord had shown him, and how the Lord supported and sustained him through this terrible, tragic time meant so much to this man that he did not care what anyone thought about it. He shared openly what God had brought him through. We lose our fear of ridicule and shame and we speak up and share out of the reality of our experience of what God has brought us through.

Paul goes on to explain why hope does not disappoint us. He says it is "because God has poured out his love into our hearts by the Holy Spirit, whom he has given us." Now, to my mind, this is one of the most important verses in the Book of Romans. It is a significant verse because it is adding a thought that we have not had in this Book up to now. It is the explanation, above all else, of how to rejoice in suffering. This is the first mention in the Book of Romans of the Holy Spirit. It is also the first time in this Book that the love of God is brought in. Up to now Paul has not said anything about the love of God, but now it is "God has poured out his love into our hearts by the Holy Spirit, whom he has given us."

We must be careful to see how Paul presents this concept here because the love of God is the subject he develops in verses 6 through 10. That connection is important because these verses have been extracted from their context and used for evangelistic preaching so many times that we may have forgotten what they originally meant. Paul uses them here in connection with suffering.

> . . . God has poured out his love into our hearts by the Holy Spirit, whom he has given us. You see, at just the right time, when we were still powerless, Christ died for the ungodly. Very rarely will anyone die for a righteous man, though for a good man someone might possibly dare to die. But God demonstrates his own love for us in this: While we were still sinners, Christ died for us. Since we have now been justified by his blood, how much more shall we be saved from God's wrath through him! For if, when we were God's enemies, we were reconciled to him through the death of his Son, how much more, having been reconciled, shall we be saved through his life! (Rom. 5:5–10)

The argument here is extremely important. It will explain to us how to rejoice in suffering. I know Christians who are suffering but are not being made steady and reliable and confident. Instead, they are being made bitter and resentful and angry, even to the point of denying their faith. Suffering, you see, does not produce these qualities automatically. We can go through suffering as a Christian and be filled with anger and rage and resentment against God. What makes the difference?

Evidence of Love

As Paul explains here, the difference lies in seeing our suffering as evidence of God's love, and not his wrath. Then we will experience that love in the midst of the suffering. The Holy Spirit will shed abroad in our hearts an experience of the love of God so rich and radiant and glorious that we will not be able to do anything but rejoice in our suffering. But, if we see our suffering as evidence of God's wrath, we will be frustrated, angry, and miserable. That is why Paul brings in this description of God's love for us.

Anyone who has gone through any degree of suffering knows that in the moment of pain and hurt it is easy to feel that God does not love you. It is easy to feel rejected, unloved. We are so used to thinking that love is something which blesses us and warms us and takes care of us, it is almost impossible for us to think we are being loved when we are hurting. It is hard for us to believe that the one who is bringing the hurt is doing it out of genuine love for us. We feel broken, worthless, and forgotten. That is why we need to understand the argument in verses 6 through 10.

Paul says there is a place where every Christian knows that God loves him, even though he himself feels worthless, useless, and forgotten. What is that place? It is the cross. In the cross of Jesus Christ we always see two things. First, we see ourselves. We see, as Paul puts it here, that we are helpless. If there were any other way to get to God, then there never would have been a cross. But the cross is God's testimony that there is no other way. That is why the verse says, "At the right time, in due time, Christ died." At that time in history God amply demonstrated to all the world that man could not save himself.

The great Hebrew prophets had spoken, and that did not help. Greek philosophers had taught, and that did not help.

The Romans had come in with their military might, and law and order was imposed over the course of the whole world of that day, and that did not help. But at the right time, Christ died on the cross so that men could see how helpless and powerless they were to save themselves.

As we look at the cross we see how ungodly we are. We are not like God, we do not act like God. We have the capacity to do so, but we do not. We even want to at times, but we do not. Therefore, we see in the cross how unlike God we are. We see that we are sinners, destroying ourselves and others. We find ourselves lawless and selfish at times, and we know it was man's sin—our sin, yours and mine—that nailed Jesus to that cross. It was not his own sin, but yours and mine. There we learn that we are enemies of God, enemies sabotaging God's plan to help us, wrecking everything he tries to do to reach us. For years we fight back and resist God's efforts to love us and to draw us to himself.

We are the enemies of God. And yet we know, if we are Christians at all, that in that place where man's inadequacy is so fully demonstrated, we also have the clearest testimony that God loves us. "God so loved the world that he gave his only begotten Son." Jesus came to break through all our despair, weakness, shame, sorrow, and sin, all man's ruin and disaster. He came to demonstrate a God who loved mankind and would not let it perish.

Now we come to the force of Paul's argument. If I clearly knew God's love when I became a Christian—when I was an enemy and helpless and powerless—how much more can I count on the fact that God loves me now that I am his child? Even though I am suffering, even though I do not feel loved right now, even though it seems as though God is against me, how much more can I count on the fact that God loves me now!

Paul is arguing from the greater to the lesser. If God could love me when it was so evident that I did not deserve it, how much more must I reckon upon his love now that I know I am dear to him and loved by him. Therefore, this suffering is not coming into my life because God is angry with me; it is coming because God loves me. It comes from the heart of a Father who is putting me through some development that I desperately need to grow into the kind of a person I desperately want to be. And he loves me enough that he will not let me off, but will take me through it. Therefore it is not his anger I am experiencing, but his love.

That is what Hebrews 12 argues, isn't it? If we have been disciplined by the fathers of our flesh, and we know they love us, why can't we believe that God loves us when he puts us through times of testing, pressure, and suffering? When I see that truth, then I can rejoice, because I know that suffering will produce the things that make me what I want to be. There is a hymn that I think expresses this idea beautifully. It goes like this:

When we have exhausted our store of endurance,
When our strength has failed, 'ere the day is half done.
When we reach the end of our hoarded resources,
Our Father's full giving is only begun.

His love has no limit, His grace has no measure;
His power no boundary known unto men.
For out of His infinite riches in Jesus,
He giveth, and giveth, and giveth again.
                                                            —*Annie Johnson Flint*

12

Rejoicing in God

The one clear mark of a true Christian is that he always rejoices. Three times in Romans 5 we, as believers, are given reasons for rejoicing. First, we rejoice in our spiritual position. "Having been justified by faith, we have peace with God through our Lord Jesus Christ. We have access by faith into this grace wherein we stand, and we rejoice in hope of the glory of God." That is our spiritual position. The moment we believe in the Lord Jesus, we can rejoice in the hope of sharing the glory of God.

Then we are to rejoice in our growing conformity to the character of Christ. This is produced by suffering. Suffering helps us to become like Jesus now. And as we suffer, knowing we are undergirded, protected, and covered over by the love of God shed abroad in our hearts by the Holy Spirit, we learn to rejoice in our sufferings.

In verses 11–21, we learn to rejoice in our great and glorious God. Verse 11 tells us:

Not only is this so [Paul has said that twice in this chapter], but we also rejoice in God through our Lord Jesus Christ, through whom we have now received reconciliation.

In my book *Authentic Christianity*, I call this rejoicing "an unquenchable optimism." Christians always have grounds for rejoicing. No matter what happens, we have a ground for rejoicing. The three kinds of rejoicing described in Romans 5 represent three levels of maturity. They are not necessarily chronological levels, but they are levels of understanding and responding to truth that reflect a continually growing and deepening maturity. The third level is rejoicing in God through our Lord Jesus Christ, through whom we have now received the reconciliation.

Notice again that Paul, as he so frequently does, reminds us that everything that comes to us comes "through our Lord Jesus Christ." Christ is the way to God. He himself said so: "I am the way, the truth, and the life. No man comes to the Father but by me." Therefore, when we see the greatness of Christ, we have seen the greatness of God. It is he who reveals the Father. Remember how John begins his gospel?

> In the beginning was the Word, and the Word was with God, and the Word was God . . . The Word became flesh and lived for awhile among us. We have seen his glory, the glory of the one and only Son, who came from the Father, full of grace and truth (John 1:1,14).

That is the way we see God. When we see the greatness of Jesus, we see the greatness of God. When we see and know the love of Jesus, we know the heart of God. Therefore, we are to rejoice in God through our Lord Jesus Christ.

Record of Achievements

How do you do that? How do you see the greatness of Christ? Paul says it is by understanding the reconciliation. If you want to know how great a person is, you look at the record of his achievements. What has he done? From verse 12 of Romans 5 to the end of the chapter is a record of the greatness of Christ, his achievement of what Paul calls "the reconciliation."

This passage is one of the most theologically important chapters in all of the Bible. In this passage is the clearest statement in the Bible on what is called "original sin," that is, the blight that has been passed on to our whole race as the result of the sin of our father Adam. Also, here is the complete answer to those who doubt the historicity of Adam and Eve. There are some who claim that the first chapters of Genesis are merely legend, or myth, that Adam and Eve were not real people. But this chapter shows that belief to be false. All through the passage, Adam, as an individual, is contrasted and compared with the person of the Lord Jesus. This section also lays the groundwork for all that Paul is going to say in chapters 6, 7, and 8. So it is a tremendously important passage.

I have found that if we get involved in the details of the passage—and it is easy to do so—we invariably get lost in the argument and lose the main point the apostle wants to make, which is the greatness and the glory of the Lord Jesus, the reason we can rejoice in God through him. So instead of dwelling on the argument in detail, I want to summarize it for you.

There are four movements in this section. First, in verses 12–14, Paul begins with us "in Adam," which is where we start as a human race. Then, verses 15–17 give us a great parallel of what we are if we are "in Christ," as contrasted with what we were in Adam. Verses 18 and 19 give a concise summary of this truth by this master logician, and the chapter closes with a brief explanation of how the law fits in (verses 20 and 21). Verse 12, then, shows us where we begin, "in Adam."

> Therefore, just as sin entered the world through one man, and death through sin, and in this way death came to all men, because all sinned—

The NIV has a dash here, which means it is an incomplete sentence. I do not agree with this translation. Notice that Paul starts out by saying "Therefore, just as . . ." When you get a "just as," you have to have an "even so" a little later. Paul is making a comparison here. The Greek text actually has an "even so," but for some reason the New In-

ternational Version doesn't translate it, so we'll correct it.
This is the Stedmaniac version:

> Therefore, just as sin entered the world through one man,
> and death through sin, [so also (or, even so) through one
> man] death came to all men, because all sinned.

Two Evils

Paul's argument begins with two undeniable, indisputable
facts: the universality of sin and the universality of death.
We cannot deny these. Everywhere we look there is evidence that what he says is true, that we are victims of the
twin evils of sin and death.

There are some who may not accept the idea of sin. There
are people today who do not like this word. Call it anything
we like, the fact remains that there is clear evidence wherever we look in the human race that something has gone
wrong with our humanity. Call it karma, destiny, fate, evo-
lutionary darkness, or whatever—but it is clearly evident
that something is wrong. G. K. Chesterson said, "Whatever
else may be said of man, this one thing is clear: He is not
what he is capable of being." I think any line of evidence
will substantiate that. Some kind of twist has come in,
something that we cannot explain—a taint, a moral poison
that makes us act in irrational ways—so that even when we
know something is wrong or hurtful, we want to do it anyway.

I do not have to go any further than my own heart to find
evidence of that. There are things that I know would destroy me and my family, and yet at times I catch myself
wanting badly to do them. And so do you, so don't feel so
pious! That is what is called "original sin." And it is not only
evident in adults. The striking and remarkable thing is that
it is found in babies. Sin is there at the beginning of life;
babies are born with it, which is conclusive proof of what
Paul is saying here. It is something that has gripped the
race.

My two-year-old grandson comes over to our house frequently and tears up the place. It takes us two days to get it back in shape after a visit from him. His mother tells us that if she says to him, "Now, eat your food," that's the one thing he doesn't want to do. So she has learned how to make him eat his food. She says, "Now, don't eat your carrots," and he gobbles them up. Anything that is prohibited, that is what he wants to do. No one had to teach him that. We have never sent him to school to learn how to disobey. He is only two years old, but he knows how to resist instruction and command; he wants to do what he ought not to do.

Perhaps this universal tendency to evil has been stated most clearly by a totally secular agency. The clearest statement on original sin that I have ever read comes from the report of the Minnesota Crime Commission. In studying humanity the commission came to this frightening and factual conclusion:

> Every baby starts life as a little savage. He is completely selfish and self-centered. He wants what he wants when he wants it—his bottle, his mother's attention, his playmate's toy, his uncle's watch. Deny him these wants, and he seethes with rage and aggressiveness, which would be murderous, were he not so helpless. He is dirty. He has no morals, no knowledge, no skills. This means that all children, not just certain children, are born delinquent. If permitted to continue in the self-centered world of his infancy, given free reign to his impulsive actions to satisfy his wants, every child would grow up a criminal, a thief, a killer, a rapist.

This is a clear statement on the universality of sin and of the fact, as Paul says here, that by one man, sin entered the world. And along with sin came death. Everyone acknowledges the universal presence of death in our society. We look at a newborn child and say, "Here is someone who is starting to live." But it is equally true to say of that child, "Here is someone who is starting to die." Death is at work in that child from the moment of birth. We are born to die. This is the story of our race. We do not need to argue it; it is evident on every side. Later on in this passage Paul says, "Death reigned." Still later on, he says, "Sin reigns." So in these two forces that have been introduced into humanity, we have a pair of royal tyrants who rule over men. King Sin and his evil and cruel consort, Queen Death, hold in their remorseless hands every human being, without exception.

Through One Man

How did sin and death get control of our race? The apostle answers: through one man. That is the key to this whole section. Again and again Paul rings the changes on that phrase: through one man, by one man. Paul is contrasting two men, actually, Adam and Jesus. But in either case, what comes to us comes from one man, either Adam or Jesus.

It was through Adam that sin and death gripped our race. We sin because we are sons and daughters of Adam, and we die because we are sons and daughters of Adam. We don't die for our own sins. Normally, we would die for our own sins; but, as Paul goes on to argue, there are even some—babies, for instance—who haven't deliberately sinned at all, and yet they still die. Therefore, Paul traces the reign of sin and death back to Adam. This is the argument of verses 13 and 14.

> For before the Law was given, sin was in the world. But sin is not taken into account where there is no law. Nevertheless, death reigned from the time of Adam to the time of Moses, even over those who did not sin by breaking a command, as did Adam, who was a pattern of the one to come (Rom. 5:13,14).

Paul's argument is simply this: Death is the punishment for breaking a command. In the Garden of Eden, God said to Adam, "Do not eat of the fruit of the tree of knowledge of evil. In the day that you eat thereof, you shall surely die." Adam broke that specific, clear-cut command; he ate of the fruit. That was not merely a little incident, a peccadillo; Adam actually was choosing to be an independent creature and denying his dependence upon the God who made him. It was an act of rebellion; it was an act of idolatry. He was enthroning himself as a god, in the place of God. Those were the implications of his action. Adam broke the command and, as a result, death and sin passed upon all his descendants.

Paul is saying that death is the result of breaking a command—and you need a law in order to be able to break a command. Perhaps we have driven down our street for years and never had to stop at a certain intersection because there was nothing that required it. Then one day a stop sign is erected. Now the law has come in. From that time on, to fail to stop at that intersection is to break a command. If we fail to stop, we are subject to a penalty, even though we have been driving through that intersection without stopping for years without any penalty. But now the law has come in, and thus we break a command if we fail to stop.

In order to have death, Paul says, there had to be a command to break. But people were dying long before the law was ever given. People died from the time of Adam to Moses, even people who never had a command to break. How could that be, if death is the result of breaking a command? Paul's conclusion is: The whole race actually sinned when Adam sinned. We broke the command in Adam. Adam broke a direct command and we were present in him; therefore we die as he died because of a broken command.

At this point many people say, "Well, that isn't fair! God is punishing us for Adam's sin!" People who argue that way are revealing how little they understand the nature of our humanity. They think of themselves as individuals quite separate from other people when, as a matter of fact, we are tied in together, all a part of one great bundle of life; we share life together. We recognize this fact when we speak of the brotherhood of man and when we say, "No man is an island." But at other times we choose to think that we have a right to stand alone, as though no one else exists. Whether we understand it or not, this passage reveals the fact that when Adam sinned, he plunged the whole race into disaster. We are all born with sin at work in us and, as a result, death is taking its toll. We sinned in Adam.

Pattern and Contrast

The most important phrase in this paragraph is the last one: Adam was a pattern of the one to come. Through the rest of this passage, the apostle is going to show us how Adam is a kind of picture of Christ; and yet there is a great contrast between the two. So the verses that follow draw both a comparison and a contrast between Adam and Jesus. First, verse 15:

> But the gift is not like the trespass.

The gift, what every human being is always looking for, is the gift of righteousness, a sense of worth, which comes as a gift from the Lord Jesus. The trespass is Adam's disobedient act in the Garden of Eden. The gift, Paul says, is not like the trespass.

> For if the many died by the trespass of the one man, how much more did God's grace and the gift that came by the grace of the one man, Jesus Christ, overflow to the many!

Adam brought a single experience of death to all people. We only die once, don't we? Adam brought that death to us. But Christ brought a repeated and ever-growing experience of life to all who are in him. That is the contrast. We can take life from Jesus a thousand times a day. We can take the gift of worth over and over again. Whenever our spirit feels put down, crushed, insignificant, inadequate, or insecure, we can be renewed, we can take again the gift of life and righteousness from him. So Jesus Christ is greater than Adam; for though the trespass of Adam brought death once, the sacrifice and the death of Jesus brings life a thousand times. Verse 16:

> Again, the gift of God is not like the result of one man's sin:
> The judgment followed one sin and brought condemnation,

but the gift followed many trespasses and brought justification.

Adam's single trespass brought in judgment, i.e., death, Adam trespassed once and brought death to all who were in him. Christ died once and, despite thousands of trespasses, brought justification to all who are in him. That is the contrast. Adam trespassed once and brought death to all. Jesus died once and brought life—despite thousands of trespasses. One trespass brought death; the death of Jesus brought forgiveness for thousands of trespasses. All my life, as many times as I sin, I cannot out-sin the grace of God. No matter how many trespasses are involved in my record, there is freedom in Christ and forgiveness for all of them.

Now let's look at verse 17:

> For if, by the trespass of the one man, death reigned through that one man, how much more will those who receive God's abundant provision of grace and of the gift of righteousness reign in life through the one man, Jesus Christ.

Adam's transgression permitted sin to reign over the whole race. This is talking about more than just the funeral at the end of my life. True, that funeral happens because of Adam's trespass, but there is more to it than that. Not only does death come to us at the end of our lives because of Adam, but it reigns throughout our lives because of Adam. Paul is talking about forms of death other than the mere cessation of life.

What is life? Life is love, joy, and excitement. It is vitality, enrichment, power; it is fulfillment in every direction, in every possibility of our being. Death is the absence of life. Death is emptiness, loneliness, misery, depression, boredom, and restlessness. How much of your life is made up of death? Most of it, right? Some people never seem to have anything but death in their lives. Death reigns because of Adam's transgression.

Paul is saying that Christ's death provides such abundant grace and loving acceptance, which are available again and

again and again, that all who are in him can reign in life—
now! I can have life in the midst of all the pressures and
circumstances and suffering and troubles. My spirit can be
alive and joyful—experiencing fulfillment and delight. Life
in the midst of death! We are to reign in life now. Love,
joy, peace, glory, and gladness fill our hearts even in the
midst of the heartaches and pressures of life.

Paul is drawing this parallel so that we might see how
much more we have in Jesus than we ever had in Adam.
What we lost in Adam, we regain in Jesus, plus much more.
Just as a climber on a mountaintop can dislodge a pebble
which rolls on and accumulates others until it begins an
avalanche that will move the whole side of a mountain, so
Adam's sin in the Garden of Eden dislodged a pebble that
has built into an avalanche of sin and death which has
swept through our entire race. But, Paul tells us, Jesus has
launched another avalanche of grace, and in him there is
ample counteraction of all that Adam has brought.

Verses 18 and 19 are a summary of this truth. First,
verse 18:

> Consequently, just as the result of the one trespass was
> condemnation for all men, so also the result of one act of
> righteousness was justification that brings life for all men.

Paul is saying that death, i.e., judgment or condemnation,
comes to us not because of our own sins, but because of
Adam's. It is a gift from Adam. What a terrible gift it is!
And thus the acceptance and worth that we need to have,
the love that we human beings desperately crave and must
have in order to function, is also a gift, a gift from the Lord
Jesus Christ. We can have all that we want, anytime we
need it. Verse 19:

> For just as through the disobedience of the one man the
> many were made sinners, so also through the obedience of
> the one man the many will be made righteous.

Some people claim that we are righteous because God declares us righteous. But here it is stated plainly that we are

made righteous in Jesus Christ. Paul is saying that when we were in Adam, sin and guilt were not an option with us— we had no way of choosing. We sin because that is part of our nature. And so, when we are in Christ, having worth and love is not something that we have to earn—it is a gift from the Lord Jesus. It is part of our new, true nature.

The Law Was Added

In verses 20 and 21, the apostle briefly deals with the place of the law in this matter:

> The law was added so that the trespass might increase. But where sin increased, grace increased all the more, so that, just as sin reigned in death, so also grace might reign through righteousness to bring eternal life through Jesus Christ our Lord.

Someone might raise the question, "Why then did the Ten Commandments have to be given?" Paul's answer is, "The Ten Commandments never were given to make men do right." That is what we think they were given for, but they were actually given to show men how wrong they already are, and to make men sin more, to increase the trespass. Isn't that strange? As in the example of my grandson, the law makes you want to do wrong even more. It increases the trespass.

But a strange thing happens at that point. Paul tells us that the worse we get—the more we fling ourselves into the rebellion, sin, and evil that we know to be wrong—the closer we are to being broken, to coming to the end of ourselves and discovering the grace of restoration, cleansing, and forgiveness in Jesus Christ.

I listened recently to a tape by Charles Colson (called the "hatchet man" of the Nixon administration) in which he told of his experience in prison. In that dark and lonely place, crammed in with forty other men, he found a brother in Christ. The two of them met together and began to pray for others in that prison. They didn't know what God could

do—they almost despaired that anything could happen—
but as they began to pray, God began to work. They found
that the Spirit of God swept through that prison in a remarkable way, and men were broken. Hardened, violent,
brutal men, who had spent their lives in resistance to right,
truth, and good, and had given themselves over completely
to hardness, cynicism, and brutality, began to break and to
find forgiveness.

Do you know that there is a spiritual awakening going on
in our prisons today? I read that in one year, in the Los
Angeles County jails, 256 prisoners received the Lord. Prisoners are open to Christ because the law has driven them
into trespass to such a degree that they are ready to hear
the gospel. Sometimes this happens without outward rebellion. Sometimes we become frustrated, hard, and cynical.
When that happens we learn that the grace of God will
abound more and more, for the increase of sin only increases the grace of our Lord Jesus.

The point of all this is that the one who breaks through is
Jesus. Adam ruins us all. Only Christ can set us free. Sin
and death will never loose their filthy hold on us except at
the command of Jesus Christ. Therefore, the One to whom
we look is the Lord Jesus, the One who broke the terrible
death grip on us and set us free—Jesus, the head of a new
race, the beginning of a new humanity. Jesus is Lord. As
we see him thus, we discover what the Scriptures say, that
the blessed Lord, who broke through death and sin, has
come to live within us, to give himself to us, and to infuse
us with his strength and purity, his wisdom and power. All
that he is is available to us. Thus we rejoice in God through
our Lord Jesus Christ, who has made for us the reconciliation.

13

Can We Go On Sinning?

Let me ask you a question. Now that you are a Christian —now that you understand that the grace of God forgives your sins, past, present, and future, that the sacrifice of Jesus Christ on your behalf settles the debt for sin, no matter when sins occur—do you then have the right to go on sinning, living as you were, knowing that the grace of God will cover those sins?

That is a highly relevant question; many people today are asking it, and many are saying that we can go on sinning. Many claim that they have the right to go on living in a blatantly sinful way because, they say, their sins are forgiven. A man in our congregation admitted to me that he was a homosexual but claimed that he did not need to make any change in his life because, as a Christian, his sins were forgiven. This is not an out-of-date question, but one we all wrestle with and must resolve. The apostle Paul faces this question in the sixth chapter of Romans.

In chapters 6 and 7 he interrupts his argument temporarily to deal with two very practical questions. In chapter 6 Paul deals with the question, "What about the sins of believers?" In chapter 7 he takes up the matter of the Ten Commandments and their demands upon us. Then, in chapter 8, Paul picks up his argument again and begins to carry on with the description of the tremendous results of being in Jesus Christ, as opposed to Adam.

We will study only two verses of chapter 6 for the moment. As we have seen before, the apostle Paul always states the truth first, in a kind of nutshell summary, a pithy statement of what he wants to say. Then he takes up his argument, step by logical step, and explains and expounds it until it is perfectly clear. That is what he does here. The whole truth that answers the question, "Can we go on sinning?" is dealt with in the first two verses of chapter 6. Paul says,

> What shall we say, then? Shall we go on sinning so that grace may increase? By no means! We died to sin; how can we live in it any longer? (Rom. 6:1,2)

This is the whole argument, right there: We died to sin; how can we live in it any longer?

An Appropriate Question

Let us observe three things about this brief statement. First, notice that the question is logical. Shall we go on sinning that grace may increase? That is a good question to ask. If my teaching or preaching of the gospel does not arouse this question in someone's mind, there is probably something wrong with my teaching, for it is the kind of question that ought to be asked at this point. There is something about the grace of God and the glory of the good news that immediately raises this issue. If sin is so completely taken care of by the forgiveness of Christ, then we don't really need to worry about sins, do we? They are not going to separate us from Christ, so why not keep on doing them? It is a perfectly logical question. It was raised everywhere Paul went, and it is a question that must be faced.

But second, notice that it is not only logical; it is also natural. That is because sin, basically, is fun, isn't it? Oh, come on—admit it! Sin is fun. We like to do it. Otherwise we would not keep on doing it; we would not even get involved in it. We know sins are bad for us. Our minds tell us, our logic tells us, our experience tells us sin is bad for us. Nevertheless, we like to sin. Otherwise we would not. Therefore, any suggestion that we can escape the penalty for our sin and still enjoy the action arouses a considerable degree of interest in us. It does in me, anyway.

We must clearly understand that the apostle Paul is talking about a life style of sin, not just a single failure or two. He is talking about Christians who go on absolutely unchanged in their life style from what they were before they were Christians. The word for "go on sinning" is in the present continuous tense. It means the action keeps on happening. The question is, "Can we go on sinning?" Verses 15 and following of this chapter deal with the effects of a single act of sin in a believer's life and what happens when we fail even once. We will come to that in due course. But here Paul is talking about habitual practice, or something that frequently occurs in a believer's experience, something that was there before he became a Christian. Can we go on living this way?

Finally, notice that this question is put in such a way as to sound rightly motivated and even pious. Shall we go on sinning, so that grace may increase? This suggests that our motivation for sinning is not just our own satisfaction—we are doing it for the glory of God, so that grace may increase. God loves to show his grace. Therefore, if we go on sinning, he will have all the more opportunity. What a chance for God to show his grace! It is clear that this question is not asked by a complete pagan or by a worldling, but by someone who seems intent on the glory of God.

Having said that, we come now to the answer, the positive answer of Paul.

> What shall we say then? Shall we go on sinning so that grace may increase? By no means!

Paul immediately reacts with a very positive statement, bluntly put: "By no means!" Or, as it is literally in the

Greek, "May it never be!" Absolutely not! It is interesting to me to see how the other versions translate this phrase. The King James Version sounds horrified: "God forbid!" Phillips seems to catch this same note of horror: "What a ghastly thought!" The New English Bible puts it very simply, "No, no." So here is a no-no in the Christian experience. Can we sin? No-no. I gather from all this that the apostle Paul simply does not agree with this philosophy that we can go on sinning and be forgiven. Why? In his inescapable logic, Paul answers in just four little words: "We died to sin."

We died to sin. How can we live in it any longer?

Here is the whole truth that Paul wants to confront us with in answer to this question. The rest of the chapter is but an exposition of what he means by that. We will take that exposition step by step because there is tremendous understanding involved in it. But Paul does not make any logical advance on his original statement. When we get to the end of the chapter, he has simply made clear what he means by "We died to sin." There is the whole argument, and if we understand what he means, we will see why he asks, "How can we go on living in it any longer?"

What It Doesn't Mean

Now let's look at this phrase, "We died to sin." First, it does not mean that sin is dead in me. It does not mean that, as a Christian, I have reached the place where I cannot sin, although many people take it to mean that.

Some years ago I was living in the city of Pasadena and one day went to get a haircut. I soon found that the barber was a Christian. As we began to discuss some things he started to tell me about his Christianity. He told me that seventeen years before he had been sanctified, as he put it, and he was no longer able to sin. For seventeen years he had lived without sin. He made it very clear that he had done no sin at all.

So I began to discuss this with him, and I brought in certain other passages, and we got into an argument. The longer we went, the hotter he got—all the while he was cutting my hair. He worked himself up into such a lather that I finally said to him, "Look, if you can get so upset, so angry, when you have no sin in you, what would you be like if you were a sinner like the rest of us?" It was two weeks before I dared to appear in public after that haircut! Surely such a claim to total sinlessness carries its own rebuttal with it.

So this passage does not mean that sin is dead in us; nor does it mean, as some have taken it, that we should die to sin. There are movements and churches based upon this idea. They say Paul is teaching us that we ought to die to sin. One can attend meetings, conferences, and camp meetings where he will be exhorted to die to sin. We are told this is the way by which we come to a victorious life. We are told we ought to begin to crucify ourselves and die to sin. Now I submit that Paul is not saying we ought to do this; he is telling us it has been done. We died to sin.

Third, neither does Paul mean by this that we are dying to sin. There are some people who take it that way. They say this means the Christian is gradually changing and growing, and the more he does so, the more he is dying to sin, and there will come a time when he will outgrow all his evil. But it does not mean that at all. Once again, we must face clearly the flat statement the apostle makes: We died to sin. It is past tense. It has already happened.

If we go back into chapter 5, we have that great contrast with what we were in Adam, and what we are now as Christians in Christ. "In Adam," he says, "we will sin." There is no way we can escape it because Adam has passed on the taint of sin and death as his heritage. Therefore, in Adam, we will sin. We all do. But then he says, "If we are in Christ (and the implication is clear that we are), we will not go on sinning." Look at verse 21 of chapter 5:

. . . so that, just as sin reigned in death, so also grace might reign through righteousness to bring eternal life through Jesus Christ our Lord.

Now whatever else those words mean, it is clear that what happens in Christ cancels out what happened in Adam. If death and sin come to us from Adam, then life and deliverance come from Christ. You can see already one reason why the apostle would add, "If this is true, how can we go on sinning?" We need to clearly understand his line of argument in chapter 5. When you become a Christian, if you have by grace received the gift of God—which is Jesus himself—and the gift of righteousness which he brings, then you are no longer in Adam, but in Christ.

And yet, having said that, we have to face the fact that Christians, who are no longer in Adam but are now in Christ, do sin, and they do die. Chapter 5 told us that sin and death are the results of Adam's transgression. How can we be free from Adam and still suffer the results of Adam's transgression? That, I think, brings us to what we clearly need to understand—the nature of our humanity.

The first thing the Scriptures tell us about ourselves is that the most important part of us is our spirit. We *are* spirit; we *have* bodies and souls, but we are spirit. That may sound a bit spooky to you. The reason we struggle with this is that we can see our bodies, and feel our souls. We have been brainwashed by the world, which says only those things that can be seen and felt are real—and who can see or feel a spirit? So we have a struggle at this point. But the Scriptures clearly tell us that basically, down deep, the very nature of our being is spirit, even as God is Spirit. You can't see your spirit, nor can you feel it, but that is who you are.

Made to Hold Something

The Scriptures help us to understand the nature of that spirit by a beautiful symbol. Since we cannot see our spirit, we have to view it through a symbol, a visual aid. The most common visual aid in Scripture to describe our human spirit is that of a vessel. You can think of your spirit as a little cup inside of you, made to hold something.

The Scriptures tell us that in the beginning this cup was made to hold none other than God himself. All the greatness and glory of God could be poured into that tiny human cup. That is what Adam was, as he came fresh from the hand of God, a cup filled with God himself. But in the Fall that cup was emptied, and filled again with a kind of poison. A satanic twist began to poison all our humanity. We find in our experience that when the poison that Adam brought in fills our spirit, it spreads into the soul. Now the soul is the realm of our experience. It is the functioning of thè mind (the reason), the will (the power to choose), and emotion (the power to feel). Scripture tells us that this poison has touched us in all those areas, so that we do not think rightly, we do not feel rightly, we do not choose rightly. That is why things go wrong wherever human beings are involved.

What the spirit and the soul feel will be expressed finally in the body's action. That is the way we are made. What the body does is always the reflection of what the spirit and soul are doing. That is, if we have fear (one of the forms of evil and death within us), it will express itself in several ways. Shyness or timidity may be one way; anxiety and worry, another; bluster and boasting, still another way. All these reflect the fear inside.

If we feel angry and hostile, it comes out in sharp words, or even violent actions. We poke someone in the jaw, or we yell at the top of our voice, or storm out of the house and slam a door. All this is revealing what is inside, what is filling the cup of the spirit. If it is self-love that is there, as it certainly is, it comes out in terms of greed, possessiveness, and selfishness, or in terms of sexual promiscuity, satisfying self, despite the exploitation of another person. Or it may be ambition, power-hunger, whatever. All of this comes out from within. Remember, this is saying nothing more than what Jesus himself told us in Mark 7.

"What comes out of a man is what makes him 'unclean.' For
from within, out of men's hearts [that is a word for spirit],
come evil thoughts, sexual immorality, theft, murder, adultery
. . . [Ho, you say, you haven't got me yet! Well, hang on!]
. . . greed, malice, deceit, lewdness, envy, slander, arrogance
and folly. All these evils come from inside and make a man
'unclean' " (Mark 7:20–23).

Paul is saying the same thing that Jesus said. It all depends on what is filling the cup of the spirit. If it is Adam's
life, then that is what is going to come out. There is nothing
we can do to stop it. All we can do is to try to pretend that
it is something else, and we are all adept at doing that.

But what happens when that spirit fully and truly turns
to Christ, when it receives the gift of God's grace, the gift
of worth? Then, according to this argument in Romans 5,
the tie with Adam is broken. The spirit is emptied of its
satanic content—sin—and it is filled again with the Holy
Spirit, who releases to it the life of Jesus. That is what the
Holy Spirit has come to do. Our human spirit, our essential
nature, is no longer in Adam, in any sense at all. It is now in
Christ. We are tied to Christ. That is the teaching of Scripture from beginning to end, from Genesis to Revelation.

But the problem comes because our souls and bodies,
which have been functioning for years under the control of
sin in the cup of our spirit, are still going on in the same old
way, functioning according to those patterns built up under
the control of sin. Our habits, thoughts, and actions, are already established along wrong lines. That is where the evil
and sin in a believer's life is coming from. His spirit is
freed from sin; his soul and body are yet under its control.

Righteousness Is Inevitable

It is a struggle to reeducate the soul and the body, and
we experience many failures until we allow the Holy Spirit
to bring it under the control of the new life of Jesus Christ
in the cup of our spirit. But it will happen, and it must
happen, Paul argues. If Christ is in the cup of the spirit,

then just as we could not evade sin because we were in Adam, so in Christ we cannot evade righteousness.

The life of Jesus is more powerful, more persistent, more insistent than the life of Adam ever was. That is the meaning of all the "much mores" in this section. If we had to sin in Adam, then for the very same reason we have to begin to practice righteousness in Christ. It is not something we can help; it will just happen. That is why Paul asked the question, "Having died to sin, how can we live any longer in it?" Why, it is impossible. It is not a question of should we; it is a question of can we. His answer is, "No, it can never be."

In our neighborhood, right next door to us, is a home that was built a number of years ago and has been inhabited now by two different families. The first was a rather difficult family, the kind of people who would never keep a yard or house in order. Soon after they moved in, the brand new home began to show the effects of their style of life. The yard was littered with trash and garbage, the lawn was dead for lack of care. When it was replanted, it died out again. To enter their house was to enter a shambles. It was never clear or in order.

These neighbors moved out, and new neighbors moved in. It wasn't long until it became evident that a different kind of people lived there. They cleaned up the house and painted it. The yard was cleaned up, the lawn was dug up and replanted, and it has been cared for adequately ever since. Things are completely different. What happened? It is impossible that there would not be a change, because there was a change in those who dwelt inside. This is what Paul is telling us here. There has to be a change.

Self-Deceived

Now someone asks, "What if a Christian does go on sinning, living in sin, claiming forgiveness, but goes on without any change in his life whatever?" What about that? There are people who are doing this. The answer, in light of this scripture, is simple. These people are simply revealing that they have never truly been justified by faith. They are not Christians. Let's put it as bluntly as the apostle himself put it. They are deceiving themselves and deceiving others. Though they may do so with good intent, and with utter sincerity as far as they know—nevertheless the case is clear.

It is impossible for your life style to continue unchanged when you become a Christian. It is simply impossible, because a change has occurred deep in the human spirit. Those who protest and say they can go on living in sin are revealing that there has been no change in their spirit; there has been no break with Adam. They are still in the same condition. The apostle Paul makes that plain in a couple of places. The first is in Ephesians:

> For of this you can be sure: No immoral, impure, or greedy person—such a man is an idolator—has any inheritance in the kingdom of Christ and of God. [He is not a Christian yet. He is claiming to be, but he is not. And lest we be fooled by his claims, the apostle goes on to say,] Let no one deceive you with empty words, for because of such things God's wrath comes on those who are disobedient (Eph. 5:5-7).

In very much the same terms, Paul puts it again in 1 Corinthians:

> Don't you know that the wicked will not inherit the kingdom of God? Do not be deceived [there it is again]: Neither the sexually immoral nor idolators nor adulterers nor male prostitutes nor homosexual offenders nor thieves nor the greedy nor drunkards nor slanderers nor swindlers will inherit the kingdom of God. And that is what some of you were. [They were; they are no longer. Some of them are still struggling, and some of them do occasionally fail and go back to some of these things. But there's a vast difference. They no longer are that way at heart; there has been a break, a change in their life style.] But you were washed, you were sanctified, you were justified in the name of the Lord Jesus Christ and by the Spirit of our God [and therefore there cannot follow the same style of life] (1 Cor. 6:9-11).

I think Paul is clear and fully answers the question, doesn't he? He is saying there is great hope for those who are caught up in any of these things. There is a way of deliverance. It is not a way that permits going on with the same style of life. Jesus Christ came to free us from sin, not to allow us to continue in it.

The question we must face about ourselves is, Have we really begun to hate sin deep inside—our own sin, the things we do wrong and, for the moment, choose to do? Have you begun to hate it? Do you want to be free from it, want to be delivered, want the power of it broken in your life? You can only want that because there has come into your heart a new Spirit; into the cup of your human spirit has come the grace of the Lord Jesus Christ. And from that vantage point, he is beginning to assert the control of his purity throughout your whole life. You cannot settle for sin any longer.

In the rest of the chapter Paul helps us to understand more about how this works, but here he makes it unquestionably clear. Can we go on sinning? May it never be!

14

The True Baptism of the Spirit

When a person becomes a Christian, when he really, truly receives Jesus Christ as Lord, something happens that makes it impossible for him to go on living a life style of evil, because he died to sin. The apostle now uses two marvelous visual aids to help us understand this truth. One of them is baptism, and the other is grafting, as a plant or a branch is grafted into a tree. Here is what the apostle says about baptism:

> What shall we say, then? Shall we go on sinning so that grace may increase? By no means! We died to sin; how can we live in it any longer? Or don't you know that all of us who were baptized into Christ Jesus were baptized into his death? We were therefore buried with him through baptism into death in order that, just as Christ was raised from the dead through the glory of the Father, we too may live a new life (Rom. 6:1–4).

When I was a boy in Montana I had a horse that could smell water from farther away than any animal I ever saw. You could be riding across the dry, parched plains, when suddenly he would prick up his ears, lift his head, and quicken his pace, and you knew he smelled water somewhere and was heading for it. Some people are like that. Whenever they read these passages and see the word "baptism," they smell water. You can just see them prick up their ears, lift their heads, and head for it. But there is no water here. This is a dry passage.

More Potent Than Water

This passage is dealing with the question of how we died to sin, how we became separated from Adam and were joined in Christ. No water can do that. That requires something far more potent than water. It is, therefore, a description for us of the baptism of the Holy Spirit, as it is called elsewhere in the Scriptures. John the Baptist, who made his reputation because he baptized in water, said, "I indeed baptize you with water, but there comes One after me, greater than I, who will baptize you with the Holy Spirit." That is what Paul is talking about here—the baptism of the Holy Spirit, which places us into Christ.

Paul says exactly the same thing in 1 Corinthians 12:13: "For we were all baptized by one Spirit into one body— whether Jews or Greeks, slaves or free—and we were all given the one Spirit to drink." Notice how he emphasizes that all believers were baptized into one body. We were placed into Christ. You are not a Christian if that is not true of you. Therefore, people today who say you need to experience the baptism of the Holy Spirit *after* you become a believer do not understand the Scriptures. There is no way to become a believer without being baptized with the Holy Spirit.

The baptism of the Spirit happened first, historically, on the day of Pentecost, when the Holy Spirit came upon 120 people who were gathered in the temple courts, fusing them into one body, joining them to the head, which is Jesus. Thus the church was formed, one body in Christ, all members one of the other and members of the Lord Jesus himself. That is the baptism of the Holy Spirit. It is not something that is felt; it is not something we can know

through our senses when it takes place; it is something the
Spirit does to our human spirit. Yet this baptism is essential
to becoming a Christian. It is part of the process by which
we share the life of Jesus Christ.

Notice some things that Paul says about the baptism of
the Spirit in this passage. First, he says that we are expected to know about it. "Don't you know that we were all
baptized into Christ, into his death?" Paul asks. He expects
these Roman Christians, who had never met him or been
taught personally by him, to know this fact. It is something
new Christians ought to know.

Shadow on the Sand

Now, how would they know this? Here is where water
baptism comes in. Water baptism teaches, by symbol, the
meaning of this baptism of the Spirit. The one is the
shadow, or figure, of the other. The people to whom Paul
was writing had been baptized in water after their conversion and regeneration, and Paul supposes that their water baptism had helped them to understand the reality of
what the Spirit had already done to them.

Some time ago, my fellow-pastor, Ron Ritchie, told me of
an experience he had one Easter Sunday during a baptism service in the ocean near his home. You really have to
love Christ to be baptized in the frigid waters of the Pacific!
A woman came up to him and asked him to baptize her
nine-year-old daughter. Ron was reluctant to do so without
finding out whether the girl really understood what was
happening, so he began to question her and to teach her
about the reality behind the water baptism. He was gestur-
ing as he talked to her, and noticed the shadow of his hand
as it fell on the sand. So he said to the little girl, "Do you
see the shadow of my hand on the sand? Now that is just
the shadow; the hand is the real thing. And when you came
to Jesus, when you believed in Jesus, that was the real
baptism. You were joined to him, and what happened to
him happened to you. Jesus was alive; then he died, was

buried, and then he arose from the dead. And that is what happened to you when you believed in him." He pointed to the shadow on the sand and said, "When you go down in the water and are raised up again, that is a picture of what has already happened." The girl immediately caught on and said, "Yes, that is what I want to do because Jesus has come into my life." So water baptism is a shadow, a picture, a symbol worked out for us, to teach us what happened to us when we believed in the Lord Jesus.

Notice also that the apostle explains how we died to sin. The Spirit took us and identified us with all that Jesus did. Now, I do not understand that, because that means the cross is a timeless event. The Spirit of God is able to ignore the two thousand years since the crucifixion and resurrection and somehow identify us, who live in this twentieth century—as he has all believers of past centuries—with that moment when Jesus died, was buried, and rose again from the dead. We participate in those events. That is clear.

But I do not think we need to struggle with this, because something similar has already been referred to in chapter 5. There we were told that by being born into this human race we became part of what Adam did. Way back at the dawn of history, Adam sinned, and we sinned in Adam. I do not fully know how that is true, but I certainly believe it. Every evidence of history demonstrates it to be true. This is not theological fiction; it is fact. Adam sinned, and so we sin. Adam died, and men ever since have died. The apostle is now saying that what was true in Adam has now been ended and now we are in Christ, by faith in Jesus Christ. Once Adam's actions affected us; but now Christ's actions become ours as well. Christ died, and we died; Christ was buried, and we were buried with him; Christ rose again, and we rose with him. So what is true of Jesus is true of us.

Here Paul is dealing with what is probably the most remarkable and certainly the most magnificent truth recorded in the pages of Scripture. It is the central truth God wants us to learn. We died with Christ, were buried, and rose again with him. That union with Christ is the truth from

which everything else in Scripture flows. If we understand
and accept this as fact, which it is, then everything will be
different in our lives. That is why the apostle labors so to
help us understand this.

Notice one other thing about this paragraph—the purpose for which all this happened. Paul says, "We were
therefore buried with him through baptism into death *in
order that,* just as Christ was raised from the dead through
the glory of the Father, we too may live a new life." Remember, Paul is answering the question, "Can a believer go
on sinning?" His answer is, "Absolutely not." We cannot
because we have died, have been buried, and have risen
again with Jesus, and therefore we, too, may live a new life.

Nectarines and Peaches

Verses 5 through 10 introduce a new figure for us and
reveal a deeper revelation of what has happened to us. Paul
now uses the figure of grafting.

> If we have been united with him in his death, we will cer-
> tainly also be united with him in his resurrection (vs. 5).

In other words, you cannot pick and choose. You cannot die
with Christ and not be risen with him. If you died with him,
you must be risen with him as well. Paul uses a word from
botany here. The word "united" means "to graft a branch
into another." If you have fruit trees, you may have done
grafting. Perhaps you have taken a branch from a nectarine
tree and grafted it into a peach tree. The branch is tied together in such a way that the life from the trunk of the tree
flows into the branch and they grow together until finally
you can't tell the difference between the graft and the natural branch. The life is fully shared. This is the figure Paul
is using here to describe our tie with the Lord Jesus. His life
becomes our life. We are no longer in Adam, in any sense.
The tie is totally broken. We are now in Christ, and he is
our life from now on.

This is a most important concept for us to understand. To help us further, Paul now gives us both sides to this parallel—death and resurrection. Verses 6 and 7 explain what it means to die in Christ; verses 8–10 explain what it means to be risen with him. Verses 6 and 7:

> For we know that our old self was crucified with him so that the body of sin might be rendered powerless, that we should no longer be slaves to sin—because anyone who has died has been freed from sin (Rom. 6:6,7).

In this parallel that Paul is tracing, Jesus was crucified, and we were crucified, too. Our old self, the old man, the man who was in Adam, is dead, and the tie has been broken. All that we were as a natural-born human being ended when we believed in Jesus.

Paul is referring to the essential "you," the spirit within you. Biblical psychology tells us that basically we are spirits, as I have already discussed, dwelling in human bodies. Your body is not you. Even your soul, which is produced by the union of the body and the spirit, is not wholly you. You are your spirit.

Until the Cross

Next, Paul explains that Jesus was crucified in order that the sin which was in his body on the cross should come to an end, that his body be rendered powerless with respect to sin. You say, "Now, wait a minute. There's something wrong here. There was no sin in Jesus." That is true. Scripture is careful to teach us that in Jesus there was no sin. He did not sin; there was no sin in him until the cross. But this tells us an amazing thing about our Lord when he was on the cross. There, Paul says, he was "made sin" for us. Sin, in the believer, is located in the body. (I will expand upon that in a moment.) Therefore, it was described in Jesus in terms of the body. His body became possessed and controlled by sin. That is why his body died. And by his death his body was thus rendered powerless with regard to sin.

Why do we bury a corpse? We bury it because it is useless, inert, inactive. There is nothing it can do any longer,
and so we bury it. That is why Jesus was buried—to prove
that the sin in his body was ended. The body was useless,
unresponsive. Paul says that is what happens to us. When
our spirit has died in Christ, then the body of sin will be
rendered powerless.

What does Paul mean by this term, "body of sin"? He
means the physical body that is dominated and controlled
by sin. In Adam, sin filled the whole of man—his spirit, his
soul, and his body. Therefore, his descendants had to sin.
That is why, before I became a Christian, even when I tried
to be good, I couldn't. Something always went wrong and I
ended by fouling up in some way. I was a slave to sin, and
no matter how much I wanted to be different, I couldn't be.

But now that bond has been broken. In Christ my spirit
is freed. It has been united with Jesus; it has risen with him,
and it is free from sin. This explains that rather interesting
passage in 1 John 3:9, which says, "No one who is born of
God will continue to sin, because God's seed remains in
him; he cannot sin, because he has been born of God." John
is talking about the spirit, the essential me. In that sense, it
is proper to say of believers, "We cannot sin."

What Paul makes clear in Romans 6 is that sin remains
as an alien power trying to dominate and control our
bodies and our souls. It is the presence of the spirit in the
body that produces the soul, just as electricity in a light
bulb produces light. The soul is our conscious experience
and is produced moment by moment as we live, as light
comes from a light bulb moment by moment. Paul makes it
clear that in Christ our spirits were freed from sin. They do
not sin, and cannot sin, because they are linked with Christ,
so that we may be able to control the sin which is in the
body.

From here on, we do not have to sin. If we do, it is because we allow it to happen. But we are no longer slaves to
sin. Throughout the rest of this account Paul deals with this
theme. The body is the means by which we are tempted to

sin. There is nothing inherently sinful about our bodies—they are perfectly all right—but somehow an alien power remains in them, and that is where we are tempted all our life long. The body is the seat of sin.

Sin in the Body

I think I can illustrate this for you. When you sit at the table to eat, you are satisfying a normal appetite that God gave to your body. It needs food; it needs replenishment of energy. There is nothing wrong with eating. But when we get to the table and find plenty of food on it, each one of us has something within us that makes us want to eat too much. We often eat more than we should. We say that we have a weight problem. What we really have is a sin problem. There is sin within us that wants to take a natural function of the body and push it beyond what it ought to do—and thus it becomes sin. That is why, when we sit at the table, many of us are going to sin by becoming gluttons and gourmands. A gourmand is someone who eats greedily, who delights in luxurious food, who lives for the taste of food. We are all tempted this way because sin, as a principle, is still in control of the functions of the body. But our spirit opposes it, and we do not have to give in. That is the point.

From time to time the body requires rest. The body of Jesus grew weary and needed rest. But there is in us a principle that wants to overindulge, and we become lazy, slothful, apathetic. We want other people to work and to serve us while we rest. This is so natural that it is even hard to know when we go over the line.

The mind, that amazing instrument of the body, functions in such a way as to reason and to logically deduce and to produce an amazing variety of inventions and technological advances. Yet the mind, with its ability to think and reason, can easily move beyond what it should into evil thoughts and prideful reactions, and attitudes of jealousy and lust. We can sin with our minds.

Consider the tongue, that member of the body that is so little, James says, yet can be set on fire by hell. With our tongues, designed to be that by which we bless God, we curse him instead. The tongue is like the rudder of a ship. It turns the whole life in the wrong direction because of the words that we speak.

Consider the glands and hormones. Physiologists tell us that they are linked somehow with our actions. Just as the brain is linked with the mind, so the glands are linked with our emotions. They are often responsible for the way we feel. They pour out hormones into the bloodstream and affect the body. Some hormones make us over react. Instead of experiencing normal fears that are designed to protect us from evil, we become paranoid, worried, filled with anxiety. Or, we become lustful and indulge in wrongful attitudes. We become angry, so that we hate and feel jealousy. We indulge in what the Bible calls "inordinate affections." Even our loves become twisted. That is sin in the body—no longer in the spirit, but in the body. I do not have to describe this in terms of our sexual appetites. These are normal, legitimate, valid appetites, made by God to be satisfied; but something within us wants to satisfy them too soon, or with the wrong person, or sometimes in the wrong way.

That is where evil comes from—the body, not the spirit. I hope this is clear, because it is a very important picture, and one that governs the rest of the Book of Romans, as well as all the New Testament. The regenerated spirit cannot sin. It is born of God and it cannot sin. It has been set free from sin in order that we may begin to exercise control over the body of sin, so that it may be rendered inactive; we no longer need to be slaves to sin.

Not only have we been set free to choose not to sin, but a new power to resist sin has been given to us:

Now if we died with Christ, we believe that we will also live with him. For we know that since Christ was raised from the dead, he cannot die again; death no longer has mastery over him. The death he died, he died to sin once for all; but the life he lives, he lives to God (Rom. 6:8–10).

Once we have reckoned ourselves dead to sin with Christ, there is nothing left but to go on to life. Jesus does not go back into sin; he does not go back into death. Sin and death are over, as far as we are concerned, because that is what is true of Jesus. He lives now, and he lives under the will and by the power of God. Therefore, Paul says, the same thing is true in our lives. Not only do we need to recognize that we died to sin with Christ, but also that his life is in us now. His power is available to us. When we decide not to sin, we have the power to carry it out, because Christ is living in us.

The Two-Step

Therefore, it all comes down to the two simple steps described in verse 11. This is the first time in the Book of Romans that we are asked to do anything; this is the first exhortation in all of Romans. Up to now, everything Paul has written has been about what God has done for us. Now in verse 11 we are asked to do something. What is it?

In the same way, count yourselves dead to sin but alive to God in Christ Jesus.

When you feel temptation in your body or your mind, then there are two things you are to do. First, remember that you do not have to obey sin. You are free to refuse it, free to say, "No, you don't have the right to use that part of my body for a sinful purpose." And second, remember his power in you to enable you to offer that same part of your body to God, to be used for his purposes. Now that may mean a struggle, because the strength of sin is very strong. When we start to turn away from evil in our bodies, the habits of our lives are so deeply engrained that often it is very difficult, and we struggle. But we have the power not to sin because we have God himself within us, the living God.

There is a group of ex-homosexuals who live in San Ra-
phael, California, and have a great ministry with those who
are involved in homosexuality. I was struck by this paragraph from one of their papers. The writer is describing
how tough it is to turn from these evil practices and be different once you have been deeply involved in them. He
says:

> This very weekend one of our brothers said to me, "How can
> I last through even one more year of this?" I said in response,
> "How can I last one more week?" But I will last, and so will
> he. For we have each other, and the sharing and fellowship
> and caring are God's ingredients to healing—long-lasting
> healing—that will impart strength beyond endurance, as God
> does it in His time, and in His way.

That says exactly what Paul says in Romans 6. There will
be a struggle; it is not always easy, but we have the strength
to do it and we have the right to do it. We have the freedom not to sin and the desire not to sin. That is what God
has brought to us in Christ.

Now you will see how the rest of this fits in. Paul is describing the two steps that we are to repeat over and over
again, in dealing with evil in our lives. First, in verses 12–
13a, Paul explains how to count yourself dead to sin:

> Therefore, do not let sin reign in your mortal body so that you
> obey its evil desires. Do not offer the parts of your body to
> sin, as instruments of wickedness. . . .

Step number one is to reckon yourself dead to sin, to choose
to deny its power over you. Step number two is found in
verse 13b: offer yourself to God.

> . . . but rather offer yourselves to God, as those who have
> returned from death to life; and offer the parts of your body
> to him [your tongue, your mind, your stomach, your hands,
> your feet, your sex organs—offer them to God] as instruments
> of righteousness.

That is the way to win over temptation. Then Paul closes
with this fantastic statement in verse 14. This, to me, is one
of the greatest verses in all Scripture:

For sin shall not be your master, because you are not under law, but under grace.

Why does Paul bring in the law? He brings in the law because he is dealing with one of the most basic problems of the Christian struggle, the thing that often depresses and discourages us more than anything else—the sense of condemnation we feel when we momentarily yield to sin. The law produces condemnation. The law says that unless I live up to this standard, God will not have anything to do with me. We have been so influenced by this idea that when we sin, even as believers, we think God is angry and does not care about us. We also think that way about ourselves, and become discouraged, defeated, and depressed. We want to give up. "What's the use?" we ask.

But Paul says that is not true. We are not under law. God does not feel that way about us. We are under grace, and God understands our struggle. He is not upset by it; he is not angry with us. He understands our failure. He knows that there will be a struggle and there will be failures. He also knows that he has made full provision for us to recover immediately, to pick ourselves up and go right on climbing up the mountain. Therefore we don't need to be discouraged, and we shouldn't be. Sin will not be our master because we are not under the law and condemnation, but under grace. And even though we struggle, if every time we fail we come back to God and ask his forgiveness, and take it from him, and remember how he loves us, and that he is not angry or upset with us, and go on from there, we will win.

I will never forget how, as a young man in the service during World War II, I was on a watch one night, reading the Book of Romans. This verse leaped out of the pages at me. I remember how the Spirit made it come alive, and I saw the great promise that all the things I was struggling with as a young man would ultimately be mastered—not because I was so smart, but because God was teaching me and leading me into victory. I remember walking the floor, my heart just boiling over with praise and thanksgiving to

God. I walked in a cloud of glory, rejoicing in this great promise: "Sin shall not have dominion over you, for you are not under law, but under grace." Looking back across these more than thirty years since that night, I can see that God has broken the grip of the things that mastered me then. Other problems have come in, with which I still struggle. But the promise remains: "Sin shall not have dominion over you. You are not under law, but under grace."

15

Whose Slave Are You?

Surely believers ought not to sin, but unfortunately, they still do. In verses 1–14 of chapter 6, we looked at the answer to the question, Can I go on living as I once did? Can I continue on in a life style of sin, just as though nothing had really happened to me except that I will go to heaven when I die?

Paul's answer is: "Absolutely not! You cannot do that; if you do, it is proof that you never really participated in the death and resurrection of Jesus." In other words, you are really not a Christian. Anyone who goes on in an unchanged life after having professed that they have come to Christ is simply giving testimony to everyone that he really has not been changed in his heart at all. Paul has just declared, "For sin shall not be your master, because you are not under law, but under grace."

In verse 15, he raises the question again, but in a slightly different way:

What then? Shall we sin because we are not under law but under grace?

Now the question is not "can we" but "shall we?" Paul is raising the question of whether a Christian ought to choose to sin occasionally because of the momentary pleasure involved.

Every one of us faces that situation from time to time. Sometimes we run up against some especially delicious temptations. At times, we are all confronted with the suggestion, "Why not give in? After all, I'm not going to hell because of this. My salvation rests on Christ and not on me. And actually, God is not going to reject me because of this, for the law does not condemn me any longer. I am not under law. It is love that will discipline me; law will not condemn me. I can be forgiven; I can be restored—so why not sin?" I have heard many Christians talk that way, and I have felt the full force of this confrontation in my own experience. Why not give in and enjoy a sin—we are not under law, but under grace? Do you see the thrust of the apostle's question?

In the verses that follow, Paul answers that question, beginning with an emphatic "No. By no means!" If I, as a Christian, go on and sin deliberately, even if it is only occasionally, I must face what sin will do to me. We believers must face the full results of what will happen when we choose to do what we know to be wrong, even though we have been set free in Christ and need not do these things.

Paul's answer is threefold. Shall we sin because we are not under law but under grace? By no means! First, sin makes one a slave (verses 16 through 19). Second, sin will make one ashamed (verses 20 and 21). Finally, sin will spread death throughout our whole existence (verses 22 and 23).

Made to Be Mastered

Let's look at the first part of Paul's answer. In verses 16 through 19 he tells us that sin will make slaves out of us:

Don't you know that when you offer yourselves to someone to obey him as slaves, you are slaves to the one whom you obey—whether you are slaves to sin, which leads to death, or to obedience, which leads to righteousness? But thanks be to God that, though you used to be slaves to sin, you whole-heartedly obeyed the form of teaching to which you were committed. You have been set free from sin and have become slaves to righteousness. I put this in human terms because you are weak in your natural selves. Just as you used to offer the parts of your body in slavery to impurity and to ever-increasing wickedness, so now offer them in slavery to righteousness and holiness (Rom. 6:16–19).

Paul goes into the common experience of the world of his day to give us a picture of what humanity is like. He uses the phrase "slaves" to describe us. In doing so, he is dealing with a profound psychological fact: human beings are made to be mastered. Someone has to master us.

Several years ago in Los Angeles I saw a man walking down the street with a sign hung over his shoulders. The front of it said, "I'M A SLAVE FOR CHRIST." On the back of it, as he passed, it read, "WHOSE SLAVE ARE YOU?" It is a good question. All of us are slaves to one or the other of these two masters—sin or righteousness. We have no other choices. By the very nature of our humanity, we are made to serve and to be controlled by forces beyond our power.

We think we are creatures of sovereign choice, but we are not. Our choices are narrow and limited. The great question is: Who controls the choices in that narrow band? What forces are at work to limit us to such a narrow range throughout our lives? The answer is that something beyond us controls these choices. God is at work; Satan is at work. We are given a limited ability to choose.

Paul then speaks of these two kinds of slavery. He says that we Christians have been set free from the slavery to sin. Once we had to sin. Before we came to Christ, there was no choice; no matter whether we chose what we thought was good or chose what we thought was wrong, we ended up making a choice that led to evil. There was no other way. Even the right things we tried to do were tainted with evil, with selfishness.

Well then, what happens when we sin as believers? Now we are free, and yet we go back and choose to do something that is wrong. We are confronted with this temptation to give way for the moment and indulge ourselves in some sin. Most of us try to kid ourselves into believing it is not very serious. "It won't hurt us anyway," we reason, so we make the choice.

Paul says, "Let's look at what happens. First of all, don't you know that you have set in operation a basic principle of life?" The principle is this: If you yield yourself to sin, you become the slave of sin. Jesus stated this in John 8:34: "Verily, verily, I say unto you [that is a little formula that means he is stating basic, fundamental, absolutely foundational truth], 'He that commits sin is the slave of sin.'"

No Ultimate Control

Now, what does this mean in practice? A slave, of course, is someone who is not in ultimate control of his own actions, someone who is at the disposal of another person, someone who has to do what that other person says. When we choose to tell a lie, we give one of the clearest evidences of the operation of this principle in our lives. Have you ever noticed what happens when you tell a lie?

A man said to me one day, "I told what I thought was a little white lie. I thought that would handle the matter. But, you know, I found out that I had to tell 42 other lies— I counted them—before I finally woke up to what I was doing and admitted the whole thing and got out from under." We can't tell just one lie. We are not in control of the events. If we choose to tell one lie, before we know it, we have to tell another.

The same thing is true with anger. I decide I am going to put a little sharpness in my voice when I answer someone. I want to cut him down just a little. I don't want it to go too far—after all, I do like him—I just want to hurt him slightly. So I do. What happens? He answers back in kind. So I cut a little deeper, and before I know it, I am embroiled in an argument and a battle that I did not want. It happened because I became a slave to sin. Sin pushed me further than 1 wanted to go. There was no way I could escape.

Secondly, sin not only takes me further than I desire to go, but it also infects others with the same attitude. Notice how it works. I wake up in the morning feeling surly and grouchy, and I snap at someone. Then the other person snaps back, and soon the whole household is reflecting my attitude. I choose to do something a little shady in my business, and soon others begin to do the same thing. So sin begins to spread, like an infection. Years ago I heard a little rhyme:

1 said a very naughty word, only the other day.
It was a truly naughty word I had not meant to say.
But then, it was not really lost, when from my lips it flew;
My little brother picked it up, and now he says it, too.

That is the way sin begins to spread. Part of the slavery is that when I yield myself to something (and do it two or three times before I wake up to what is going on so that it gets out of control and goes beyond what I wanted), it becomes difficult to begin to change. Something resists every opportunity I take to change because a habit has begun. Just as an illustration, someone said to me the other day, "It's easy to quit smoking; I've done it dozens of times!" What a testimony that is to the power these things have to grip us and to control us. Paul is right: we become slaves of that which we obey.

In verses 20 and 21 Paul continues:

When you were slaves to sin, you were free from the control of righteousness. What benefit [or what fruit] did you reap at that time from the things you are now ashamed of?

Each of us can look back in our lives at something we are ashamed of. It leaves a stain in our minds when we think about it. Shame is the awareness of unworthy actions and irreparable damage that we do to others and our painful feeling about them. We have all experienced shame at times. Sin—no matter what it is or how small it seems—always leads to shame. Our memories of the past are stained and blotted by the sense of shame that we experience. We all know what it is like—those shameful deeds that we would like to forget, but can't; hurtful words that we wish we had never said; strained relationships that go on for years, so that whenever we meet certain people we feel uncomfortable in their presence.

This is the inevitable fruit of sin, something of which Paul reminds us many times. In Galatians he says, "Do not be deceived [don't kid yourself]: God cannot be mocked. A man reaps what he sows. The one who sows to please his sinful nature, from that nature will reap destruction. . . ." I can't drop the seed of evil into my heart without reaping from it the harvest, the fruit of corruption. But "the one who sows to please the Spirit, from the Spirit will reap eternal life" (Gal. 6:7,8). That is exactly what we see here in Romans 6.

The End of Light

The third reason we should not give way to sin is found in verses 21 to 23:

> Those things result in death! But now that you have been set free from sin and have become slaves to God, the benefit you reap leads to holiness, and the result is eternal life. For the wages of sin is death, but the gift of God is eternal life through Christ Jesus our Lord (Rom. 6:21–23).

Life and death are the two results. When Paul talks about death here, he is talking about something that you experience right now while you are alive. Death is both physical and moral; the one is a picture of the other. Physical death always involves darkness, the end of light and life. It involves limitation, for a corpse is helpless—what can it do for itself? And it involves, ultimately, corruption—the corpse begins to stink and smell, it becomes foul and decayed, rottenness sets in.

When we sin as believers, these same elements of death

are present. There is, first of all, darkness. I can look back in my own life and see how, as a young Christian, there were times when I struggled and struggled to understand passages of scripture. I could not seem to grasp them; they were closed to me. Others understood them and seemed to be rejoicing in them, but I could not—until God, in his mercy, began to deal with me about things that I was doing that I knew were wrong. Finally, God led me to the place where I could be free. I would repent and turn from these things and come into the freedom that God had given me in Christ. Then I would discover that the Scriptures began to open up, and light came into my darkness.

I meet Christians all the time who do not seem to understand many of the truths of the Word of God. I do not know if this is always the explanation, but in many cases it is because they are deliberately allowing things in their lives that they know are wrong. They do not realize that these things spread death. Darkness sets in, and they cannot see the light. Paul reminds us in 2 Corinthians, "The god of this age has blinded the minds of unbelievers, so that they cannot see the light of the gospel of the glory of Christ" (2 Cor. 4:4).

Not only does darkness set in when we sin, but there are limitations, too. Remember the account in the Old Testament about Moses in the wilderness? He became angry one day when the people tested him and frustrated him. God told him to speak to the rock and it would give water. Instead, in his anger, Moses struck the rock with the rod. That was just a little thing, a momentary blowup. For a few seconds, he lost his temper. But God said, "Moses, because you have done this, you will not be able to enter the Promised Land. When the people enter the land, you must stay behind because you have done this thing."

I am not suggesting that there are things we do that forever limit the opportunities God gives us. But I know that as long as we cling to things that we know are wrong, justifying them in our lives and refusing to enter into the freedom that God gives us, there is loss of opportunity.

That is why many Christians never seem to discover the adventure of serving God. They sit with folded arms, watching other people having fun and excitement, while nothing opens for them. Often it is because of this very thing—the choices of sin that they make. Death means a lessening of our experience of freedom and delight in the things of God and an increase in boredom and banality. Sometimes our lives become utterly nauseating to us. Have you ever felt that way? Sometimes your whole Christian experience almost stinks in your own nostrils. That is a sign of the death brought in by sin.

Now throughout this account, Paul stresses over and over again the words "set free." "You have been set free," he says. "You no longer are the slaves of sin. When you came to the Lord Jesus, a change occurred; you have been freed. You are no longer a slave to evil, but a slave to righteousness." Paul says, "Just as you used to offer the parts of your body in slavery to impurity and to ever-increasing wickedness, so now offer them in slavery to righteousness and holiness."

Now that you have been set free from sin and have become slaves to God, all this business of being limited, of experiencing death and shame, is totally unnecessary to a believer. That is the tragedy of sin in a believer's life. We do not have to experience death in our lives; we only have it because we choose to. Therefore, any experience of these things in our lives is something that has come because we have chosen to let it, although we were free to choose otherwise.

Useless Unless Used

A member of our family is currently learning to ride a bicycle. She is learning how to balance herself and pedal down the street. And she is doing very well at it. But so far, the only way she has found to stop is by running into something, and I am constantly picking her up out of bushes and off the sidewalk.

The other day, while I was helping her, I said, "You don't have to run into things to stop; there is another way to do it. A provision has been made so that you can stop this bicycle without having to run into things." I showed her that all she had to do was to reverse the pedals and the coaster brake would bring her to a stop. But I had shown her this before, so when I said that to her, she looked at me and said with just a bit of sarcasm, "Well, I am sure relieved to know that there's another way to stop!"

I realized that she didn't need me to tell her that. What she did need was to actually do it when it was time to stop. What good is it to have a bicycle that has a provision for stopping if you never use it? You might just as well not have it. The question the apostle raises in this passage is: "What good is it to be set free from sin by Jesus Christ and have every opportunity and every possibility of walking in holiness (wholeness) and in righteousness (a sense of worth, a sense of security and assurance that you are loved by God and are valuable to him), if, at the moment of choice, we ignore these things and go right on as though we were slaves to sin?"

As I travel across America, I am often struck by the fact that the various cities I visit are filled with churches. On almost every corner you can find a church. And those churches are often filled with Christians. This country would appear to have a fantastic opportunity to witness a new quality of life—a quality of life so uniquely different from that of the world that people ought to be stopping us on the street to ask, "What goes with you? How come you have such peace in your eyes? How come you have such love in your heart? Why are you so different?" Instead, with our cities filled with churches and our churches filled with people, all the world sees is the same old, tired reactions with which they themselves are so familiar.

The challenge of Romans 6 is this: Christ has made us free, free to be kings, free to have a sense of worth, free to be secure in our own personhood, knowing who we are before God. He set us free to be whole people, so that we are not torn by a dozen different conflicting interests, but, with a single eye, can live to the glory of God, free from the control or the blame or the censure—or the praise—of men. We are free at last to respond to the greatest calling that a man can have—the call to know God.

That is what this closing verse means. "The wages of sin is death, but the gift of God is eternal life." Jesus described eternal life in John 17:3: "Now this is eternal life: that they may know you, the only true God, and Jesus Christ, whom you have sent." Here we are, called to this kind of living, called to this quality of existence, and yet, because of the foolishness of our hearts and the weakness of our faith, we choose to give way to these momentary indulgences that lock us into slavery, shame, and death. May God help us to set sin aside and to live as the free men and women God has made us to be! As Paul said in Galatians 5:1: "It is for freedom that Christ has set us free. Stand firm, then, and do not let yourselves be burdened again by a yoke of slavery." We have been freed from the slave market; now we are to walk as new men.

16

Free to Win or Lose

Romans tells us that God's solution to the problem of man is to begin a whole new race. He does not start with halfway measures, or try to patch up the old; he does not try to improve what is there until it gets good enough to live with. He cuts us right off at the root and begins a new race. But the wonder and the glory of it is that he starts the new race within the shell of the old. Outwardly, we remain unchanged. Our bodies are still subject to decrepitude, decay, and death. Yet within, a new man has begun if we have exercised faith in Jesus Christ. God's solution is to end the curse of Adam and to release within us the power of a new life, the life of Jesus himself. When we put our faith in our Lord and what he has done, we enter into an identification with his death and his resurrection, and the death of Jesus cuts us off from the old Adam with whom we all began life. The resurrection of Jesus, Paul says, introduces us to a whole new power—the life of Jesus, available to us.

The radical transformation within us, then, is going to result in some change in our attitude, outlook, and value system, and, therefore, it will result in a change of life style. But we can still sin as believers, if we choose to. If we choose to sin, however, we cannot escape the enslavement that sin will bring. It will involve us more deeply than we would like; it will spread darkness and corruption throughout our lives; it will lead us to do things of which we will be terribly ashamed. Though we can choose to sin, we will not escape the effects of sin in our experience.

That brings us to chapter 7, in which the apostle deals with still another question before he goes on to develop more fully this wonderful, glorious gospel. The question is this: Does the law help us, as believers, to handle the problem of sin in our lives? Here, the answer is both yes and no. Yes, the law does help us—but only up to a point. It will help us to define the problem. But no, the law is no help at all when it comes to delivering us. In fact, it will only make things worse.

Paul deals with the last part of this question first. In verses 1 through 6 he shows the necessity of being freed from the law in order to handle the problem of sin. We cannot handle our problem with the law hanging over our heads; we must be freed from that. This is a very pertinent problem in our day. Every Christian believer rejoices in what he reads in the Scriptures about our identification with Christ and about these tremendous terms—being freed from sin, dead to sin, and alive to God, alive to righteousness, wholeness, power. Yet our experience tells us that we do not often achieve this. We are aware that we all have a problem with sin in our lives. We still like it, and we still do it. We experience what Paul says we will experience (enslavement, death, darkness, unhappiness, and shame) as a result of our sin. This is true in all of Christendom today. Churches everywhere are filled with Christians who are struggling with this.

What is wrong? Basically, it is the very problem that Paul describes in Romans 7. We still have not learned how to handle the law. We still want regulations and detailed instructions to follow so we can be freed from our problems. Yet, when we try, even with the best of intentions, it still doesn't work. That is what Paul is dealing with in this chapter. Now, let's see what he has to say in verses 1–3:

Do you not know, brothers—for I am speaking to men who know the law—that the law has authority over a man only as long as he lives? For example, by law a married woman is bound to her husband as long as he is alive, but if her husband dies, she is released from the law of marriage. So then, if she marries another man while her husband is still alive, she is called an adulteress. But if her husband dies, she is released from that law and is not an adulteress, even though she marries another man.

This is a simple illustration taken right out of life. This situation occurred again and again in Paul's day, and it occurs again and again in ours. It is intended to clarify this whole problem of our relationship to the law. But before we get into the illustration and its application, let's first notice that Paul carefully underlines for us to whom this passage is addressed. In the first verse, he says, "Do you not know, brothers—for I am speaking to men who know the law. . . ." In other words, if we are to understand this paragraph, we must know something about the law—its function, its purpose, and its effect. If we don't, we will end up in confusion.

What Do You Know?

We must take a moment to ask ourselves if we understand the law. First, do we know that the law Paul mentions here is a reference to a standard of conduct, or behavior, which is expected of men? There are other uses of the word "law." Sometimes it is used in reference to a principle that governs our lives, such as the law of gravity. But here Paul is talking about a standard of conduct that we are expected to live up to.

The most obvious and perfect expression of that standard of behavior is the Ten Commandments, with which everyone is familiar. The Ten Commandments tell us, "You shall have no other gods before me. You shall not make for yourselves a graven image . . . You shall not take the name of the Lord your God in vain . . . Remember the sabbath day, to keep it holy. Honor your father and mother . . . You shall not kill. You shall not commit adultery. You shall

not steal. You shall not bear false witness against your
neighbor. You shall not covet . . ." (Exod. 20:3–17 RSV).
That is a standard of conduct, isn't it? That is the law that
Paul talks about here—the law that was given to Israel.

But Paul has already made clear in chapter 2 that, in a
wider sense, the law is present among men everywhere.
Have you ever heard people talking about their experiences
and relationships with other people? Listen for a while, and
you will hear a phrase like this: "I don't think that is fair."
What do these people mean? What is it that determines
whether a thing is fair or not? It is obviously some unspoken
standard of conduct or behavior that both the speaker and
the listener have in mind which is universally understood.

Some might put it this way: "I think this is the right thing
to do." There again is an unspoken standard of behavior.
Someone says, "I'm going to get even!" How do you know
when you are "even"? There is clearly a measure, a standard
in mind. So, as Paul points out in chapter 2, the law really
is everywhere; it is embedded in the hearts of men. There
is an undescribed, unspoken standard of conduct to which
we all refer. Every man everywhere thinks in these terms,
no matter what his background may be. Now, that is the
law. It is the unspoken agreement that we all understand
and which we must measure up to. This is what Paul calls
"the law."

Let's see what more we know about the law. The purpose
of the law is to condemn failure. The law never pats us on
the back when we do right. It takes for granted that we
ought to do right anyway, and it never says thank you for
doing right. But if we do wrong, the law condemns us. In
one way or another, it points out and punishes wrongdoing.
It does this in the laws of our land, in traffic laws, and even
in our so-called "moral" laws. Evil and wrongdoing always
take their toll. Therefore, the nature of law is that it condemns failure.

Why is the effect of the law to discourage people? If law
condemns—and no one likes to feel put down and condemned—then the effect of the law, invariably, is to discour-

age, to produce a sense of defeat, and, ultimately, a sense of despair. That is what the law does. That is why, in our land and in all the nations of the earth, law is producing a sense of despair. That is a major problem with which people wrestle today.

People under the Law

No one likes to feel despairing, and so we react in various ways. There are certain invariable signs that reveal the people who are still under the law. Paul is writing this to those believers in Christ who were still under the law. In their minds, at least, they thought they had to live under the law, and there are certain signs of people who live like that.

One of the first signs is that they are always proud of their record. You say, "Wait a minute! I thought you said the law's effect was to make you discouraged and defeated. Someone who is proud of his record is not discouraged or defeated." Well, that is a diversion. The law is making them discouraged, and they don't like it. In certain areas of their lives they see defeat, and so they attempt to get people's attention off this area of failure and onto areas where they feel they have succeeded. That is why they are always pointing out the areas of their success and boasting about how well they are doing. They want to keep us from looking at that other area where they are failing. The law produces failure. Therefore, one of the first marks of a person who is living under the law is that he is always pointing out how well he is doing. Isn't that strange?

Another mark of people who are living under the law is that they are always critical of others. This is another diversionary tactic. Why are people critical of others? Well, if I succeed in getting my friends' eyes fastened on other people, they won't look at me. And I feel justified because the faults I point out in other people aren't the same faults of which I feel guilty. God plays some amazing tricks with us. He so blinds our eyes, or allows Satan to do so, that in-

variably the things for which we criticize others are the
very things of which we are guilty. But we don't know it!
The law produces a sense of failure and defeat, and we constantly adjust to it and compensate for it by criticizing
others.

Another mark of those under the law is that they are always reluctant to admit any error or fault in their own lives.
I was interested in Chuck Colson's characterization of
former President Richard Nixon. One of Nixon's problems
was that he could never admit he was wrong in anything. In
fact, in his book *Born Again,* Colson said that even when
Nixon obviously had a cold—nose running, face red, sneez-
ing, all the symptoms of a cold—he would never admit it.
That is the mentality of those who are under the law. They
feel very heavily the standard of conduct they are expected
to have, so they pretend they are living up to it, even
though they don't. They hate to admit defeat because that
means they must change.

Another symptom of those under the law is that they are
subject to times of inner boredom and depression, and often
display outward symptoms of depression and discouragement and defeat. The law is doing its work of condemning,
and that sense of condemnation produces depression of
spirit. Did you know this? Remember, you can't understand
this passage unless you know what the law does. If you
know this, you can see that this is a major problem in the
church. This is what has gone wrong with so much of the
church in America today.

Her Tie to the Law

Let's go back to the illustration: you and I are the woman
in Paul's little story. She has two husbands, one following
the other. Now, the point of this little story is not that the
woman has two husbands. Although that is important, it is
not the major point. What Paul is getting at here is what
the death of the first husband does to the woman's relationship to the law—not what it does directly to the woman

herself, but what it does to her tie to the law. Notice that verse 2 tells us the place of the law in this story:

> For example, by law a married woman is bound to her husband as long as he is alive, but if her husband dies, she is released from the law of marriage [or, the law of her husband].

Notice three factors here: First, there is the law; second, there is a woman; and third, there is the husband. It is the law that binds the woman and her husband together. The law is outside their relationship, saying, "You two must stay together because you are married." The law is not the husband, as it is often interpreted to be; that is clear.

If the first husband dies, Paul says, the woman is released from *the law*. Not only is she released from her husband, but she also is released from the law. If her husband dies, the law can say nothing to her as to where she can go and what she can do and who she can be with. She is released from the law. The death of the husband makes the woman dead to law.

Now, who is this first husband? According to the context, it is quite clear. We have been looking at it all along. The first husband is Adam, this old life into which we were born. We were linked to it, married to it, and couldn't get away from it. Like a woman married to an old, cruel, mean husband, there is not much we can do about it. While she is married she is tied to that husband. In verse 3, Paul says:

> So then, if she marries another man while her husband is still alive, she is called an adulteress. But if her husband dies, she is released from that law and is not an adulteress, even though she marries another man.

Now, that is plain, isn't it? The woman cannot have two husbands at once. She cannot have a second husband while she is married to the first. She is stuck with number one and she has to share his life style. As we have already seen, that life style is one of bondage, corruption, shame, and death. That is why we who were born into Adam have to share the life style of fallen Adam. It fits perfectly, doesn't it?

Now, if this woman, while she is married to her first husband, tries to live with another—for her husband's life style is sickening to her—she will be called an adulteress. Who calls her that? The law does. The law says, "You are a hypocrite." That, you see, is the spiritual counterpart of the physical term "adulteress." The law condemns her; it points out her failure; it calls her an adulteress. It is only when the first husband dies that she is free from that condemnation of the law and thus can marry again. When she does, the law is absolutely silent; it has nothing to say to her at all.

You Also Died

Now look at verse 4:

So, my brothers, you also died to the law through the body of Christ, that you might belong to another, to him who was raised from the dead, in order that we might bear fruit to God.

What a fantastic verse! Here is the great, marvelous declaration of the gospel of our Lord Jesus. Notice how Paul draws the parallel: "So . . . you also." We fit right into this. The key thought here is "you died to the law through the body of Christ," and the body of Christ refers to the death of the Lord Jesus on the cross. He died in a body. He came to take a body upon himself, so that he might die.

Paul is referring to what the Scriptures say in many places—that on the cross the Lord Jesus was made sin for us. He took our place, as sinful humanity, on the cross. I don't know how, but he did. In other words, he became that first husband. It is extremely important to grasp that truth. On the cross, he became that first husband, that Adamic nature to which we were married. And when he became that, he died. And when he died, we were freed from the law.

The law has nothing to say to us anymore. We are free to be married to another. Who is this? It is Christ risen. Our first husband is Christ crucified; our second husband is Christ risen from the dead. We now share his name, we share his power, we share his experiences, we share his position, his glory, his hopes, his dreams—all that he is, we now share. We are married to Christ, risen from the dead. The law therefore has nothing to say to us. Isn't that clear?

> For when we were controlled by our sinful nature, the sinful passions aroused by the law were at work in our bodies, so that we bore fruit for death. But now, by dying to what once bound us, we have been released from the law so that we serve in the new way of the Spirit, and not in the old way of the written code (vv. 5,6).

While we were married to sin (the old Adamic life), we often tried to act as though we were married to someone else, didn't we? We tried to act righteous and loving and kind. Many of us did. We really tried to behave ourselves, but we found we couldn't. The law refused to go along with us. The law judged us. It said, "You are really not that way, you are just acting like that. You are pretending." The law called us hypocrites, and it was right. That is what we were. We were religious hypocrites, attempting to give the impression that we were okay, right, loving, moral, kind, and good, when we weren't at all. Inside, all our attitudes were selfish and self-centered and loveless; but we were pretending. And the law saw through it and named us what we were: hypocrites!

No Longer Hypocrites

But, according to this, we died to the law through the death of our first husband. When Jesus was crucified, that first husband died. And now we are free from the condemnation of the law. We are married to another, Christ risen from the dead. So now, when we seek to be righteous and to do righteous things, to be loving and kind, we are no longer hypocrites. This is the point Paul wants to make. We are doing what we really are. We are tied to Jesus. His life is now ours, and we are acting according to our true nature.

We are married to a new husband. And because we share his life and power, we are not only able to be what he is, but we are also free from any condemnation or failure in our struggle along the way. We don't always act right, but the law doesn't condemn us. The law's purpose was to condemn, and we can't be condemned anymore because we are not hypocrites. We are doing what we were designed to do. We have a new identity. No longer bound to our failures, we can admit them and forget them. We don't have to have them clinging to us; we no longer have to believe that God is unhappy with us because we don't always live exactly right. He has made provision for this. It is not a fraud when we go back to God again and again, and accept his forgiveness from his hand.

Therefore, it is not law that straightens us out, it is love. We no longer need the law to straighten us out, for we have love to do so. We are free to fail and still be loved. And we are also free to win in the new power given to us. The next question Paul asks is, "Is the law worthless, then, and contemptible?" His answer, of course, is no. Some Christians talk that way about the law, but Paul never does. There is a place for it, and it is valuable in a certain way, but it can do nothing to deliver us from evil. Only our relationship to love can do that.

17

The Continuing Struggle

The gospel of Jesus Christ is able to set men free. This is the central declaration of the gospel: Christ has come, he has died, he has risen again, and he has come into our hearts by means of the Holy Spirit so that we who believe in him might be free.

That is what the gospel is all about—freedom! Freedom from self-centeredness, freedom from hostility and bitterness, freedom from anxiety and all kinds of fears, freedom from bondage to evil habits of any type—this is the freedom Christ has come to give us. He has come to release us, to free us to be the men and women whom God has designed us to be, living in the midst of (as Paul describes it) "a generation of crooks and perverts," yet being lights shining in the darkness of our day. As we have seen all the way through this Book, and especially in Romans 5 and 6, this kind of life is totally possible in Jesus Christ. Yet there are at least two ways we can miss this, even though we are Christians.

Paul has dealt with one of these in Romans 6. In the last half of Romans 6 he has pointed out that, even though one is a Christian, he can give himself over to the bondage and

slavery of sin. He can continue to give way to sin. He may
think it is not worthwhile to fight or he may enjoy the
pleasure that sin gives him, so he keeps on doing the things
that are wrong. This is what theologians call "antinomian-
ism," which means, simply, "against the law." Antinomian-
ism reflects an attitude that unfortunately is common among
us—the idea that God, in his grace, will forgive us, so why
not indulge in sin? I will go ahead and sin because I know
God will forgive.

The answer to that attitude is found in Romans 6:15–22.
The scripture says that if you do live on that basis, sin will
enslave you, it will shame you, it will limit you, it will defile
you, it will spread corruption and death in your experience.
And though you may be a Christian, you will have a miserable Christian life because you cannot give way to sin without being enslaved by it.

The second way we can miss God's freedom for us is
exactly the opposite. It is by attempting to handle this problem of sin by trying our best to do what God wants. By
discipline and dedication of heart, and the exercise of determined will power, we try our best to do what God asks,
to live according to the law, and to fulfill the requirements
of the law.

Now, this takes many forms. Sometimes it comes as a
challenge to take certain steps by which to overcome certain problems. Such a program may sound good, because
it is an appeal to do that which is right, but it is what the
Scriptures call legalism—the exact opposite of antinomian-
ism. It is a wholehearted attempt to do what God wants—
with the end result that we become defensive, self-
righteous, critical of others, proud of our own record. Furthermore, we become unaccountably bored, discouraged,
depressed, and even frequently despairing. That, basically,
is the story of Romans 7.

We have already seen in Romans 7:1–6 that there is no
need to be like this. Legalism is not the answer; we are not
under the law, but under grace. Romans 7 is a commentary
on Paul's great declaration of Romans 6:14: "Sin shall not

have dominion over you: for ye are not under law, but under grace" (KJV). Not only are we freed from sin, as Paul points out, but we are freed from the law, as well. The law condemns us, but we are no longer under law if we are resting in Christ. Therefore, the law does not serve any useful purpose in delivering us from sin.

To Drive Us to Christ

That raises the question: "What, then, is the purpose of the law in a Christian's life? Is the law really contemptible and worthless? Ought we to just dispense with it?" There are many Christians around who say, "I'm a Christian, saved by grace. The law has no meaning to me at all. The law was given to Moses for the Israelites, but it doesn't apply to a Christian. Let's dispense with it." But Paul never speaks this way, and neither does Jesus. In fact, Jesus tells us in the Sermon on the Mount that if anyone disparages the law, changes it, or waters it down in any degree whatsoever, he is under the curse of God. The law abides forever.

Therefore, we must clearly understand what Paul is teaching here about the function and purpose of the law. We must know (1) that the law cannot deliver us from sin. It simply cannot do so. But (2) it can always do one thing well—even with Christians—it can expose sin in us and drive us back to Christ. That is what the law is for, and that is the story of Romans 7:7–25.

This section divides into two parts. In verses 7 through 13, Paul discusses how the law exposes sin and kills the believer. That is the term he uses: the law kills us. Then, in verses 14 through 25, he takes up exactly the same theme—how the law exposes sin and kills us—but this time it is not explained, it is experienced. In the first section Paul tells us how it works; in the second section he tells us how it feels. This is a feeling generation; therefore, this is a passage that ought to strike a responsive chord in many hearts, for Paul describes just exactly how it feels to be under the law as a Christian.

In verses 7 through 11, the apostle begins to describe his own experience in relationship to the law:

> What shall we say, then? Is the law sin? Far from it! Indeed I would not have known what sin was except through the law. For I would not have known what it was to covet if the law had not said, "Do not covet." But sin, seizing the opportunity afforded by the commandment, produced in me every kind of covetous desire. For apart from law, sin is dead. Once I was alive apart from law; but when the commandment came, sin sprang to life and I died. I found that the very commandment that was intended to bring life actually brought death. For sin, seizing the opportunity afforded by the commandment, deceived me, and through the commandment put me to death (Rom. 7:7–11).

This is Paul's experience. It is clear that he is describing something he himself went through. But also, note that Paul employs the past tense throughout this passage, which suggests that he is describing his experience before he became a Christian. This probably happened not long before he became a Christian, and it is common to the experience of many today. Paul, as we know, was raised in a godly home. He was a Jew, raised in the city of Tarsus. As a typical Jewish son, he was taught the law from birth. So when he says he lived "apart from the law," he does not mean that he didn't know what it was. He simply means a time had to come when the law came home to him. "The commandment came," he says.

We have all had that experience. We have read much scripture that was just words to us—beautiful words, perhaps, but we didn't understand them. Then, years after, an experience that we went through made those words come alive. This is what Paul is talking about here. He knew the law from birth, but he did not know it in the sense of understanding what it was saying until he went through a certain experience. Here he describes that experience, one that he had before he became a Christian.

Protected from Temptation

In his home Paul, like many of us today, was protected and sheltered, kept from exposure to serious temptations. He was raised in the Jewish culture, where everyone around him was also sheltered. Therefore, he grew up relatively untroubled with problems of sin. Now, there are many people like that in our churches today. They have grown up in a home where they have been protected and sheltered. They have run with a crowd of friends who, likewise, have been kept from exposure to various temptations. They have not fallen into evil.

Many young people, like Saul of Tarsus, think they have handled the problem of sin. What about keeping the law? It's not hard! Hardly any temptations come, under these circumstances. These people do not feel struggle along this line. They have the world by the tail—they can handle it. As Paul describes it, "they are alive apart from the law." But then comes a time when they are exposed. They are thrust out into a different life style, a different crowd of people. They move out on their own and suddenly find themselves removed from the shelter, protection, love, and cultural defenses that have been theirs from childhood on. Perhaps the new crowd—as a way of life—does things that these sheltered young people have been taught are wrong. Now, for the first time, they feel the force of the prohibition of the law. The law says, "Thou shalt not—covet, commit adultery, murder, steal"—whatever it may be. And yet the crowd around them says, "Let's do it—it's fun!" For the first time, they begin to feel the prohibition of the law. Then a strange phenomenon happens. Something about that situation arouses within them a strong desire to do the things that are prohibited. Maybe they are able to resist for awhile, but eventually they find themselves pressured, pushed by something within them that wants very badly to do these things.

That is what Paul discovered. It was the tenth command-

ment, "Thou shalt not covet," that got to him. He thought
he had been keeping all the law because he had not done
some of the external things prohibited in the other commandments. But this one commandment talks about how
you feel inside, your desires, your imagination, your ambi-
tions. It says, "Thou shalt not desire what another has."
Paul found himself awakened to this commandment and
discovered that he was coveting, no matter where he turned.
When the law came, he found himself aroused by it,
brought under its power. It precipitated an orgy of desire.
Many of us have felt this same way.

Power at a Touch

Not long ago I had an opportunity to go up into the
Colorado Rockies for a conference. As I came out of my
hotel, the man who was to drive me there was waiting in
his powerful, shiny, new Lincoln Continental. I got into the
car and expected him to turn on the ignition. But to my
amazement, he started driving without turning on the
engine—or at least that's how it seemed to me. I suddenly
realized that the engine had been running all the time. It
was so quiet I hadn't heard it. As we moved up into the
Rockies, the power of that engine became manifest. We
traveled up the steep grades in those great mountains without difficulty because of the power released by his touch on
the accelerator.

That is something like what Paul is describing here. Sin
lies silent within us. We do not even know it is there. We
think we have hold of life in such a way that we can handle
it without difficulty. We are self-confident because we have
never really been exposed to the situation that puts pressure
upon us—we never have had to make a decision against the
pressure of the commandment, "Thou shalt not . . ."

But when that happens, we suddenly find ourselves filled
with attitudes that almost shock us—unloving, bitter, resentful thoughts, murderous attitudes—we would like to get
hold of someone and kill him, if we could. Lustful feelings

surface that we never dreamed were there, and we find we would love to indulge in them if only we had the opportunity. We find ourselves awakened to these desires. As the great engine surges into life at the touch of the accelerator, so this powerful, idling beast within us called sin springs into life as the law comes home to us.

Now, is this the law's fault? No, Paul says, it is not; he goes on in verses 12 and 13:

> So then, the law is holy, and the commandment is holy, righteous and good. Did that which is good, then, become death to me? By no means! But in order that sin might be recognized as sin, it produced death in me through what was good, so that through the commandment sin might become utterly sinful [exceedingly sinful].

That is what the law is for. It is to expose the fact that this evil force is in every one of us, waiting only for the right circumstance to spring into being, overpower our will, and carry us into things we never dreamed we would do. According to this passage, the great power of sin is that it deceives us. We think we have life under control—and we are fooled. All sin is waiting for is the right occasion when, like a powerful, idling engine, it roars into life and takes over at the touch of the accelerator of the law, and we find ourselves helplessly under its control.

The law is designed to expose that sin so that we begin to understand what this evil force is that we have inherited at birth. The law shows sin up for what it is, something exceedingly powerful and dangerous, something that has greater strength than our will power and causes us to do things that we are resolved not to do.

Present Tense Experience

In verses 14 through 25, the same experience is described again, but this time in terms of how we feel when it happens. There is only one major difference between this section and the previous one. In this section, Paul switches to the present tense. That is significant because it means he is now describing his experience at the time he wrote this letter to the Romans. This, then, is a description of the law as it touches the Christian's life. It does exactly the same thing as it did before we became a Christian, only now we have it from the point of view of the Christian, the believer who is deceived by the sin that is still resident within.

> We know that the law is spiritual; but I am unspiritual [carnal, fleshly. Paul gives us now an excellent definition of carnality], sold as a slave to sin. I do not know what I am doing. For what I want to do I do not do, but what I hate I do.

Some have been convinced, from this verse alone, that Paul was a golfer. If you have ever tried golf, you know that this is the very thing that happens. What you want to do, you do not do. What you do not want to do, this is the very thing you do. Of course, Paul has a much greater problem than playing golf. The key to this whole passage is verse 14: "The law is spiritual," Paul says. "It deals with my spirit. It gets right at the very heart of my being." Fundamentally, as we have seen, human beings are spirits. The law is spiritual, and it touches us in that area. "But I am carnal," Paul says. "I can't respond to it. I am sold as a slave to sin."

Now, this always raises a problem. Compare this with chapter 6, verse 17, where Paul is speaking of slavery and says, "But thanks be to God that, though you used to be slaves to sin, you wholeheartedly obeyed the form of teaching to which you were committed. You have been set free from sin and have become slaves to righteousness." If he could write that to the Romans, surely it was true of him as well. Yet how could he write that he had become in Christ a slave to righteousness, and just a few paragraphs later write, "I am carnal, sold under sin, a slave to sin"?

In spite of what many have said, Paul is not confused here, but is simply describing what happens when a Christian tries to live under the law. When a Christian, by his dedication, will power, and determination, tries to do what is right in order to please God, he is living under the law. And Paul is telling us what to expect when we live like that

—for we all try to live that way from time to time. Sin, you see, deceives us. It deceived Paul as an apostle, and he needed this treatment of the law. It deceives us, and we need it, too.

Now, Paul tells us what happens. There are two problems, basically, which he gives us in verse 15: "I do not know what I am doing. For what I want to do I do not do. . . ." That is problem number one. I want to do right— there are things I would love to do, but I cannot do them. The second problem is: ". . . but what I hate I do." There are some things I don't want to do—yet I find myself doing those very things.

In the verses that follow, Paul takes the second problem first, and shows us what happens in our experience.

And if I do what I do not want to do, I agree that the law is good. As it is, it is no longer I myself who do it, but it is sin living in me (vv. 16,17).

That is an extremely important statement. Paul makes it twice in this paragraph, and it is the explanation of and the answer to how we can be delivered from this condition.

I know that nothing good lives in me, that is, in my sinful nature [or my flesh]. For I have the desire to do what is good, but I cannot carry it out. For what I do is not the good I want to do; no, the evil I do not want to do—this I keep on doing. Now if I do what I do not want to do, it is no longer I who do it, but it is sin living in me that does it (vv. 18–20).

Let's examine this carefully. Paul says that as a Christian, redeemed by the grace of God, there is now something within him that wants to do good, that agrees with the law, that says the law is right. There is something within that says what the law tells me to do is right, and I want to do it. But also, he says, there is something else in me that rises up and says, "No!" Even though I determine not to do what is bad, I suddenly find myself in such circumstances that my determination melts away, my resolve is gone, and I end up doing what I had sworn I would not do. Have you ever felt that way?

The "I" and the "Me"

So, what has gone wrong? Paul's explanation is, "It is no longer I who do it; it is sin living in me." Isn't that strange? This indicates a division within our humanity. There is the "I" that wants to do what God wants, and there is the sin which dwells in "me," which is different than the "I." We must understand what this is.

As we have seen, human beings are complicated creatures. We have within us a spirit, a soul, and a body. These are distinct, one from the other. What Paul is suggesting here is that the redeemed spirit never wants to do what God has prohibited. It agrees with the law that it is good. And yet there is an alien power, a force that he calls sin, a great beast lying dormant within our soul and body. When it is touched by the commandment of the law, it springs to life, and we do what we do not want to do.

Jesus himself agrees with this. On one occasion he said, "If your right hands offends you, cut it off." He did not mean that one should actually chop off his right hand, because that would be a violation of other texts that indicate that God made the body and made it right, and it is morally neutral. What he means is that we should take drastic action because we are up against a serious problem. He indicates there is a "me" within us that runs our members, that gives orders to our hands, our feet, our eyes, our tongue, our brain, our sexual organs, and controls them. That "me" is giving an order to do something wrong, but there is another "I" in us who is offended by this. That "I" does not like it, does not want it. And so, Jesus' words are, "Cut it off." In a moment we are going to see how that happens, what it is that cuts it off and thus enables me to handle the problem. Man is made in such a way that his will power is never enough; sin will win, and we will do the evil we swore not to do.

Now look at the other side of this problem in verses 21 through 23:

> So I find this law at work: When I want to do good, evil is right there with me. For in my inner being I delight in God's law; but I see another law [another principle] at work in the members of my body, waging war against the law [or principle] of my mind [my agreement with the law of God] and making me a prisoner of the law [principle] of sin at work within my members.

Here is the same problem exactly. I want to do right and determine to do right, knowing what it is and swearing to do it, only to find that under certain circumstances all that determination melts away and I do not do what is right. I do exactly what I did not want to do. So I come away angry with myself. "What's the matter with me? Why can't I do what is right? Why do I give way when I get into this situation? Why am I so weak?" This is right where we live, isn't it? This is what we all struggle with. The cry of the heart at that moment is:

> What a wretched man I am! Who will rescue me from this body of death? (vs. 24)

What is this? Well, right here we arrive at the place where the Lord Jesus began the Sermon on the Mount: "Blessed are the poor in spirit, for theirs is the kingdom of heaven." Blessed is the man who comes to the end of himself. Blessed is the man who has arrived at spiritual bankruptcy, who cries, "What a wretched man I am!" Why? Because this is the point—the only point—where God's help is given.

This is what we need to learn. If we think we have something in ourselves with which we can work out our problems, if we think that our wills are strong enough, our desires motivated enough, that we can control evil in our lives by simply determining to do so, then we have not yet come to the end of ourselves. And the Spirit of God simply folds his arms and lets us go ahead and try it on that basis. And we fail, and fail miserably—until, at last, out of our failures, we cry, "O wretched man that I am!" Sin has deceived us, and the law, as our friend, has come in and exposed sin for what it is. When we see how wretched it

makes us, then we are ready for the answer, which comes
immediately:

Thanks be to God—through Jesus Christ our Lord! (vs. 25)

Who will deliver me from this body of death? The Lord
Jesus has already done it. We are to respond to the feelings
of wretchedness and discouragement and failure, to which
the law has brought us because of sin in us, by reminding
ourselves immediately of the facts that are true of us in
Jesus Christ. Our feelings must be answered by facts.

Free Sons of God

We are no longer under the law. That is the fact. We
have arrived at a different situation; we are married to
Christ, Christ risen from the dead. That means we must no
longer think, "I am a poor, struggling, bewildered disciple,
left alone to wrestle against these powerful urges." We must
now begin to think, "No, I am a free son of God, living a
normal human life. I am dead to sin, and dead to the law,
because I am married to Christ. His power is mine, right at
this moment. And though I may not feel a thing, I have the
power to say 'No' and walk away and be free, in Jesus
Christ."

I recently met a pastor from Canada who had been reared
in Russia. With a burden on his heart to get the Word of
God into Russia, he joined an organization (among several
that exist today) to get Bibles into Russia. His first experience of crossing the Russian border with a load of Bibles in
the trunk of the car was a thrilling one. He wasn't going to
try to smuggle them in; he was just counting on God to get
him through somehow.

He and a friend loaded the boxes of Bibles into the car,
and as they drove up to the border, all his resolve and
courage began to drain away. Within a mile or so of the
border his friend asked, "How do you feel?" He replied, "I

feel scared." So they stopped alongside the road and there they simply told the Lord how they felt. "Lord, we are scared. We didn't get into this situation because we want to be here. It isn't we who want to get this Word into Russia; it is you. This is your project, and this is your situation. We are willing to take whatever risks you ask, but you have got to see it through. We are scared and we don't know what to do. We don't have any wisdom, we don't know how to handle this situation when we get to the border, but we expect you to do something." He said that as they prayed that way, totally bankrupt, wanting to do good, unable to do it, but committing the matter to the Lord Jesus, they felt the inward sense of the Spirit of God witnessing to them that God would act. They didn't know how or what he would do, but they felt a sense of peace.

They drove on to the border, and when the guard asked for their papers, they gave them to him. He examined them, then said, "What do you have in the trunk?" They said, "Some boxes." He said, "Let me see them." So they opened up the trunk, and there were the boxes of Bibles. They expected surely that his next question would be, "What's in them?" But he didn't ask it. He simply said, "Okay," shut the door, gave them their papers, and on they went.

That is what this passage is describing for us. This is the way we are to live, the way we are to face every challenge, large or small. "Thanks be to God, it is through Jesus Christ our Lord."

There are teachers who teach that this passage in Romans 7 is something a Christian goes through but once. Then he gets out of it and moves into Romans 8, never to return to Romans 7 again. Nothing could be further from the truth! Even as mighty a man as Paul went through it again and again. This is a description of what every believer will go through many times in his experience because sin has the power to deceive us and to cause us to trust in ourselves, even when we are not aware we are doing so. The law is what will expose that evil force and drive us to this place of wretchedness that we might then, in poverty of spirit, cry out, "Lord Jesus, it is your problem; you take it." And he will.

The chapter ought to end with the exclamation in verse 25: "Thanks be to God—through Jesus Christ our Lord!" The next sentence belongs with chapter 8. It is the summarizing verse that introduces the explanation Paul gives us in chapter 8. Here, then, is the way of deliverance for Christians. We do need the law. Every time sin deceives us we need it. But the law will not deliver us from sin; the law will only bring us, again and again, to the mighty Deliverer. His life and power within us sets us free, without condemnation to us.

18

No Condemnation

The eighth chapter of Romans is the favorite of many—
and not without reason. This is one of the most significant
chapters of the Scriptures. Someone has called it "the
brightest jewel in the casket of gems of the Word of God."
I like to think of it as a great mountain, like Mt. Shasta,
rising above all the surrounding hills and capturing the
attention of all. Yet, the interesting thing about it is that
Paul does not introduce any new thoughts until the middle of the chapter (verse 17). In the opening words of this
chapter he simply gathers up what he has been saying and
brings it into focus.

To understand this chapter we must ignore the division
between chapters 7 and 8. I believe the text of the Scriptures is inspired by God, "breathed out" by him—but I
wonder if the chapter divisions were put in by the devil!
Many times they come right at a place where they actually
obscure truth. Sometimes these divisions break the continuity of a thought and take it out of the context, so that
we are likely to miss something tremendously important.
That is certainly true here. The first two verses of chapter 8
ought to be linked with the closing verse of chapter 7. They
are really all one sentence. When you read them that way,

it will help explain the struggle and darkness in Romans 7.
It is a struggle that does not have to go on, and Paul re-
solves it with this one, great, flashing word of relief:

> Thanks be to God—through Jesus Christ our Lord! (Rom.
> 7:25)

Then the rest of verse 25 belongs with the opening verses
of chapter 8. It is an explanation of what he means when
he says, "Thanks be to God—through Jesus Christ our
Lord!"

> So then, I myself in my mind am a slave to God's law, but in
> my sinful nature a slave to the law of sin. [That summarizes
> all that he has been talking about in chapter 7. But don't
> stop there, for there should not even be a period between
> that and verse 1 of chapter 8], (But) there is now no con-
> demnation for those who are in Christ Jesus, because through
> Christ Jesus the law of the Spirit of life set me free from the
> law of sin and death.

There is absolutely no question but that chapter 8 ought
to open with the word "but." It introduces a contrast that
shows the way out of the struggle of chapter 7: "But
there is now no condemnation for those who are in Christ
Jesus. . . ."

Linked by the Body

What is Paul saying in this passage when it is all taken
together like that? First, he makes clear that there is a struggle in the Christian life. There is a struggle between what
he calls "the sinful nature" and the Spirit. I am not sure I
like that term "sinful nature" too well, however. The Greek
word is "flesh," and, as the word is used in the Scriptures,
it not only means the body, but it also means the sin that
finds its seat in our bodies. It is by the body that we are
linked to our father, Adam. Genetically, all that we have
in our bodies is traceable back through the stream of human history to Adam. God made a body for Adam that is

like ours—with two eyes, two ears, a nose, and so on, and we have these characteristics because Adam had them. But we also have inherited from Adam the principle of sin.

Now, it is hard to define that principle. In some way, it describes the access that the devil has to our humanity. It is the means by which Satan is able to implant in our minds "the fiery darts of the wicked one," as Paul calls them in Ephesians. This refers to obscene and lustful thoughts, selfish attitudes, and hostile, bitter feelings that we have toward others—thoughts that come suddenly, unbidden, into our minds when we least expect them. They come from this root of sin that is in our bodies, the flesh. As Christians, we must expect to be caught up in a struggle between the flesh and the Spirit.

In Galatians 5 Paul describes this struggle between the Spirit and the flesh:

> For the sinful nature [or the flesh] desires what is contrary to the Spirit, and the Spirit what is contrary to the sinful nature [the flesh]. They are in conflict with each other, so that you do not do what you want (Gal. 5:17).

That really is a verse of hope. Paul says the Spirit struggles against the flesh, so that we *cannot* do the things that we would. That is what Paul is describing here in Romans 7. In verse 25 he says, "I myself in my mind am a slave to God's law." That is, as he said earlier, "I want to do good, I believe in it. I delight in God's law in my inner being. I am changed; I agree that the law is good. But I find I can't do it."

In his mind he is awakened to the value and the righteousness of God's law, and this has come about by means of the Spirit in his life. How else can we ever come to the place of agreeing that God is good and holy, his Word is right and the law is good, except by the Spirit of God in us? It is only when a man is filled with the Holy Spirit that he is able to talk like that. Therefore, it is the Holy Spirit, within Paul's human spirit, agreeing with God's law. But set against that is this sin that is in his flesh that takes hold of him and makes him a slave to the law of sin, even though he does not want to be.

How does he break this hold? He breaks it, as he says, by relying upon a new view of himself that is true because he is in Jesus Christ. That is what Romans 8 declares to us. The life of Jesus in him, released to him by the Holy Spirit, sets him free from the law of sin and death.

But there is a struggle to believe that great fact. If you ever have watched an alcoholic, or perhaps have struggled with alcoholism yourself, you know it is an intense struggle. An alcoholic can come to the place where he can see everything evil happening to him because of alcohol. He wants to quit; he determines to quit. He knows he is going to lose his wife, his children, his reputation, and everything if he doesn't quit. I have seen these people resolve never to drink again. Yet, in a moment of temptation, the very struggle of Romans 7 comes in, and suddenly they find themselves overpowered by sin. They give in, and then they hate themselves for it.

Those who struggle with homosexuality feel the same way. Habits of reaction have settled in and they find it very difficult to say "no," even though they want to. Born again, they want to be delivered—but it is hard to believe in their new identity in Christ.

And it is not only such things that can grip us like this. A hot temper or a habit of overeating can do the same thing. Perhaps right now you are saying, "For dinner I am going to take just a very light meal." And someone will spread out a beautiful roast and apple pie and, before you know it, your resolve is gone—and so is the food.

This is a problem of the will, isn't it? Our wills are weak, and we know it. This is what Paul is describing here. This is the struggle of the Christian life. It comes again and again, but it does not have to continue. Some Christians resent the fact that the struggle is there at all. They have a false idea of Christianity. They think Christianity means that God takes all struggle away and removes the temptation so they never have to struggle again. Unfortunately, that is not true; and many people have been hurt and have become angry with God because he does not do that. I have seen young Christians become extremely upset at times because they thought they were free from struggle and then found that they were not.

The text tells us that this struggle can cease only when we reckon on who we really are in Christ. Basically, what we need is a new self-image; that is what will deliver us. When we see who we really are, we can say "no" to the flesh and "yes" to the Spirit—and discover a whole new way of life.

No Condemnation

The second major thing the apostle is saying is that not only is there a struggle, but (and this is very important) the struggle is without condemnation. Though we may struggle at times, Paul says, there is no condemnation to those who are in Christ Jesus. The reason there is no condemnation is given in just one little phrase: "in Christ." That goes right back to our justification by faith. We came out of Adam, we are in Christ, and God will never condemn those who are in Christ.

Now, we have to understand what "no condemnation" means. What is Paul talking about? Certainly, the most basic element in it is that there is no rejection by God. God does not turn us aside, he does not kick us out of his family. If we are born into the family of God by faith in Jesus Christ, the Holy Spirit has come to dwell within us and he will never, never leave us. No matter what we do, he will never leave us. God will never cut us out of his family or treat us as anything less than sons and daughters.

One of the most beautiful stories of the Scriptures is that of the prodigal son who left home, got into deep difficulty, wasted his life in riotous living, and ended up in the pigpen. On this subject Dr. Vernon McGee asks, "Do you know the difference between the son in that pigpen and the pig? The difference is that no pig has ever said to himself, 'I will arise and go to my father.'" He is right; only sons say that. Thus there will be no condemnation, no rejection, by God. He will always treat me as his child, not as his enemy.

The second thing "no condemnation" means is that God is not angry with us when struggle comes into our lives. We want to be good; we want to stop doing bad. But when the moment of temptation comes, we find ourselves overpowered and weak, and we give way. Then we hate ourselves. We go away frustrated, feeling, as Paul described, "Oh, wretched man that I am, what's the matter with me? Why can't I do this thing? Why can't I act like I want to?" But though we may condemn ourselves, God does not. He is not angry with us about that. He sees us, as the Scriptures show us, as a child in his family, learning to walk.

No father ever gets angry with his little son because he doesn't get right up and start running around the first time he tries to walk. If the child falls and stumbles and falters, the father helps him; he doesn't spank him. He lifts him up, encourages him, and shows him how to do it right. And if the child has a problem with his feet—maybe one foot is twisted or deformed—the father finds a way to relieve that condition and help him to learn to walk. That is what God does. He is not angry when we are struggling. He knows it takes awhile—quite awhile, at times. And even the best of saints will, at times, fall. This was true of Paul, it was true of the apostles, and it was true of all the prophets of the Old Testament. Sin is deceitful and it will trip us at times. But God is not angry with us when it does.

The third thing "no condemnation" means is that there is no punishment. God will never take us to the woodshed because of our struggles. He is not angry at us and he is not going to punish us. We may punish ourselves; we may be frustrated; we may cry out, "Oh, wretched man that I am!" But God does not say that—he does not punish us.

Now, a word of caution. When we deliberately decide to sin, and like it, then he will punish us. This is the discipline of a father described in the closing part of chapter 6. When we deliberately give ourselves back into sin once we have been set free from it, then, as a loving disciplinarian, God will correct us and punish us until we begin to see what has happened. He does this out of love, just as an earthly father would.

But that is a different condition than the one we are facing here. Here Paul is describing those times when we want to do good, and we are trying to do good. But we are weak, and, in a moment of temptation, we fail. And we fail again and again. Still there is "no condemnation to those that are in Christ Jesus." Even when we are being punished as disobedient sons, we still are not rejected. That remains true no matter what happens to us.

Why are we not condemned? The answer that Paul gives in verse 2 is beautiful:

. . . because through Christ Jesus the law of the Spirit of life set me free from the law of sin and death.

Paul was not left with a continuing, constant struggle; God came in and did something about it. God reminded him of what he knew to be true, and he began to believe it. When he began to think of himself as God thought of him he found he had power to say no to sin.

In summary, Paul actually brings out three reasons in this whole passage why there is no condemnation. First, look back at verse 18 of chapter 7: "I know that nothing good lives in me, that is, in my sinful nature. For I have the desire to do what is good. . . ." His heart is right, that is clear. Then again, in verse 22, he says, "For in my inner being I delight in God's law. . . ." Paul really wants to do right, his heart is right; therefore there is no condemnation.

Second, and obviously connected with this, Paul explains that sin has deceived and overpowered him. It is also too much for us. We can't handle this wild beast raging within us when it is awakened by the demands and prohibitions of the law. God does not condemn us for that; he knows that it is more than we can handle. He lets us discover that fact by our experience, but he does not condemn us when we do.

Third (and this is the most important), God has already
made provision in Christ for our failure. He knows that our
very struggle is driving us back to Christ. When I have
come to the place of saying, "Oh, wretched man that I am!"
the only thing left, if I want any escape at all, is to ask,
"Why am I thinking of myself in this way? God says I am
different." Reckoning on that difference that has come to
me in Christ, I can rise up to act differently. That is the
way out. God knows that my failures are driving me to that
moment; and, as a loving father, he is patiently waiting
for it to come. Therefore God will not condemn me.

The Spirit of New Life

We have seen two clear declarations so far: one, there is
struggle in the Christian life; two, the struggle is "without
condemnation." The third major thing Paul says is that a
provision has been made for victory. The law of the Spirit
of life in Christ Jesus will set us free from the law of sin
and death, which is in our members. That is why Paul cries,
"Thanks be to God—through our Lord Jesus Christ!" This
law of the Spirit of life is what God has already said he has
done for us in Christ. He has cut us off, made us different
creatures, brought us into Christ, and married us to him.
We are no longer the same as we were. When we believe
that we release the Spirit of life within us.

When we are failing and angry with ourselves, our natural way of thinking about ourselves is something like this:
"I'm a mess, a hopeless, helpless mess! Why can't I stop this
thing that is hurting me so, and hurting others, too?" We
are all wrapped up in our own feelings and think we deserve to be whipped and punished, and cast into hell.

At that point God says to us, "What is wrong is your view
of yourself? That is no longer what you are; that is only a
temporary condition to which you are giving in. The truth
is, you have been set free. You are married to Christ. Your
human spirit has been indwelt by the Holy Spirit and it cannot sin. It has not sinned and does not sin. Now, you your-

self, as a person, have been deceived by the sin in your flesh, and it has taken over and has led you into this difficulty. But that is not who you are. Don't believe that about yourself any more. There is a fresh provision of the forgiveness of God and the righteousness of Christ waiting for you. You are in Christ—this is who you are." Take his forgiveness, believe it, thank God for it, and go on, knowing your struggle will end.

Of course this does not mean that God has ended the temptation of the flesh in our lives. It is still there. The law of sin and death, like the law of gravity, goes on working all the time. But the moment you believe that what Jesus Christ says about you is true and you believe what he has done for you, a new law comes into effect. This new law is stronger than the law of sin and death; it even uses that law to accomplish its end.

When I was a boy, I discovered that there was a law at work in my members that was affecting my eyesight. It is what I later learned to call the law of myopia, which is nearsightedness. It was in my members, right in my eyes, so that I could not see what other people could see. Finally, I went to a doctor about it, and he told me what was wrong— and he prescribed glasses for me to correct the problem.

Later I discovered a new law, the law of contact lenses— two little pieces of plastic which I could put in my eyes every morning and which would keep working all day long. All I had to do was put them in. They did not eliminate the law of myopia—they actually used it. But the result was that I saw perfectly, with 20/20 vision. Now, if I got cocky and decided I didn't need those contact lenses anymore ("I can handle this situation without them!") and took them out, immediately the law of myopia would take over and I would have the same old problem again. But if I put the lenses in, the law of contact lenses would cancel out—overcome—the law of myopia, and I could see perfectly.

That is what Paul is telling us here. God has given us a new image of ourselves. We are not what we feel we are. When we believe that, we can be set free any time we

employ that law, any time that by faith, we reckon on what
God says as true. That is our provision for victory.

Basis for Victory

The fourth major point that Paul makes in this brief paragraph is given in verses 3 and 4. It is a review of the basis
for victory:

> For what the law was powerless to do in that it was weakened
> by our sinful nature, God did by sending his own Son in the
> likeness of sinful man [flesh] to be a sin offering. And so he
> condemned sin in sinful man [the flesh], in order that the
> righteous requirements of the law might be fully met in us,
> who do not live according to our sinful nature but according
> to the Spirit (Rom. 8:3,4).

This is a beautiful description of the good news in Jesus
Christ. There is nothing new here; we have had it all before.

Paul says the law is powerless to produce righteousness.
It cannot do it. It cannot make us good in any way. It can
demand and demand and demand, but it cannot enable and
it never will. This, by the way, is why nagging a person
never helps. Did you know that? Nagging is a form of law,
and God will not let the law nag us because it doesn't help.
It only makes it worse. If you try to nag your husband or
wife or child, you will find the same thing happens there.
Nagging only makes a person worse. Why? The reason,
Paul says, is that the law stirs up the power of sin. It releases this force, this beast within us, this powerful engine
that takes over and carries us where we don't want to go.
That is why nagging, or any form of the law, will never
work. It is not because there is anything wrong with what
is being said—it is because of the weakness of the flesh
that it cannot work. In 1 Corinthians 15 Paul says, "The
sting of death is sin, and *the power of sin* is the law" (1
Cor. 15:56). The law keeps sin going; it stirs it up.

To break through this vicious circle God sent his own
Son. There is a beautiful tenderness about this. He sent "his
own Son." He did not send an angel, he did not send a

mere man—he sent his own Son as a man, in the likeness of
sinful flesh. Notice that. He did not send him in the likeness
of *flesh* (a mirage), but in the likeness of *sinful flesh* (in the
flesh but without sin). Jesus had a real body, a body like
yours and mine. Since sin began in the body, it has to be
judged and broken in the body. Therefore, Jesus had a
body. But it was not a *body* of sinful flesh, it was the *likeness* of sinful flesh. It was like our sinful bodies, in that it
was subject to infirmities (Jesus grew weak and tired, hungry and weary), but there was no sin in him. Paul preserves
that distinction very carefully here.

In that body of flesh, without sin, he became sin. As we
read here, he was sent "as an offering for sin." In the mystery
of the cross, (which we can never, never understand, no
matter how long we live) the Lord Jesus, during the hours
of darkness, gathered up all the sins of the world, the terrible, evil, foul, awful injustices, crimes, and misery that we
have seen throughout history, from every person, gathered
it into himself, and brought it to an end by dying. The good
news is that by faith in him, we are involved in that death.
We have already seen that. In chapter 6, verse 6, Paul says,

> For we know that our old self was crucified with him so that
> the body of sin might be rendered powerless, that we should
> no longer be slaves to sin—

This is the way the Lord did it. As described in chapter 7,
he (Christ-made-sin) was the first husband to whom we
were married; and he died. When the first husband died we
were free to be married to the second husband, who is
Christ-risen-from-the-dead. Thus he has tied us to himself as
a risen, ascended Lord, and that is who we are from now on.

This is true not only for a few Christians who have gone
beyond all the rest and have some special experience; all
Christians are one with Christ. If you are a Christian at all,
this is who you are. It is always who you are. To let yourself believe anything else is to delude yourself. To believe
your feelings about yourself at any moment of evil or sin
is to fool yourself. This is who you really are. By the gift

of God, without earning it or without ever deserving it, you are righteous in his sight; just like Jesus, you are righteous with the righteousness of God. The very righteousness which the law demands is fulfilled in us the minute we believe what God has done about our evil. That righteousness becomes ours continually, as a gift.

Believe the Change

The last (fifth) thing the apostle says is that this becomes real to us when we choose to live according to the Spirit and not according to our sinful nature. When we believe what God says about us and see ourselves in a new way, then we will change the way we act. This is always God's way of deliverance. We think that we have to change the way we act in order to be different; God says, "No, I have made you different, and when you believe it, you will automatically change the way you act." Do you see the difference?

I heard a beautiful story once about a girl who was the daughter of one of the royal families of Europe. She had a big, bulbous nose that destroyed her beauty in the eyes of others—and especially in her own eyes. She grew up with a terrible image of herself as an ugly person. So her family hired a plastic surgeon to change the contour of her nose. He did his work, and there came the moment when they took the bandages off and the girl could see the results.

When the doctor removed the bandages, he saw that the operation had been a total success. All the ugly contours were gone. Her nose was different. When the incisions healed and the redness disappeared, she would be a beautiful girl. He held a mirror up for the girl to see. But so deeply embedded was this girl's ugly image of herself that when she saw herself in the mirror, she couldn't see any change. She broke into tears and cried out, "Oh, I knew it wouldn't work!" The doctor labored with that girl for six months before she would finally accept the fact that she was indeed different But the moment she accepted that fact, her whole behavior began to change.

We, too, act from what we know we are. If the evil in us deceives us into thinking we are not what God says we are, then we are going to keep on acting evilly. The way to break the power of the most vicious and evil habit is to see yourself as God sees you. Then you begin to act that way. You can't help it. As this verse makes clear, you are one with Jesus and you share his life and he himself, with all the beauty of his character, is one with you. He is married to you and you to him and there is no distinction. If you can see this when you have temporarily believed something false about yourself and are struggling, then you will be set free.

Many of us can testify to the fact that this works. God sets us free in this way. This is what Paul has been saying all along. Sin shall not have dominion over you, for you are not under the law, with its nagging demand that you be different before you can be accepted. You are under grace, with its affirmation that God has already made you different—now believe it!

19

Why Not Live?

In the epistle to the Romans the gift of righteousness is used in two ways. At this point we must make the distinction between them very clear. We have already seen that righteousness is a gift of worth that is instantly imparted to our human spirits when we believe in Jesus; and, from that vantage point within us, it is continually available to us. We can turn to it any time we feel pressure or insecurity or need. It is available continuously by faith. Up to this point in Romans this is the way the word righteousness has been used.

Now a new form of righteousness comes before us. It is what we might call "righteousness displayed." It is righteousness in the human spirit which has worked its way out to visibility. That is, it is righteousness actually seen in our actions, deeds, words, and thoughts. We begin acting like Christ. As well as being like him in the spirit, we now begin to act like him. That is what is referred to in Romans 8, verses 3 and 4:

> For what the law was powerless to do [i.e., produce righteousness] in that it was weakened by our sinful nature, God did by sending his own Son in the likeness of sinful man to be a sin offering. And so he condemned sin in sinful man, in order

[and here is the point] that the righteous requirements of the law [the right behavior which the law insisted on] might be fully met in us, who do not live according to our sinful nature but according to the Spirit.

This is what the Bible calls "sanctification," i.e., righteousness manifest. That is our new behavior. And it is ours, the apostle says, when we do not live according to our sinful nature, but according to the Spirit.

Verses 5 through 13 expound and explain that just being a Christian does not mean you automatically begin to look, act, talk, think, and react like Jesus Christ. You do not become Christlike simply by becoming a Christian. Your human spirit becomes like Christ, for it is linked with him, but you may not act that way for quite some time. It depends on whether you are walking (behaving) "according to the flesh" or "according to the Spirit." Those two choices are made crystal clear in the passage before us.

Two Possibilities

The apostle now explains to us these two possibilities in our Christian life: Are we going to live according to the Spirit, or according to the flesh? Verse 5 describes these two alternatives for us so that we can identify them and recognize them in our lives:

Those who live according to their sinful nature [i.e., according to the flesh] have their minds set on what that nature desires; but those who live in accordance with the Spirit have their minds set on what the Spirit desires (Rom. 8:5).

There is the difference. There are two possibilities before us, as Christians, that will determine whether or not we manifest the righteousness which the law demands. It depends on whether we walk according to the Spirit or according to the flesh. Notice that the difference lies in what we set our minds on. What are we thinking about all through the day; what is important to us? How do we view life? Do we have the viewpoint of the flesh, which governs the thinking of

the world? Or do we have the viewpoint of the Spirit—
God's viewpoint—on life?

Now, what is the mind-set of the person who lives according to the flesh, or, as the NIV puts it, those who have
"their minds set on what that sinful nature desires"? We
only have to look around to see what that is. Listen to the
television or radio, or read the newspapers, or observe
people—even ourselves—and we will see what this is. It is
the natural viewpoint of life. What do people want in life?
Basically, they want to make money, because money provides the comforts, conveniences, and pleasures they would
like to have. People also want to have fun. That is what
life seems to be all about—the pursuit of pleasure. We want
money, we want pleasure, and we want meaning. People
are always manipulating people and circumstances to ac-
quire some degree of fame, to be seen and known. There is
a passion in the human heart to be known and recognized.
People will give anything to gain influence, standing, pres-
tige, and following. Finally, I think people desire to fulfill
themselves. They want to manifest every capability that is
within them. They want, somehow, to feel fulfilled. That is
what the world lives for, isn't it? And it wants it all now,
not later. That is the natural point of view.

You say, "Well, what's wrong with that?" There is really
nothing wrong with that—unless that is all you want; if
that is all you want, then it is terribly wrong. This is what
the Scriptures help us to see—that there is another point
of view, which is life viewed according to the Spirit.

"Ah," you say, "I know what that means!" That means
you have to forget about making money, having fun, and
fulfilling yourself. All you do is go around memorizing scripture and thinking about God all day long. Whenever anyone asks you to do something, you're too busy thinking
about God and too involved in spiritual things to get your
hands dirty. So you become a religious recluse. You go
around reciting scripture verses and telling people what is
wrong with their lives—and that is being spiritual!

Unfortunately, many people think that this is what we are

talking about when we say we are to have our minds set on the things of the Spirit. But, of course, if you see people like that (or if you are like that yourself), you soon discover that kind of life does not produce the results this passage tells us should be there. It is really nothing but another form of being run by the flesh—it is a religious form of it, but it is actually the same thing.

What does it mean, then, to have your mind set on the Spirit? It means that in the midst of making money, having fun, gaining fame, and fulfilling yourself you are primarily concerned with showing love, helping others, speaking truth, and, above all, loving God, and seeking his glory. The only trouble with the world is that it is content with just making money, having fun, and fulfilling itself—that is all it wants. The end is man. But the mind set on the Spirit desires that God be glorified in all these things, which are proper and right. When your mind is set on the Spirit you look at the events of life from God's point of view, not from the world's. Your value system is changed and it touches everything you do. You no longer see that the important thing must be to make a lot of money. The important thing is that, in seeking to fulfill your needs, God be glorified. It is to live on the basis of a new identity and a new power. That is what makes the difference. That is the mind set on the Spirit. It does not remove you from life—it puts you right back into it. But it does so with a different point of view.

Existential Death

In verse 6 the apostle describes the results you can expect from either of the two courses outlined in verse 5. He says,

> The mind of sinful man is death, but the mind controlled by the Spirit is life and peace . . . [I am going to change this a bit to make it a little more accurate according to the original text: The thinking of the flesh is death, but the thinking of the Spirit is life and peace] . . .

214 FROM GUILT TO GLORY

What happens when you, as a Christian, let yourself live just as the world does and never bring the perspective of God into what you do? Then you are living according to the flesh. And the thinking of the flesh is death, while that of the Spirit is life and peace. This describes the results that come right now in our experience. Death, in this present experience, always consists of four basic things: fear, guilt, hostility, and emptiness. Those are the forms of death which come when you have your mind set on those things—and only those things—that the flesh desires: making money, having fun, fulfilling yourself, and gaining fame. If that is all you want out of life, then you will also have with it fear, guilt, hostility, and emptiness, in all their various forms. Fear can appear as worry, anxiety, dread, or timidity. Guilt can show up in your life as shame, self-hatred, self-righteousness, or perfectionism. Hostility will manifest itself as hate, resentment, bitterness, revenge, or cruelty. Emptiness can show up as loneliness, depression, discouragement, despair, meaninglessness. These are all symptoms of death.

As if that were not enough, these symptoms of death not only have this immediate effect upon our feelings, but they actually go on to settle into the body and affect our physical functioning. We can develop nervous twitches, tics, rashes, eczema, ulcers, stuttering, heart attacks, cancer, and many other diseases. This, literally, is death. We are producing death in our experience if, as Christians, we continue to live, think, and act as the world lives, thinks, and acts.

What, then, is living with the mind set on the Spirit? It is facing all these things—seeking to make money, having fun, fulfilling yourself, even seeking a degree of fame—but at the same time realizing that God is at work in you. He supplies the power to do these things. Expect him to be at work and to be glorified in all these things, and the result will be life and peace.

What is life? To summarize all that the Scriptures say on this, life includes four basic things that are opposites of death: If death is fear, then life is trust, hope, and confidence. If death is guilt, then life is a feeling of acceptance, security, and assurance. If death is hostility, then life is love, friendliness, kindness, and reaching out to others. If death is emptiness, then life is a sense of well-being, fulfillment, excitement, vitality, and fullness. With life comes peace, which, of course, is an inner calm, a quiet spirit, a remarkable sense of being able to cope with and to handle life. That is what comes when the mind is set on the Spirit.

But the apostle does not stop with that; he gives us the reasons why this is true. In verse 7 he explains why the mind set on the flesh produces death:

> . . . because the sinful mind [or the thinking of the flesh] is hostile to God. It does not submit to God's law, nor can it do so.

That is what is wrong. The mind set on the flesh brings death because it is hostile to God and cannot obey the law of God. It opposes it, in other words. Anyone who thinks that life consists only of making money, pleasing himself, having fun, and gaining a degree of notoriety, is hostile to God. That thinking is against God. As James 4:6 says, "God opposes the proud, but gives grace to the humble." It scares me to think that whenever I am trying to live for myself, for my own advancement, that God is lined up against me; he resists that kind of thinking. That is why James 3:16 can say that "where jealousy and selfish ambition is, every evil work is present." God resists the proud and gives grace to the humble.

Although it is not stated here, the implication is clear. The mind that is set on the Spirit pleases God. That is what God wants; and God gives grace to that end, he advances it and helps it. He works on behalf of one whose outlook on life is not that of proud confidence in self, but which shows humble trust in the living God who is ready to work with him and through him to do whatever needs to be done. That is the difference.

Who Belongs to Christ?

In verses 8 and 9 there is a parenthesis which the apostle brings in because he wants to show us the difference between a Christian who lives "according to the flesh" and a non-Christian, who is "in the flesh." These terms are entirely different and need to be carefully recognized as such.

Those controlled by their sinful nature [literally, it is those who are in the flesh, who live in the flesh] cannot please God. You, however, are controlled not by your sinful nature [i.e., you are not in the flesh] but by the Spirit, if the Spirit of God lives in you. And if anyone does not have the Spirit of Christ, he does not belong to Christ (Rom. 8:8,9).

That is as plain as you can make it. Nothing could be plainer than that. If anyone does not have the Spirit of Christ, he does not belong to Christ. Such a person is said to be "in the flesh" as contrasted with a Christian who though he is not "in the flesh" may be living "according to the flesh." You cannot tell if a person is a Christian by what he does at any given moment. He may do exactly the same thing as a non-Christian. We may be cruel, vindictive, hateful, lustful, and sinful in every way. At that moment, you cannot tell any difference between the Christian and the non-Christian. But there is a difference, Paul says. One has the Spirit of Christ in him—the Holy Spirit—and eventually that will make a fantastic difference in his behavior. The other does not, and he will continue in sin and even become worse and worse.

In fact, the apostle suggests by this that the actions of a non-Christian may actually be much better than those of a Christian. There are non-Christians who are kinder, more thoughtful, and more gracious than Christians. People say, "Look at them! If their lives are so nice and pleasant, surely they must be Christians." But it is not necessarily so. He who does not have the Spirit of Christ does not belong to Christ. The difference will show up in the ultimate tests of life. When the crunch comes one will collapse and fall, and the other will rise and eventually conquer. A Christian can live "according to the flesh" even though he is not "in the flesh." Those distinctions have to be made quite clear.

Verses 10 and 11 are the apostle's conclusion in this matter. This is what he is aiming at:

> But if Christ is in you, your body is dead because of sin, yet your spirit is alive because of righteousness. And if the Spirit of him who raised Jesus from the dead is living in you, he who raised Christ from the dead will also give life to your mortal bodies through his Spirit, who lives in you (Rom. 8:10,11).

That is a great statement. Notice first of all, the helpful teaching about the Spirit here. The term "Spirit" is used. He is called the Spirit of God and the Spirit of Christ. Then it is made clear that the Spirit actually is the means by which Jesus Christ himself is in us. All this refers to the work of the Holy Spirit. These terms all refer to the same thing. By means of the Spirit, Christ is in you. And if Christ is in you, your body is dead because of sin. You may not realize that, but it is true.

The problem is, our bodies are yet unredeemed. As a consequence, they are the seat of the sin that troubles us so. And the sin that is in us—still there in our bodies—affects the body. That is why the body lusts, the body loves comfort, and the body seeks after pleasure; that is why our minds and attitudes react with hate, bitterness, resentment, hostility. Sin finds its seat in the body. That is why our bodies keep growing old. They are dying, dead, because of sin.

I have been watching some of my friends through the years. Although I haven't noticed much change in myself, I have noticed they seem to be deteriorating. They are growing older and getting weaker. Their hair is turning gray, they groan and creak where once they leaped and ran. Their bodies are dying because of sin.

For one who is not a Christian, that is the whole story. The body is dead, and so is the spirit. It is falling apart, and will continue to do so. But that is not the final answer

for the Christian. The human spirit of the Christian is alive
because of the gift of righteousness. Christ has come in and
we are linked with him. Paul puts it beautifully in 2 Corinthians 4:16: "Though outwardly we are wasting away, yet
inwardly we are being renewed day by day." That is the
joy of being a Christian. Though the body, with the sin that
is within it, is giving us trouble and difficulty, tempting us,
confounding us at times, nevertheless, the spirit is alive because of righteousness. Sin has its seat in the actual physical
body, and it rises up (as Paul describes in Romans 7) like
a powerful beast. Stimulated by the law, it can rise up and
attack us, overwhelm us, and conquer us. But we have an
answer. It is put so clearly in 1 John 4:4: "The one who is
in you is greater than the one who is in the world." In other
words, the Spirit of God within us is stronger than the sin
that is in our bodies. Therefore we have strength to control
the body. That is what Paul is saying in verse 11: "And if
the Spirit of him who raised Jesus from the dead is living in
you, he who raised Jesus from the dead will also give life
to your mortal bodies through his Spirit, who lives in you."

Strength to Say No

Unfortunately, many of the commentators say that this
verse refers to the promise of resurrection at the end of life,
when God is going to make our bodies alive. But that is not
what Paul is saying. He is talking about the Spirit in us,
giving life to our *mortal* bodies. Now, a mortal body is not
yet dead. A mortal body is one that is subject to death. It
is dying, but it is not yet dead. Therefore, this is not talking
about the resurrection. Later on Paul will come to that, but
in this chapter he is talking about what the Spirit does in
us now. He says that though sin in our mortal bodies is going
to tempt us severely, and at times rise up with great power
(we have all felt the power of temptation in our lives, this
urgent, almost irresistible desire to do something that we
know is wrong), we must never forget that because our
human spirit has been made alive in Jesus Christ, and the

Spirit of God himself dwells in us, we have the strength to say no to that expression of evil.

We cannot reverse the processes of death—no one can. Our bodies are going to die. But we can refuse to let the members of our bodies become the instruments of sin. By the power of the Spirit within, we can refuse to give in or to let our members be used for that purpose. We don't have to let our eyes look at wrong things. Nor do we have to let our tongues say evil, hurtful, sarcastic, and vicious things; we don't have to let them lie. We don't have to let our ears hear things that are hurtful or let our minds give way to thinking about things in a wrong and vicious fashion. Nor do we have to let our hands be used for wrong purposes. We don't have to let our legs and feet lead us into places where we ought not to be, nor do we have to let our sexual organs be used for wrong purposes. We don't have to let the members of our bodies be used wrongly. That is what Paul said back in chapter 6, verse 12:

> Therefore, do not let sin reign in your mortal body so that you obey its evil desires. Do not offer the parts of your body to sin, as instruments of wickedness, but rather offer yourselves to God, as those who have returned from death to life; and offer the parts of your body to him as instruments of righteousness.

That is as plain as can be. We don't have to sin. By resurrection power, by the power of the one who raised Jesus from the dead, and who lives in us, we can say no to these temptations and desires for evil that are expressed within us. That is why, in chapter 12 of this letter, Paul says, "Therefore, I urge you, brothers, in view of God's mercy, to offer yourselves as living sacrifices, holy and pleasing to God—which is your spiritual worship." And we can do that.

In verses 12 and 13 Paul gives his conclusion. He tells us we have only one obligation:

> Therefore, brothers, we have an obligation—but it is not to our sinful nature, to live according to it. For if you live according to the sinful nature, you will die [literally, you are

about to die; death becomes your experience in your present existence]; but if by the Spirit you put to death the misdeeds of your body, you will live (Rom. 8:12,13).

You will live, with all that that means in terms of security, trust, fulfillment, vitality, joy, and peace. Notice that Paul stresses this must be done by the Spirit, that is, simply by believing what the Spirit of God has said. That is the way you act by the Spirit—by faith. When you believe that God has said these sins in your body do not need to be there—that they can be controlled, they have been crucified with Christ, they are worthless, they cannot help you, nothing worthwhile can come from them—then you can say no to sin and you can live by the Spirit. Then you can make money, have fun, gain fame, and fulfill yourself. And through it all, God will be glorified. You will manifest, in your present experience, love, joy, peace, and the grace of Jesus Christ. The very righteousness which the law demands is fulfilled in those who walk not after the flesh but after the Spirit. That is beautiful, isn't it?

At the close of World War II, a picture appeared in a magazine showing a soldier in conflict with a tank. I remember the picture vividly; it was in color and it showed a huge army tank bearing down on the tiny figure of the soldier, about to crush him. How frightened he was, as this massive tank was about to overwhelm him. The picture was designed to show the odds involved when a foot soldier with a rifle faced a tank. Then another picture showed what happened to that soldier's odds when the bazooka (a rocket launcher) was invented. It showed him standing with a bazooka in his hands. It was the same soldier, but he had a different weapon. The next picture showed the tank, shrunken in size, with the soldier at least equal in size, if not a little larger.

This is what Paul is saying to us. Without the power of God released in our lives, we are like an infantry soldier in the presence of a tank. We cannot do a thing. It is too much for us. But by trust in the power of the living God at work in us, we can rise up in the face of temptation and, armed with the bazooka of the Spirit, we can say no and make it stick. We can turn and begin to live as God intended us to live.

The question this raises, then, is this: Why not live? Why spend most of your Christian life in weakness, constantly experiencing guilt, fear, loneliness, depression, and discouragement? Why not live? Jesus said, "I am come that they might have life and that they might have it more abundantly." Paul is simply describing how we might, indeed, find that life.

20

The Sons of God Among Men

In the second half of Romans 8, Paul gives us a further revelation of what being in Christ and in the Spirit actually means. The apostle has been leading us step by step to understand more fully our new identity in Jesus Christ. The more we understand that identity, and the more we believe it to be true, under all circumstances, the more quickly we will begin to act that way. In verses 14 and 15, Paul uses a term he has never used before in this letter. He says,

> Those who are led by the Spirit of God are sons of God. For you did not receive a spirit that makes you a slave again to fear, but you received the Spirit who makes you sons. And by him we cry, "*Abba*, Father."

For the first time in this letter Paul uses the phrase "the sons of God." Now, I want to make something clear. This is a generic term that includes both sexes. All believers in Christ who really trust him and have received the gift of righteousness by faith are sons of God—regardless of whether they are male or female. There is no need for any differentiation of the sexes here. That is why the Scriptures speak of us—all of us—freely as the sons of the living God. This speaks of something that is true of our spirit, and our spirit is sexless. Spirit is not identifiable by male or female, so what is true of the human spirit is quite apart from what is true of the body.

Offspring and Sons

It is important in understanding this to recognize right away that not everyone is a son of God. According to Galatians 5, we are sons of God *by faith in Jesus Christ*. Faith is what makes you a son of God—nothing else. It is true that we are all creatures of God by natural birth. When Paul was preaching in Athens, that great intellectual center, he mentioned to the Athenians that even their own poets recognized that men came from God. We are the offspring of God, and in him "we live and move and have our being," he said. That is true of all human beings everywhere in the world at all times. They are creatures of God. They are the offspring of God.

But Paul is careful to use quite a different word in Romans. Here the word is "sons of God." We are in the family of God, and this is a distinctive term. I want to underscore how important this is, because it is something that God desires us to return to when we are in trouble. If you are having difficulty handling your behavior—whether you are not doing what you want to do, or doing what you don't want to do—the way to handle it is to remind yourself of what God has made you to be. This terminology is therefore tremendously helpful.

In other words, in the struggle that you have with sin within you, you are not a slave, helplessly struggling against a cruel and powerful master; you are a son, a son of the living God, with power to overcome the evil—even though it is a struggle to do so. And though you may be temporarily overcome, you are never ultimately defeated. You cannot be, because you are already constituted children of God. That is why Paul could say in Romans 6, "Sin shall not have dominion over you, for you are not under law but under grace." In this gracious relationship we are made and constituted sons of the living God. No matter what happens to us, that is what we are. Nothing can change that. This is the place from which we start.

It is important also for us to see how we become sons of God. Paul says, "You did not receive a spirit that makes you a slave again to fear." When the Spirit of God came into your heart, he did not make you a slave to fear. Remember how Paul puts that in 2 Timothy 1:17: "You have not received a spirit of fear, but of power and of love and of a sound mind." That is the nature of the Holy Spirit. What did the Spirit do? Paul says, "You received the Spirit who makes you sons," or, literally, "the Spirit of adoption, who adopted you as sons." How did you become a son of God? Well, the Spirit of God found you, and he found me, and he adopted us into God's family.

I was with a family the other night where there were two adopted or "chosen" children and two children born to the parents. I watched all evening long to see if I could tell the difference between them. I finally had to ask the parents because I could not tell any difference—even from their looks. Two were adopted into the family and two were born into it, but they were all treated so beautifully and so naturally that I could not tell the difference.

Some of you may be saying at this point, "Look, you are confusing me. What do you mean when you say we are adopted into the family of God? I have been taught from the Scriptures that I was born into the family of God. I have been born again." That is the term that is being bandied about these days. Even politicians are boasting, "I've been born again." Thank God, some of them are. "But," you say, "some passages talk about the new birth, about being born into the family of God. I thought we were born, not adopted. What do you mean by 'adopted'?"

Aspects of Belonging

I am glad you asked that question. You see, the truth is that both of these are true. We are both adopted *and* born into the family of God. As Jesus said on another occasion, "With men that is impossible, but with God, all things are possible." We can't be both adopted and born into a human family, but we can in God's family. God uses both these terms because he wants to highlight two different aspects of our belonging to the family of God.

We are said to be adopted because God wants us to remember always that we are not naturally part of the family of God. We have been seeing all along in this letter that we are born into Adam's family, and we are all children of Adam by natural birth. We belong to the human family, and we inherit Adam's nature. All his defects, all his problems, all the evil that came into his life by his act of disobedience—all these were passed along to us by natural birth. So by nature we are not part of God's family. In the same way, some people were born into one family, and then, by a legal process, were taken out of that family and were adopted into another family. From then on they became part of the family that adopted them.

This is what has happened to us. God has taken us out of our natural state in Adam and, by the process of the Spirit, has made us legally sons of God, and we are part of his family. But he reminds us that we are in his family by adoption so that we might never take it for granted, or forget that if we were left in our natural state we would not have a part in the family of God. It is only by the grace of God that we come into his family.

But it is also true that we are born into God's family. Once we have been adopted, it is also true that, because God is God, he not only makes us legally his sons, but he makes us actually share his nature. It is an astounding truth! This tie with Jesus is so real that we are seen to be actually one with him, and as Peter puts it, "We have been made partakers of the divine nature." So we are as much a part of God's family as if we had originally been born into it, and we are born into it by the grace of God.

So both these statements are true. There is nothing more wonderful to remind yourself, morning by morning and day

by day, than this great fact: If you are a Christian, you are
a son of the living God, adopted and born into his family.
Because you are his son, God loves you, God protects you,
God provides for you, God plans for you, God hears you,
God claims you and openly acknowledges you. He chastens
and corrects you, and he honors you. All of that is true because you are his son.

We know how we treat our natural children. There is a
difference between them and the neighbors' children. Our
children are considerably superior, of course. We may love
the neighbors' children—they may be delightful, but they
are not our children. We have a special relationship with
our own children. We care for them, hurt for them, love
and protect them, plan for them, and watch out for them.
There are special ties with them. That is what this truth is
saying to us. God has a special relationship to us. We are
the sons of God turned loose among the sons of men.

It would be helpful, I know, if God would put a little
mark on us that would indicate that we are his sons. If we
had a little red star on our foreheads, then we could recognize all the other sons of God. Or, perhaps if we had a special glow. (Sometimes that does show, anyway.) But there
is no special mark. Outwardly, there is no distinction; but
inwardly, there is a tremendous distinction, and that is what
we need to understand. We can't tell by looking at anyone
whether he is a son of God or not, though often there is an
underlying sensitivity that identifies brothers and sisters in
Christ to one another. But there is a vast difference within,
and because of that difference, there is a special relationship that God has with us.

Now, the great question in all this is, "If it all depends on
my being a son of God, how can I be sure that I am a son?"
Paul has been leading up to this question all through his
letter. The thing that is going to make the essential difference in your life (not only now, in the way you behave, but
for eternity, in the destiny you are headed for) is whether
or not you are a son of God. In light of that the greatest
question in life is, "Am I or am I not a son of God?" You

can't ask for a more important question than that to settle.
Your whole behavior, your happiness as an individual, your
ultimate destiny, your whole relationship to the greatness
and the glory of God, is all dependent on that question: Are
you or are you not a son of God? That is why the apostle
Paul in this passage gives us three very practical tests—
three levels of assurance—by which we can know whether
we are sons or not.

Proof by Observation

First, Paul says, if we are led by the Spirit of God, we
are sons of God. Now, to be led by the Spirit means that
one is under the control of a being other than himself. This,
therefore, is a level of proof which arises from our circumstances, from our experiences, from the events and reactions
that happen to us, over which we have no deliberate control. Paul is saying that we can learn the answer to this
question by observation. This is proof addressed to the
mind. We can reason it; we can observe it. We can look
around in our lives and see if we are being led by the Spirit
of God. If there is proof that we are, then we are sons of
God.

What are some of these signs? There are certain things
that the Scriptures tell us the Spirit of God is going to do
when he comes into a life. If he has done them, and we can
see that he has, we have immediate assurance that we are
sons of God. "Those who are led by the Spirit of God are
the sons of God." So let's look at the signs of being led by
the Spirit.

I think the most evident sign, at least one of the most
important to me and obviously something that does not
come from man, is that when I read the Scriptures I am
taught by the Spirit. He opens my mind to an understanding of the Word of God. He is called the Spirit of truth.
Therefore, when he comes into my life, the first thing he
will do is to make the Bible a living Word to me. We see
it as truth—we know it as truth. Our eyes are opened to

understand that here at last is reality. This is the work of the Spirit of God.

Have you ever been reading a passage of scripture when suddenly something just leaped out at you? The passage takes on a new, fresh, and glowing meaning. If that has happened, you are being led by the Spirit of God. He is doing his work of opening the truth to your mind and heart. This, of course, is what Paul refers to in verse 13: "If *by the Spirit* you put to death the misdeeds of the body, you will live." He is talking about our understanding of what the Spirit of God has already done with the flesh within us, how it was crucified with Christ, and how, therefore, we can be freed from it. We can rise up and refuse to obey that flesh because its connection with us has been broken. If you understand that, you are being led by the Spirit of God, and, therefore, you are a son of God.

Some years ago when I was in a city some distance from home, I was rather discouraged. I opened the Scriptures and read one of Paul's letters. I was so impressed with a statement he made about Christians. He said, "Remember that you are chosen of God, and precious in his sight." It came home to me suddenly that this applied to *me. I* was chosen of God and precious in his sight! That kind of experience is given by the Spirit of God within us, teaching us the truth.

The Spirit also arouses us to pray. Have you ever felt that you just had to pray, that you just had to get away somewhere and have a few moments of quiet? You may not have prayed for several days, but suddenly you can't stand it any longer. You have to find some time when you can open up and talk to your Father. Now, that is being led of the Spirit of God. It is he who arouses in us the desire to pray. Those who have had these experiences can know by them that they are children of God.

Another thing the Spirit does is awaken a love for the brethren. When you meet someone and learn he is a Christian, do you ever feel a special bond with him right away? Have you ever longed to be with Christians? Sometimes do you get tired of even the closest of friends who are not Christians? Do you long to be with brothers and sisters in the family? The Spirit awakens within us a love for the brethren. John says in his first letter that if you have a love for the brethren it is a sign that you are in Christ.

Another sign is that the Spirit makes the world empty, and he makes God real. The Spirit directs us and checks us at times. Do you ever feel this? These are signs that we are being led by the Spirit of God.

Of course, ultimately, the Spirit produces the fruit of the Spirit in us. If we have evidence at all that we are truly loving—especially when it is hard to be loving—if we feel love, joy, peace, gentleness, compassion, goodness, and faith, then we know these have all been awakened by the Spirit of God. "As many as are led by the Spirit of God, they are the sons of God." That is one test by which we can know if we are sons of God.

An Emotional Response

There is another level of assurance of our sonship mentioned in the closing part of verse 15: "And by him we cry, 'Abba, Father.'" "Abba" is the Aramaic word for father. Of course, the Greek word is translated "father" here, also. So, by means of the Spirit, we are given an emotional response to God in which we are aware of his fatherhood, and our soul cries out within us, "Abba, Father." "Abba" is a baby's word.

I remember years ago hearing a story about Dr. Alan McRae, the great Bible student and Hebrew scholar. Some time after the McRaes' baby boy was born, Dr. McRae had to go away for three or four weeks. When he came back, his wife was showing him how the baby had learned to say a few words. When this eminent Hebrew scholar came in, his little son stretched out his arms and said, "Ab-Abba, abba!" Dr. McRae said, "Look, he's speaking Aramaic already!" The closest and most intimate relationship you can have is the awareness that you belong to a father, with a

father's arms around you, a father's heart concerned for
you, a father's wisdom planning for you, and a father's love
protecting and guarding you. If you have ever sensed the
fatherhood of God, the brotherhood of Jesus, it is because
the Spirit of God has awakened your heart to sense that you
belong to the family of God.

I have seen tears come to people's eyes when something
from the Scriptures reminds them of their relationship to
God the Father. It can happen when you are driving your
car, or sitting with your family, or going through a time
of sorrow. Suddenly and unexpectedly, that wonderful sense
that you belong to the Father comes, and you cherish that
relationship. Your soul cries, "Abba, my Father!" This, by
the way, is the word Jesus himself used in the agony of
Gethsemane. As he knelt to pray in his hour of anguish, he
cried out, "Oh Abba—my Father!" Even in his anguish he
was aware of that relationship.

Verse 16 tells us of still another level of assurance that
the Spirit is in us:

> The Spirit himself testifies with our spirit that we are God's
> children.

This is the deepest level of assurance. Beyond the emotions, beyond the feelings, is a deep conviction born of the
Spirit of God himself, an underlying awareness that we cannot deny that we are part of God's family. We are the children of God. I think this is the basic revelation to which
our emotions respond with the cry, "Abba, Father." That is
our love to him, but this is his love to us. It is what Paul
refers to in Romans 5 when he speaks of the love of God
"which is shed abroad in our hearts by the Holy Spirit
which is given unto us."

As I look back on my own life, I can understand how
this is true. I think I became a Christian when I was about
eleven years old, in a Methodist brush arbor meeting. I
responded to the invitation and, with others, came and knelt
down in front and received the Lord. I had a wonderful
time of fellowship with the Lord that summer and the next
winter, and there were occasions when I would be over-

whelmed with the sense of the nearness and dearness of God. I used to sing hymns until tears would come to my eyes as the meaning of those old words reflected on the relationship that I had with God. I used to preach to the cows as I brought them home. Those cows were a very good audience, too, by the way; they never went to sleep on me.

Seven-Year Prodigal

But that fall we moved from the town where I had Christian fellowship to a town in Montana that did not even have a church. Gradually, because of that lack of fellowship, I drifted away from that relationship with God into many ugly and shameful things—habits of thought and activity that I am now ashamed of. I even developed some liberal attitudes toward the Scriptures. I did not believe in the inspiration of the Bible. I argued against it, and during high school and college I was known as a skeptic.

But all through those seven years there was a relationship with God I could not deny. Somehow I knew, deep down inside, that I still belonged to him; and there were things I could not do, even though I was tempted. I could not do them because I felt I had a tie with God. This is that witness of the Spirit—Calvin called it "the testimonium"—which we cannot deny and which is especially discernible in times of gross sin and despair. 1 John 3:20 says, "If our hearts condemn us, God is greater than our hearts." He knows all things. There is a witness born of the Spirit which you cannot shake, which is there with the ultimate testimony that we belong with the children of God.

Now, this is where to begin when you get into trouble. Go back to this relationship. Remind yourself of who you are. You can see it in your experience as you look around. You are led by the Spirit of God. You can feel it in your heart. There are times when your emotions are stirred by the Spirit, and you can also sense at the level of your spirit that you belong to God.

In verse 17 the apostle goes on to mention an even

greater and deeper relationship. This verse introduces the
next section in the passage, but I want to set it before you
now:

> Now if we are children, then we are heirs—heirs of God and
> co-heirs with Christ, if indeed we share in his sufferings in
> order that we may also share in his glory.

These words introduce the very climax of this epistle. We
learn of the glory that is awaiting us and its tie with the sufferings that we go through now. We started in Adam; we
are now, by faith, in Christ, we are in the Spirit; if we
are in the Spirit, we can walk according to the Spirit; if
we are in the Spirit, we are therefore led by the Spirit; and
if we are led by the Spirit, we are the sons of God; and if
we are the sons of God, we are heirs of God. All that God
owns is to be committed to us.

That is a staggering, mind-blowing thing, but that is
what the apostle writes, and it runs all the way through
the Scriptures. There is a thread that runs all the way from
Genesis right through Revelation. In subtle and sometimes
open ways it is constantly hinting that something fantastic
is coming. What God has in mind for this beguiled and
driven race of men who are now redeemed by faith in
Christ is beyond description! That is what Paul is going
to bring before us now, as we consider the heritage waiting
for us in Jesus Christ.

But all this is for us to remember when we get into trouble. This is not just hope for the future; it is deliverance for
the present. If we remember who we are, by an absolute
psychological certainty we will start acting like who we are.
When we do, we will find there is power available to say
"no" to the flesh, to say "yes" to the Spirit, and to walk in
a way that glorifies God.

21

The Agony and the Ecstasy

The apostle John says, "Beloved, now are we the sons of God; but it does not yet appear what we shall be" (1 John 3:2). That is the theme that Paul brings to a focus in verses 18–28 of Romans 8. He actually deals with two themes: the sufferings of believers, and the glorification of believers.

As a pastor I have always found comfort in 1 John 3:2. Sometimes when I am beset by saints who come to me and criticize various things that are going on, I have a difficult time relating to them. Then I have to remind myself, "Well, they are still children of God even though it does not yet appear what they shall be." I also see the increasing decrepitude in people's deteriorating physical bodies as they grow older. I have to say again, "It does not yet appear what we shall be." Things are moving toward a great day, but it is not here yet; and until that day, we have to put up with the difficulties, the hardships, and the sufferings to which our current situations bring us. These are the themes that Paul links together in this great section of Romans 8.

He stated this very plainly earlier, in verse 17:

> Now if we are children, then we are heirs—heirs of God and
> co–heirs with Christ, if indeed we share in his sufferings in
> order that we may also share in his glory (Rom. 8:17).

This verse links two things that we would probably not put together: sufferings and glory—hurts and hallelujahs. They belong together, and you find them together in almost every passage of scripture that deals with the suffering of the Christian. In fact, in 2 Corinthians 4:17 the apostle Paul links them directly: "For our light and momentary troubles are achieving for us an eternal glory that far outweighs them all." So, our sufferings as believers—physical, emotional, whatever they may be—are directly linked with the glory that is coming. The important thing we need to see is that both the sufferings and the glory are privileges given to us.

It is easy for Christians reading these passages to get the idea that we earn our glory by the sufferings that we go through. Those who go through the greatest suffering will earn the greatest degree of glory. But it is wrong to see it that way. We never earn glory. As this passage makes clear, glory is given to us as part of our inheritance in Christ. And suffering, also, is our inheritance in Christ. Suffering is a privilege committed to us. Paul says this very plainly in Philippians 1:29:

> For it has been granted to you on behalf of Christ not only to believe on him, but also to suffer for him [or, for his name's sake] . . .

In the early part of Acts, it is recorded that the early Christians actually rejoiced in their sufferings. They rejoiced because they were counted worthy to suffer for the sake of the Lord. And though they were beaten and mistreated, they went away rejoicing because God had counted them worthy to bear suffering for his name's sake. This is the transforming view that makes it possible for us to endure suffering and, more than that, to actually rise above it with triumphant rejoicing. We can do this when we see that our sufferings are privileges committed to us. Our Lord Jesus said this himself: "Blessed are you when people insult you, persecute you and falsely say all kinds of evil against you because of me. Rejoice and be glad, because great is your reward in heaven, for in the same way they persecuted the prophets who were before you" (Matt. 5:11,12).

Nothing will help us more to endure suffering than a clear view of the glory that is linked to it. That is the theme of this section in Romans 8, beginning with verse 18:

> I consider that our present sufferings are not worth comparing with the glory that will be revealed in us (Rom. 8:18).

The theme of that verse and the next nine verses is that incomparable glory lies ahead—glory beyond description, greater than anything you can compare it with on earth. A magnificent and fantastic prospect awaits us. All through the Scriptures there has been a rumor of hope that runs all through the Old Testament, through the prophetic writings, and into the New Testament. This rumor speaks of a day when all the hurt, heartache, injustice, weakness, and suffering of our present experience will be explained and justified and will result in a time of incredible blessing upon the earth. The whisper of this in the Old Testament increases in intensity as it approaches the New Testament, where you come to proclamations like this that speak of the incomparable glory ahead.

We tend to make careful note of our suffering. Just the other day I received a mimeographed letter from a man who had written out in extreme detail (even though rather humorously) a report of his recent operation. He said he'd had to listen to all the reports of other people's operations for years, and now it was his turn! We make detailed reports of what we go through in our sufferings. But here the apostle says, "Don't even mention them! They are not worthy to be mentioned in comparison with the glory that is to follow."

Now, that statement would be just so much hot air if it did not come from a man like Paul. Here is a man who suffered intensely. No one of us has gone through even a fraction of the suffering that Paul endured. He was beaten, stoned [with rocks!], chained, imprisoned, shipwrecked, starved, often hungry, naked, and cold. He himself tells us this. And yet it is this apostle who takes pen in hand and says, "Our present sufferings are not worth comparing with the glory that shall be revealed in us." The glory that is coming is incomparable in intensity.

Our sufferings hurt us, I know. I am not trying to make light of them or diminish the terrible physical and emotional pain that suffering can bring. It can be awful, almost unendurable. Its intensity can increase to such a degree that we actually scream with terror and pain. We think we can no longer endure. But the apostle is saying that the intensity of the suffering we experience is not even a drop in the bucket compared with the intensity of glory that is coming. Paul is straining the language in trying to describe this fantastic thing that is about to happen.

United with Beauty

This glory is not only incomparable in its intensity, but it is also incomparable in its locality. It is not going to be revealed to us, but in us. The word, literally, means "into us." This glory is not going to be like a spectator sport, where we will sit up in some cosmic grandstand and watch an amusing or beautiful performance in which we actually have no part. We are to be on the stage. We are going to be involved in it. It is a glory that will be "revealed into us," and we are part of it. I think that incomparable spokesman, C. S. Lewis, has explained this more accurately than anyone else. I would like to share with you a paragraph or two from his message, *The Weight of Glory*:

We are to shine as the sun. We are to be given the morning star. I think I begin to see what it means. In one way, of course, God has given us the morning star already. You can go and enjoy the gift on many fine mornings, if you get up early enough. "What more," you may ask, "do we want?" Ah, but we want so much more. Something the books on aesthetics take little notice of. But the poets and mythologies know all about it. We do not want merely to see beauty, though God knows even that is bounty enough—we want something else

which can hardly be put into words—to be united with the beauty we see, to pass into it, to receive it into ourselves, to bathe in it, to become part of it. That is why the poets tell us such lovely falsehoods. They talk as if the west wind could really sweep into a human soul. But it can't. They tell us that beauty, born of murmuring sound, will pass into a human face. But it won't—or not yet, at least.
[Lewis sums it up in a previous sentence in this way:] The door on which we have been knocking all our lives will open at last.*

That is what Paul says is about to happen. This is the incredible glory that God has prepared for those who love him, that he has given to us—not because we have been faithful, not because we earn it, but because we are heirs of God, and co-heirs with Christ.

Thus we are called and entrusted with the privilege of suffering for humanity. All Christians suffer. There are no exceptions. If you are a true and genuine believer in Jesus Christ, you will suffer. But we are not only given the privilege of suffering with him now, but also sharing in his glory that is yet to come. We can endure the suffering, and even triumph in it, because we see the glory that is to follow.

In the paragraph that follows, the apostle shows us two proofs that confirm this hope of glory. The first one is that nature itself testifies to it, and the second is our own experience. Paul says the whole created universe bears witness to this day to come. Verses 19 through 22 explain the testimony that is found in nature. First, nature is waiting for something:

The creation waits in eager expectation for the sons of God to be revealed.

The word in the original language which is translated "eager expectation" is an interesting word. It is a word that pictures a man standing and waiting for something to happen, craning his head forward. That is why I think Phillips

* C. S. Lewis, *The Weight of Glory* (Grand Rapids: Eerdmans), pp. 12, 13.

translates this correctly when he says, "The whole creation is standing on tiptoe, eagerly awaiting the revelation of the sons of God." The word means "to crane the neck, to look on with a visible display of anticipation that something is about to happen." That is what Paul says the world of nature is doing. It is eagerly awaiting this remarkable event toward which the world is hastening, and has been hastening since the beginning of time.

Paul goes on to explain why he makes such a statement in verses 20 and 21:

> For the creation was subjected to frustration, not by its own choice, but by the will of the one who subjected it, in hope that the creation itself will be liberated from its bondage to decay and brought into the glorious freedom of the children of God (Rom. 8:20,21).

Creation not only is waiting for something but it is doing so because it is linked with man. Creation fell with man, the apostle declares. Not only did our whole race fall into the bondage of sin and death, as the earlier chapters of Romans explain, but the entire physical universe fell as well. It was man's sin that put thorns on roses. It was man's sin that made the animals hate and fear each other and brought predators and carnivores into being. With the fall of man came the spreading of fear, hostility, and hatred in the animal world, and the whole of nature testifies to this fact. It is, as Paul describes it here, subjected to frustration.

Futility Prevails

Recently we have been hearing a lot about how plants are sensitive to people, how they even understand something of what we say, and how our attitudes are conveyed to them. Can you imagine how frustrated a plant can get when it wants to produce and grow, and yet it is always treated in such a manner that it cannot? Some of us have to live with these frustrated plants in our homes! Think of the beauty of nature—and yet every area is spoiled by thorns and thistles, and various things that mark decay. Futility prevails in the natural world.

This phrase, "the bondage to decay," is an accurate description of what scientists call the second law of thermodynamics. This is the law of infinite increase of entropy. Everything is decaying; everything, without exception, is running down. Though for a while something may seem to grow, eventually it dies. Even human life dies, and so does all that is with it. All of this is because of the fall of man.

I recently spent a few days in the beautiful High Sierra where the great sequoia trees grow. As I walked about, I was sad to see how the crush of man has spoiled what is left of the beauty of creation. In the area where I was there had been a great forest—the world's greatest forest of sequoia trees, those great redwoods. But man came in, and in less than a decade there was nothing but blackened stumps and rotting logs where once there were thousands of trees. It is ironic that although the forest was razed in the name of profit, no one made a dime on the whole operation. At least half of the lumber that was cut was never removed and was left to rot. This is how man despoils creation wherever he goes. He pollutes the air and ruins the environment. This is all a part of the bondage to decay that we see all around us.

But the apostle argues, if that is true, it is also true that when man is delivered from this decay, nature will be delivered as well. Therefore, when the hour strikes when the sons of God are to be revealed—when it shall appear what we truly are, as John would say; when what we have become in our spirits, sons of the living God, shall become visibly evident to all—in that hour, nature will be freed from its bondage. It will burst into a bloom and fecundity that no one can possibly imagine now. The desert will blossom like the rose, the prophet says, and the lions will lie down with the lambs. None shall hurt and destroy in all of God's holy mountain. Rivers will run free, clear, and sweet again.

All that God intended in nature will come into visible

manifestation in that day. Nature will be delivered into "the freedom and the glory of the children of God." That is a literal rendering of what Paul says here, and it means that glory has a great deal of freedom about it. It is a stepping into an experience of liberty such as we have never dreamed, such as has never come into our imaginations at any time. It is incomparable glory.

Now, in anticipation of that day, the apostle says, nature groans. But it groans in hope (verse 22):

> We know that the whole creation has been groaning as in the pains of childbirth right up to the present time.

As Paul has said earlier, nature groans in the hope that the creation itself will be liberated from its bondage to decay and brought into the glorious freedom of the children of God. Someone has pointed out that all the sounds of nature are in a minor key. Listen to the sighing of the wind. Listen to the roaring of the tide. Even most of the sounds of birds are in a minor key. All nature is singing, but it is singing a song of bondage. Yet it sings in hope, looking forward to the day, Paul says, when it will step into the freedom of the glory of the children of God.

The Groan and the Glory

Not only does nature testify to this bondage, bearing witness to the hope that is waiting, but, Paul says, we ourselves have this testimony. Our present experience confirms that this glory is coming. Paul sets this evidence before us in verse 23:

> Not only so, but we ourselves, who have the firstfruits of the Spirit, groan inwardly as we wait eagerly for our adoption as sons, the redemption of our bodies.

In some ways, I think that is the most remarkable statement in this whole remarkable paragraph. Paul says here that though we ourselves are redeemed in spirit, our bodies are not yet redeemed; therefore we, too, are groaning. All through this paragraph there is a constant contrast between the groan and the glory; yet there is a link between the two. Nature groans; we groan. And yet the groan is producing the glory. I remind you again of what Paul said in 2 Corinthians 4:17:

> For this slight momentary affliction is preparing for us an eternal weight of glory beyond all comparison.

Have you ever thought of afflictions in that way? Our afflictions are working for us. Every time we groan, it is a reminder to us of the promise of glory. I do not think anything will transform our sufferings more than remembering that.

Our lives consist of groans. We groan because of the ravages that sin makes in our lives, and in the lives of those we love. Also we groan because we see possibilities that are not being captured and employed. And then we groan because we see gifted people who are wasting their lives, and we would love to see something else happening. It is recorded that, as he drew near the tomb of Lazarus, Jesus groaned in his spirit because he was so burdened by the ravages that sin had made in a believing family. He groaned, even though he knew he would soon raise Lazarus from the dead. So we groan in our spirits—we groan in disappointment, in bereavement, in sorrow. We groan physically in our pain and our limitation. Life consists of a great deal of groaning.

But the apostle immediately adds that this is a groaning which is in hope:

> For in this hope we were saved. But hope that is seen is no hope at all. Who hopes for what he already has? But if we hope for what we do not yet have, we wait for it patiently (Rom. 8:24,25).

As nature groans in hope, so we believers groan—but we groan in hope, too. For in this hope we were saved, in the anticipation that God has a plan for our bodies as well.

Among the Greeks it was taught that the body was evil, and that the best thing was to get out of it, to get away from it, to escape into whatever glory awaited the human spirit, for the body was a prison, holding us in.

I am afraid this pagan concept is more prevalent among Christians than we like to think. Many Christians have an ejection-seat mentality. As soon as they get into difficulty, they want to pull the ejection cord and zip off into glory. They want to get away from it all. We are all tempted to feel that way, but that is not the Christian point of view.

The Christian viewpoint is that, though the body is in pain and suffering and is limited now, this is an important aspect of our lives. It is part of the whole program and plan of God, part of the privilege committed to us as Christians. We suffer with Christ. As he suffered, so do we, that we might also be glorified, as he is. Therefore, what is happening to us now is something that we never need to see as meaningless. It holds great meaning. That is why boredom is the most unChristian attitude we can have. Boredom is an attitude of enduring, waiting for something better to come, but seeing nothing meaningful in what you are going through at the time.

We are saved in hope, Paul says, and by that hope we live. It is true that hope, by its very nature, is something yet in the future ["But hope that is seen is no hope for what we do not yet have, we wait for it patiently"]. But what makes it possible to wait is that we already have the first-fruits of the Spirit. We know that the Spirit of God is able to give joy in the midst of heartache. He is able to make us feel at peace even when there is turmoil all around. This happens to even the weakest and newest among us. This is what Paul calls the firstfruits of the Spirit—the power of God to make a heart calm and restful and peaceful in the midst of turbulent, trying, and difficult circumstances. Because we have these firstfruits we can wait patiently for the hour when, at last, even our bodies will be set free, and we will step into an incomparable glory, such as we have never imagined or seen before No one, in all the wildest dreams of science fiction, has ever imagined or conceived of something so vast and so magnificent as the glory God has waiting for us.

More Groans

There is more involved in this program of patient waiting, as the apostle goes on to explain in verses 26 and 27:

> In the same way, the Spirit helps us in our weakness. We do not know how we ought to pray, but the Spirit himself intercedes for us with groans that words cannot express. And he who searches our hearts knows the mind of the Spirit, because the Spirit intercedes for the saints in accordance with God's will.

Now it is the Spirit that is groaning. There are three groans in this passage. Nature is groaning, we are groaning, and now the Spirit is groaning, with words which cannot be uttered. This passage helps us in our understanding of prayer. The apostle says that we do not know what to pray for. We lack wisdom. I want to point out immediately that this is not an encouragement to cease praying. Some people think this means that if we don't know how to pray as we ought, and if the Spirit is going to pray for us anyway, then we don't need to pray. But that would contradict many other scripture passages, especially James 4:2, which says, "You have not because you ask not." God does want us to pray, and we are constantly encouraged to pray. Jesus taught us to pray. In Philippians 4:6, Paul tells us that we are never to be troubled or anxious, but in everything, with prayer and supplication, we are to let our requests be made known to God.

There are many occasions when we do know how to pray. But there will come times when we won't know what to pray for. We know something is wrong, but do not know how to analyze it, or how to explain it, or how to ask God to do something about it. We are without wisdom. It is at that time, the apostle tells us, that the Spirit of God within us voices, without words, his requests to the Father.

I have always been amazed at people who emphasize the gift of tongues and take this verse as proof that the Spirit prays in tongues through us. This verse could not mean that. Paul tells us that this praying of the Spirit is done with groans which words cannot express. Now, tongues are words, words of other languages. If this referred to the gift of tongues, it would merely be putting into other languages the feelings of our heart. But this passage has nothing to do with that. This describes the groans of the Spirit within, so deep and so impossible to verbalize that we cannot say anything at all. We just feel deeply. The apostle says that when that happens, it is the Spirit of God who is praying. The Spirit is putting our prayer into a form which God the Father, who searches the heart, understands. The Spirit is asking for something concerning the situation that we are trying to pray about.

Now, what is the Spirit asking for? That is explained in verse 28:

> And we know that in all things God works for the good of those who love him, who have been called according to his purpose.

Never separate this verse from the previous two verses. The apostle is saying that what the Spirit prays for is what happens. The Spirit prays according to the mind of God, and the Father answers by bringing into our lives the experiences that we need. He sends into the life of those for whom we are concerned the experiences that they need, no matter what they may be.

Now, that means that even the trials and tragedies that happen to us are an answer from the Father to the praying of the Spirit. What we need to understand is that these things do not happen by accident. They happen because the Spirit which is in you prayed and asked that the Father allow them to happen—because you or someone close to you needs it. These are the results of praying in the Spirit.

The joys, the unexpected blessings, and the unusual things that happen to you are also the result of the Spirit's praying. The Spirit is praying that these things will happen, he is voicing the deep concern of God himself for your needs and mine. Out of this grows the assurance that no matter what happens, it will work together for good. This verse does not tell us that everything that happens to us is good. It does say that whether the situation is bad or good, it will work together for good for you if you are one who is loved and called by God. What a difference that makes as we wait for the coming of the glory! God is working out his purposes within us.

Paul is telling us here that we can wait with patience because nature testifies to his glorious coming, and our own experience confirms it as well. We are being prepared for something—we can't really tell what it is, specifically, but we are getting ready for something. And one of these days, at the end of our lives, if not before, we will step out of time into an incredible experience of glory, something that beggars description—a glory that Christ himself shares, and that we will all share with him.

That is what God is preparing us for. No wonder the apostle then closes this passage with one of the greatest paeans of praise in the Scriptures. As we face the sufferings we are going through now, what a blessing, and what a help it is to remember the glory that has been granted to us. We have been counted worthy to suffer for his name, that we may also share in the glory that is to come.

22

If God Be for Us

The glory of Christianity is that, whether our hearts are aching or rejoicing, there is no incident or circumstance— no matter how trivial—that is without purpose or meaning. God has declared that "in all things God works for the good of those who love him, who have been called according to his purpose" (Rom. 8:28).

That great statement of the apostle in this eighth chapter introduces to us the crowning concept of this letter to the Romans. We are called "according to his purpose." God has a purpose. There is purpose in life. What seems to be a meaningless jumble of events in history is not meaningless at all; there is a purpose to every event. Everything is moving to accomplish a desired end, and that end is the subject of this whole letter to the Romans. God's purpose, in effect, is to have many sons, all of whom will love him with all their hearts. That takes us back to what Jesus said. "You shall love the Lord your God with all your heart and all your mind and all your soul and all your strength. This is the first and greatest commandment." To accomplish that God called the world into being, set up the whole universe, peopled the earth with a race of men, permitted them to fall, sent into this sin-ridden earth his own beloved Son,

246

accomplished the cross and the resurrection, and now as
Paul so clearly says, "works for the good of those who love
him, who has been called according to that great purpose."

In this we have a tremendous statement of what life is
all about. We see that God's purpose is to have a race of
people, his own children, who will love him. Love is the
end and aim of life. Now Paul looks back through this letter
to the Romans and sums up in five brief steps the process
that God follows to accomplish that end:

> For those God foreknew he also predestined to be conformed
> to the likeness of his Son, that he might be the firstborn among
> many brothers. And those he predestined, he also called;
> those he called, he also justified; those he justified, he also
> glorified (Rom. 8:29,30).

These are the five steps that God takes, stretching from
eternity to eternity—far beyond the scope of any of our individual lives. I want to make clear that in this passage the
apostle Paul is not touching the question of why some people believe and some do not. That is the problem of election. All that man can comprehend about that subject is
clearly stated in the ninth chapter. But Paul is not facing
the mystery of election here. He is simply describing what
has already happened when, as Christians, we look back to
see how God brought us to the place of belief.

A Question of Existence

The first step is that God foreknew us. Many people
imagine that this means God foreknew what we were going
to do, he foreknew that we would believe in Christ. There is
a certain line of teaching that says God looked down the cor-
ridor of time and saw that we would believe in Christ, and
therefore he chose us to be part of God's elect because of
what we were going to do. But this verse, as I have already
suggested, is not dealing with that question. This verse says
those whom he foreknew," not *"that which* he foreknew."
It is concerned therefore, with the question of existence. It

is telling us that from among the tremendous number of human beings who have been born on this earth since the creation of man, God foreknew that you and I would be there—as well as all the believers who have preceded us or who will follow us in the course of history.

When you consider the fact that at every birth the chances of knowing beforehand the exact characteristics of those who will emerge from that union are somewhere in the range of one in two hundred million, this is a most remarkable statement. Because of the abundance of sperm to one ovum, doctors tell us that the possibility that any one particular person could be foretold and foreknown is fantastic—the odds are one to two hundred million for every single birth. So, when you consider that out of all those possibilities God has seen that we would be the ones who would come—and not only us, but all believers of all time, in all ages—you begin to get some faint understanding of the mind and the wisdom of God.

We are impressed by great computers that amass huge numbers of facts and put together amounts of information that none of us as individuals could ever handle. But these computers are nothing! They are children's toys, compared with the greatness of the mind of God, who saw all the fantastic possibilities and yet knew that we would be there. Not only that, but he knew it long before the world was ever called into being! That is the amazing statement of the Scriptures. Before the foundation of the earth, God foreknew that we would be here. I cannot go any further than that. That baffles and bewilders me; but, nevertheless, it is fact. This is where Paul begins.

Then, Paul says, the next step is that God predestined. "Ah," you say, "I know what that means! That means God looked over the whole group and said, 'Now these will go to hell, and those will go to heaven.'" But predestination has absolutely nothing to do with going to hell. In the Word of God, predestination is never related to that in any way whatsoever. To think of predestination in those terms is completely unbiblical. Predestination has to do only with

believers. It simply tells us that God has selected beforehand the goal toward which he is going to move every one
of us who believes in Christ. That goal is conformity to the
character of Christ. Everything that happens to us focuses
on that one supreme purpose.

If we understand that, it will help to explain some of the
conundrums of our lives. We think that God's primary objective is our happiness, but the Scriptures never say that.
God is interested in our happiness, and eventually our happiness is involved in all that God does, but that is not his
primary concern. His primary concern is for our character.
God knows we can never develop the character he wants
without times of difficulty and trial and suffering. That is
why suffering is an inevitable part of the picture. It helps us
to remember that God's primary objective is not that we be
happy all the time. He is not that kind of father. Rather, his
primary objective is that we be holy, which means "whole,"
"complete," all that we were intended to be, functioning as
God intended us to function, like Jesus.

We have all noticed that God is forming a lot of characters! In fact, he is going to end up with a heaven full of
them. But one distinctive thing about those characters is
that they are all like Jesus. They all have different person-
alities, but they will all have the same basic, fundamental
character: loving, gracious, gentle, wholesome, helpful, compassionate—all the things that marked the magnificent life
of Jesus interpreted in a thousand and one different ways in
our human lives. That is the wonder and the glory of God.
That is what he has predestined: there shall be many
brethren, and Jesus is the firstborn among many just like
him.

The Holy Spirit Gets into the Act

The third step is that God called us. "Those whom God
foreknew he also predestined; and those he predestined, he
also called." This is where we get into the act. Up to this
point, the passage has been concerned with God's mind and

purpose, but now we suddenly become involved in the picture. Those whom God has foreknown and predestined, he now calls. I could not begin to describe to you the mystery and wonder that is involved in this. This means the Holy Spirit somehow begins to work in our lives. We may be far removed from God, we may have grown up in a non-Christian family, we may be involved in a totally non-Christian faith, or we may be from a Christian home. It does not make any difference. God begins to work and he draws us to himself.

Jesus said, "All that my Father has given me shall come unto me." Not one shall be lost. The Holy Spirit begins to draw us and woo us and open our minds and create interest in our hearts. We think we are getting religious, but we are only responding to the drawing of the Spirit of God. We are not aware of this—we think it is our choice. In a sense, we do have to make a choice, and in chapter 9 Paul explains more fully this mystery of our free will and God's sovereign choice. Nevertheless, we are being drawn in ways we do not understand.

The apostle Paul was converted on the Damascus road when he saw the glory of the Lord shining about him with a brilliance greater than the sun. He heard a voice that said to him, "Saul, Saul, why do you persecute me? Is it not hard for you to kick against the goad?" By that last phrase the Lord Jesus indicated that he understood that Paul was fighting, struggling, kicking, trying to hold on to his independence—but he was being goaded relentlessly to a fate he could not escape. That is what happens to all of us. We do not understand it, but it is true.

Dr. Harry Ironside used to tell about a man who gave his testimony, telling how God had sought and found him, how God had loved him, called him, saved him, delivered him, cleansed him, and healed him—a tremendous testimony to the glory of God. After the meeting, one rather legalistic brother took him aside and said, "You know, I appreciate all that you said about what God did for you, but you didn't mention anything about your part in it. Salvation is really part us and part God, and you should have mentioned something about your part." "Oh," the man said, "I apologize. I'm sorry; I really should have mentioned that. My part was running away, and his part was running after me until he found me." That is what Paul is saying here. God called us. Those whom he predestined, he also called.

Fourth, those God called, he justified. All along in this letter we have been looking at what justification means. It is God's gift of worth. Those who are justified are rendered valuable in his sight. They are forgiven, cleansed, and given the position before him of being loved, accepted, and wanted. This is justification—being given the gift of worth without any merit on your part at all. By the cross God was freed to give the gift of righteousness. Had he given it apart from the cross he could have been properly accused of condoning sin—but the cross freed him. It established his righteous justice on other grounds, so that he is now free to give to us the gift of worth without any merit on our part.

Then, finally, those God justified, he also glorified. Paul writes as though this had already happened—and it is true that it has already begun. Glorification is what Paul calls "the revelation of the sons of God." It is the exciting day which the whole creation is anticipating, when God is suddenly going to pull back the curtains on what he has been doing with the human race. Suddenly, the sons of God will stand out in glory.

But in a sense, as we have said, this has already begun. It is what we call, in theological terms, sanctification. Sanctification is the process by which the inner worth which God imparts to our human spirit by faith in Christ begins to work itself out into our conduct. We actually begin to change. We begin to be like what we actually are. Therefore, our attitudes change, and our actions change. As our habits begin to change, we stop certain things and begin others. Our whole demeanor is different; we become much more gracious, happy, wholesome persons. That is called sanctification, and that is the process of glorification; it has already started. It is the process that Paul says is inevitable.

God has started it, that is what he is doing, and that is
what he is going to complete at the day of the revelation of
the sons of God. So Paul writes here as though it were already done: "Those whom God justified, he also glorified."

There are none lost in the process. Those whom he foreknew, before the foundation of the world, he also predestined to conform to the likeness of his Son. The same
number of people he also called; and the ones he called, he
also justified. The very ones he justified, he also glorified.
No one is lost, because God is responsible for the entire
process. It will involve pain and toil, death and tears, disappointment, bereavement, sorrow, sin, stumbling, failure,
falling, forgiveness—all these things. But it is going to happen, because what God sets out to do, he does—no matter
what it takes.

At this point Paul asks the final question:

What, then, shall we say in response to this?

What can you say? All you can say is, "Thank you. How
great thou art!" The response of the heart is, "Father, I love
you." And that is what God is after. He is after the love of
men—the uncoerced, unforced love of men, despite their
pressures, their problems, their heartaches, whatever they
go through. Therefore, the rest of this chapter is a beautiful
description of how to love God. The process of loving God
is outlined for us in three questions which the apostle asks
in this last section. The first one is found in verse 31:

If God is for us, who can be against us? He who did not spare
his own Son, but gave him up for us all—how will he not
also, along with him graciously give us all things?

If you have understood all that God has done for you, your
first response of love is to say to yourself, "If God is for me,
who can be against me?" You love God when you work out
and reflect on the implications of his saving commitment to
you. The moment you think this through and say to your-

self, "If God has done this, and God is for me, then this and this and this must be true." As you rejoice in that truth, you are loving God. You are responding as he intended you to respond to his love for you.

In the Shadow of Mike

Now, what is the effect of this realization? It is clear from this passage that it is the removal of fear. If God is for us, who can be against us? All fear of successful opposition is removed. It is not that there is no opposition. The devil is still there, his legions are still there, the communists are still there—there is still going to be opposition. But Paul is saying, "If God is for us, what difference does it make?" If God is for us, who can be against us?

One of our elders was telling us recently of the plight of his thirteen-year-old grandson. The boy's father is a Chicano, and the youngster looks like his dad. In school in Missouri where they live, the boy ran into a tremendous nest of White Supremacists. Because of the prejudice against blacks and Chicanos, that innocent lad began to suffer unjust torment and persecution. He did not understand it and he came home one day weeping, beaten up because of his looks. His mother didn't know what to do so she wrote and asked us to pray for this situation, and we did.

A week or so later a letter came back and described how one night the biggest kid in school appeared at their door and said that he was a Christian, that he knew they were Christians, and that he had come to tell them he had gone to every kid in school and told them that if they ever did anything to that boy again they would answer to him. I don't know what that boy's name was, but let's call him Mike. I can imagine this little boy going back to school, walking in the shadow of Mike, and all his tormenters looking at him. He probably would be saying to himself, "If Mike is for me, who can be against me?" That is what Paul is saying here. That is what David said in the twenty-seventh Psalm:

> The Lord is my light and my salvation;
> whom shall I fear?
> The Lord is the stronghold of my life;
> Of whom shall I be afraid?

That is what we ought to be saying when trouble strikes, when difficulty comes, and when opposition appears. We ought to think it through and say, "This is the way we love God. If God be for me, who can be against me?"

Not only does our belief in God's love for us remove our fear of opposition, but, as verse 32 indicates, it also removes our fear of want:

> He who did not spare his own Son, but gave him up for us all—how will he not also, along with him graciously give us all things?

He who has already given us the best, the greatest, the dearest, the most precious thing he has, and who did so while we were sinners—while we were enemies, while we were helpless—will he not also give us some of these trivial, piddling little things that we need? That is Paul's next argument.

If someone thinks enough of you to give you a costly, brilliant, beautiful, flawless diamond, do you think he will object when you ask him for the box that goes with it? If a mother will give up a baby, do you think she will object if they ask to take his clothes, too? And if God has given us his own Son already, do you really think he will withhold anything else that we need? Paul's argument is unanswerable. Of course he won't. We can say with David in the twenty-third Psalm, "The Lord is my shepherd, I shall not want." The first sign that we love God, then, is that all fear is removed. We begin to face our lack, to face our enemies, and to say, "If God be for us, who can be against us?"

The second question Paul asks of those who know God's love for them is found in verses 33 and 34:

> Who will bring any charge against those whom God has chosen? It is God who justifies. Who is he that condemns?

Christ Jesus, who died—more than that, who was raised to life—is at the right hand of God and is also interceding for us (Rom. 8:33,34).

This is a reminder of the work that God has done. We love God when we trust in the full effect of his work on our behalf. Paul is looking back over the letter, and sees two great works that God has done. The first is justification. "Who will bring any charge against those whom God has chosen?" Who can? It is God who justifies.

Justification means that nothing and no one anywhere can accuse us successfully before God. Now, the devil is the accuser of the brethren. He will try to accuse us constantly. This verse tells us we must not listen to his voice. We must not listen to these thoughts that condemn us, that put us down, that make us feel there is no hope for us. These thoughts will come—they cannot be stopped—but we do not have to listen to them. We know God is not listening to these accusations. Who can condemn us when God justifies us? Therefore we refuse to be condemned. We do not do this by ignoring our sin or trying to cover it over, or pretending that it isn't there; we do it by admitting that we fully deserve to be condemned, but that God, through Christ, has already borne our guilt. That is the only way out. That is why Christians should not hesitate to admit their failure and their sin. We will never be justified until we admit our need of it. But when we admit it, then we also can face the full glory of the fact that God justifies the ungodly, and therefore there is no condemnation.

In Touch with a Living Person

Then Paul raises the question, "Who is he that condemns?" Who is going to do this? The only one who has the right is Jesus—and Jesus died for us. More than that, he was raised to life for us, he is now at the right hand of God in power for us, and he is also interceding for us. So there is no chance that he is going to condemn us. This is a reference to the power that we have to take hold afresh of the life of Jesus. Not only is our guilt set aside, but power is imparted to us—his life in us, his risen life made available to us now. So we can rise up and say "no" to the temptations that surround us and the habits that drag us down; we can be a victor over them. That is not a mere dogma; we are in touch with a living person. That is the glory of Christianity. The unique distinction of Christians is that we have Jesus.

I know that every cult, every new faith, every false faith around, old and new, offers some kind of experience, perhaps a mystic experience, or some sense of peace or freedom. We must not discount these, for they can deliver some of these things. But the difference is that they do not have a grounding in history. There is no assurance that these experiences are reality. But we Christians have a grounding in the history of Jesus. He came, he died, he rose again. These are unmistakable facts. Therefore, when we come to Jesus, we come to someone we know exists. We know he is there. Therefore, the experience we go through is real. Dr. A. W. Tozer, that grand old prophet, states it like this:

The teaching of the New Testament is that now, at this very moment, there is a Man in heaven appearing in the presence of God for us. He is as certainly a man as was Adam or Moses or Paul; he is a man glorified, but his glorification did not de-humanize him. Today he is a real man, of the race of mankind, bearing our lineaments and dimensions, a visible and audible man, whom any other man would recognize instantly as one of us. But more than this, he is the heir of all things, Lord of all lords, head of the church, firstborn of the new creation. He is the way to God, the life of the believer, the hope of Israel, and the high priest of every true worshiper. He holds the keys of death and hell, and stands as advocate and surety for everyone who believes on him in truth. Salvation comes not by accepting the finished work, or deciding for Christ; it comes by believing on the Lord Jesus Christ, the whole, living, victorious Lord who, as God and man, fought our fight and won it, accepted our debt as his own and paid it, took our sins and died under them, and rose again to set us free. This is the true Christ; nothing less will do.*

Our whole relationship rests upon that magnificent person. We are freed from the condemnation of guilt because of him.

That brings us to the third and last question relating to how we love God. We love him by reminding ourselves of the implications of his continual, unchanging commitment to us. We love him by remembering and trusting the full effect of his work for us. And finally, we love God by answering this question:

Who shall separate us from the love of Christ? (vs. 35)

Is there any force, anywhere, that can come between you and Jesus? Here the apostle is facing the question that many people ask. Is there any way to lose your salvation? Who can remove us from Christ, once we fully come to him? Paul's answer is, "Let's take a look at the possibilities." First, can all the troubles and dangers of life separate us from his love?

Shall trouble or hardship or persecution or famine or nakedness or danger or sword? As it is written: "For your sake we face death all the day long; we are considered as sheep to be slaughtered" (vv. 35,36).

That is life at its worst. Will that do it?

No, in all these things we are more than conquerors through him who loved us (v. 37).

"Trouble" means catastrophe and disasters. "Hardship" refers to the tight, narrow places we have to go through sometimes. Will persecution do it? That is hurt deliberately

* A. W. Tozer, *Man, The Dwelling Place of God* (Harrisburg: Christian Publishers) p. 142.

inflicted on us because we are Christians. Will famine—
will lack of food and money do it? Will nakedness, or lack
of clothes? Will danger, or threat to our lives? Will the
sword (war, riot, uprising) do it? "No," Paul says. In these
we are superconquerors. Why? Because rather than divid-
ing us from Christ, they draw us closer to him. They make
us cling harder. They scare us and make us run to him.
When we are independent and think we can make it on
our own, these things strike, and we start whimpering and
running for home, and we cling all the closer. We can never
be defeated then, so we are more than conquerors.

What about supernatural forces? What about people and
power and demons and strange forces?

> For I am convinced that neither death nor life, neither angels
> nor demons, neither the present nor the future, nor any pow-
> ers, neither height nor depth, nor anything else in all creation
> [literally, anything even in a different creation], will be able
> to separate us from the love of God that is in Christ Jesus our
> Lord (Rom. 8:38,39).

There is nothing left out of that list, is there? Everything is
there—demons and dark powers, black magic and angels,
truth and error, death and life—whether in this creation or
any other creation. Paul takes everything in and says that
nothing, no being or force, is capable of separating us from
the love of Jesus Christ our Lord. So we love God when we
say, "If God be for us, who can be against us?" We love
God because of what he himself has done on our behalf,
and the nature of that commitment is that he loves us.
Nothing can separate us from that.

This is the highest point of the letter. Obviously, Paul
cannot go beyond this, and neither can we. What can you
say? What can you do but love when you are confronted by
a God like that?

I want to bring this study to an end by giving you a modern version of this passage, put in terms of a specific individual, Ruth Harms Calkin, who wrote:

God, I may fall flat on my face; I may fail until I feel old and beaten and done in. Yet Your love for me is changeless. All the music may go out of my life, my private world may shatter to dust. Even so, You will hold me in the palm of Your steady hand. No turn in the affairs of my fractured life can baffle You. Satan with all his braggadocio cannot distract You. Nothing can separate me from Your measureless love— pain can't, disappointment can't, anguish can't. Yesterday, today, tomorrow can't. The loss of my dearest love can't. Death can't. Life can't. Riots, war, insanity, unidentity, hunger, neurosis, disease—none of these things nor all of them heaped together can budge the fact that I am dearly loved, completely forgiven, and forever free through Jesus Christ Your beloved Son.

Can you add anything to that?